Religion and Technology in the 21st Century: Faith in the E-World

Susan Ella George
University of Wales, Australia
University of South Australia, Australia

INFOSCI Information Science Publishing
Hershey • London • Melbourne • Singapore

Acquisitions Editor: Michelle Potter
Development Editor: Kristin Roth
Senior Managing Editor: Jennifer Neidig
Managing Editor: Sara Reed
Copy Editor: Angela Thor
Typesetters: Amanda Appicello, Sharon Berger
Cover Design: Lisa Tosheff
Printed at: Integrated Book Technology

Published in the United States of America by
Information Science Publishing (an imprint of Idea Group Inc.)
701 E. Chocolate Avenue
Hershey PA 17033
Tel: 717-533-8845
Fax: 717-533-8661
E-mail: cust@idea-group.com
Web site: http://www.idea-group.com

and in the United Kingdom by
Information Science Publishing (an imprint of Idea Group Inc.)
3 Henrietta Street
Covent Garden
London WC2E 8LU
Tel: 44 20 7240 0856
Fax: 44 20 7379 0609
Web site: http://www.eurospanonline.com

Library of Congress Cataloging-in-Publication Data

George, Susan, 1967-
Religion and technology in the 21st century : faith in the e-world / Susan George.
p. cm.
Summary: "This book examines the unique synergy between religion and technology, and explores the many ways that technology is shaping religious expression, as well as ways that religion is coming to influence technology"--Provided by publisher.
ISBN 1-59140-714-1 (hardcover) -- ISBN 1-59140-715-X (softcover) -- ISBN 1-59140-716-8 (ebook)
1. Computers--Religious aspects--Christianity. 2. Internet--Religious aspects--Christianity. 3. Computers--Religious aspects. 4. Internet--Religious aspects. I. Title.
BR115.C65G46 2006
201'.66--dc22
2006009289

British Cataloguing in Publication Data
A Cataloguing in Publication record for this book is available from the British Library.

All work contributed to this book is new, previously-unpublished material. The views expressed in this book are those of the authors, but not necessarily of the publisher.

Religion and Technology in the 21st Century:

Faith in the E-World

Table of Contents

Preface

Overview of Subject Matter and Topic Content

This text examines the topic "technology and religion." There are various reasons why the intersection of these topics is of interest. This text is certainly not the first to examine the nexus, but we believe it does so from a unique perspective called "synergy." This perspective considers how each field can assist the other in their respective endeavours, how each field is furthered by the impact of the other. The dual consideration of this text is in both (1) the way that religion is being enhanced by technology, and (2) how technology may benefit from a broader basis of input.

In a significant way, this dual consideration of the nexus of technology and religion starts to answer some of the questions raised by the philosophy of technology. The philosophy of technology has raised doubts about whether technology can benefit humanity. Some see technology as "destroying" humanity. There are subtle forms of "destruction" found in the way it "lays waste" human nature through the producer-consumer society it supports; in the very real technological disasters and accidents that harm people; and in the unwitting influences technology brings to everyday life, where it is used without question. One key philosophical issue is that of technological determinism: the idea that society is driven by technology; that humanity is somehow being led by technology rapidly going out of control. Another key question is "how can we relate ourselves to technology in a way that it does not destroy us?" As technology and religion integrate, we find the synergy provides some answer to such key questions raised by the philosophy of technology.

In the analysis of how technology has impacted religion, the text demonstrates an example of how even this facet of humanity has been influenced by technology; some may say that technology has "determined" even this aspect of life. While we do see ways that technology has changed the expression of religion across various cultures, technology is not totally setting the agenda. We see the ways that technology facilitates human-connectedness and interaction; in many instances, virtual religious communities come closer to the heart of community than some expressions of organised religion. We also see interesting technical questions raised in "mediating" social and physical presence through ICT (information and communication) technologies. We are drawn to ask whether the various "Internet congregations" that exist constitute a "church," and ask of the theological validity of "virtual meetings" and "remote religion." While virtual religion may appear to be just another example of technology permeating every facet of life, we see religion as a special part of the human arena being impacted. Religion is a unique field impacted by technology because the field itself is an attempt to transcend the human condition. In this way, as others have noted, there are similarities with technology itself. If technology is accused of relentlessly determining society and the course of human life, in its application to religion, it merely sets humanity on a relentless "spiritual quest": a meta exploration of what it is to be human, answering some questions in the philosophy of technology.

However, the synergy of technology and religion, does more than answer some difficult questions in the philosophy of technology. The synergy contributes to religion itself. It does so in various ways, one of the chief means being the way that "community" is stimulated through virtual life; technology fosters interaction, engagement, participation and an "active" involvement with religion that is quite astounding compared to the worst of institutionalised religion. Moreover, the involvement with religion appears to be answering an interesting dilemma that some found to exist within Christendom, the question of how to be a Christian; how to have "faith" when the dominant institutions of society and culture itself made nominal ascent to doctrine and certain ritualistic traditions the norm and limit of faith. The virtual communities are also suggesting interesting possibilities in the contest of the emerging church and the question of how to be church in the wake of Christendom. While the mediation of physical presence through technology is currently far removed from face-to-face interaction, there are elements of community that technology enhances. Also, the simple sheer availability and presence of information, contacts, and other resources that ICT mediates is stimulating a spiritual quest among all religions, which is surprising, considering the suggestion of some that technology will quell the "spiritual."

Turning to the other side of "technology and religion," this text also examines how technology may benefit from a broader basis, and actually be impacted by religion. In particular, the way that artificial intelligence (AI) may benefit from theological input. AI also already draws upon many disciplines, from psychology to mathematics, linguistics to computer science. The broad basis of the field is required because AI aims to achieve "intelligent behaviours" in machines; it seeks to reproduce distinctively human abilities, from language to sophisticated reasoning, and in many instances not only reproduces human performance, but seeks to transcend human performance. AI is a unique technology because it intersects so closely with the human world. Intelligent technologies are not just another tool that humanity may use, but intelligent technologies are attempting to reproduce elements of human behaviour. In this way, they are "intruding" into the human world in a unique way. AI is concerned with human behaviour, with the nature and purpose of people and machines. Theology is perfectly able to address such concerns. To some extent, the chief concerns of AI are not "intelligence," but "identity." Indeed, AI might better be considered a pursuit in "artificial identity" rather than "artificial intelligence." Theology informs us of the nature of human identity, suggesting that it includes a moral, relational, and social component, as well as the creative, intellectual, logical and linguistic abilities that AI already recognises.

While AI can be informed by theology, the main synergy of technology and religion contributes to the philosophy of AI. To varying degrees, AI operates under the assumption of computationalism, the idea that thinking is a mechanistic process; that cognition is essentially computation; and that computation can be abstracted as a step-by-step deterministic procedure (most generally expressed in the Turing machine). Such conceptions make philosophical assumptions about the nature of mind, even that "mind" is a separate component of human identity. It also makes assumptions about the possibility of abstracting human identity from a physically incarnated, contextual situation, and having a step-by-step procedure to explain human "operation." It appears that such assumptions make AI practically possible. We find that they are not only unwarranted, but in many ways inhibit AI from progressing. We seek an alternative conception of computation itself in principle-based engineering (PBE). This conception of computation bears similarities with Putnam's "everything is computation," and also Searle's conception of "observer-related" computation. However, it is uniquely inspired by theological themes.

The main theological theme that informs PBE is "incarnation." Contrary to popular opinion, theology affirms the physical world. In the context of computation, PBE recognises the importance of physically situating and realising computation. Turing was not concerned whether an algorithm was implemented in silicon or bricks: the abstract model was paramount. With PBE, the implementation is paramount; the materials of the implementation are important; being situated in the world, and human context is also essential. PBE also offers AI a nonevolutionary paradigm with a constraint-based alternative. In so doing, it makes possible an alternative general mechanism from artificial life, one that is also distinct from symbolic AI, with its emphasis on formal systems, and sub-symbolic AI, with its particular "neural"-based understanding of mechanisms that are relevant to the operation of the brain. PBE so challenges the "evolutionary" and "emergent" paradigm that has come to dominate AI, reinstating the importance "design" and "purpose" within systems.

Once again, we emphasise that it is the synergy between religion and technology that we find most important and explore in this text. It is a synergy where the pursuits of each field are enhanced by a consideration of the nexus. It is a synergy that addresses particular questions within technology and particular questions within religion: a synergy that contributes to the philosophy of technology, and the questions of how technology can benefit and not destroy humanity. To the extent that technology is determined by humanity, not vice versa, humanity finds benefit.

Where Topic Fits in the World Today

The text emphasises the synergy that is produced in the nexus of technology and religion. It is not a one-sided case of "theology informing technology," nor of "technology informing theology," but is a rather unique "marriage" of two disciplines. Perhaps most generally, this text informs the philosophy of technology, having particular implications for the philosophy of artificial intelligence.

Some treatments of "technology and religion" have explored the common themes underlying the disciplines. The theme of "transcending human limitation" has been identified as a common goal of both technology and religion. Technology seeks to overcome humanity's physical and mental limitations. Religion, particularly Christianity, with its concept of resurrection, seeks to overcome human limitation, including the ultimate human limitation of death. This mutual drive to transcend has even been used to explain the emergence of a technological society from a Judeo-Christian culture. However, this text is not primarily interested in the common underlying themes.

Other treatments of "technology and religion" consider the influence of technology upon religion, and do so from a sociological perspective. For example, there is interest in the rise of "virtual religion," mediated through the Internet; how different cultures are appropriating technology for religious expression. Sometimes there is a distinctly Christian interest in religion and technology, where the focus is the analysis of contemporary technological society, and how religious themes may be mediated in that context. While we do consider how technology impacts religion, we recognise that the nexus is more than what technology does for religion.

More rarely, the treatments of "technology and religion" examine how technology is influenced by religion. Most work in this perspective considers the morality of technological application, or perhaps the ethics of scientific experiment. In this sense, religion functions as a guideline for technology, but does not fundamentally change technological practice, other than in some general ways. This text is a little more daring in its examination of theology and intelligent technologies, finding that technology may benefit from a "broader basis."

Description of Each Chapter

Chapter 1, "Technology and Religion," defines both "technology" and "religion." Technology is distinguished from science because it is applied knowledge that impacts daily life. The pervasive nature of technology means that it is technology, rather than science, that has risen to be a crucial consideration within secular society. Rather than "science vs. religion," it is "technology and religion" that is of interest. Additionally, technology can never be "neutral": there are always moral or ethical considerations, because it is applied. Religion proves hard to define. It may be seen as a social construction, as wish-fulfilment, and as alienation. It is sometimes distinguished from spirituality because of its social nature, although not all religions entail a communal aspect. Having initiated consideration of both technology and religion, we also aim to motivate why the particular combination of religion and technology is of interest. We outline how the topic is of interest to sociology, cultural anthropology, the philosophy of technology, as well as the disciplines of religion and technology themselves. We outline the proposal that the synergy between the topics is the main point of importance, as each enriches the other, and in so doing, also informs the philosophy of technology.

Chapter 2, "The Philosophy of Technology," outlines some of the considerations that philosophers of technology have made, as they reflect upon technology and what it is doing to society and humanity. One of the most poignant questions is that of "technological determinism" and the extent to which technology is "under control." The speed of change, the assumption that technology is beneficial, the uptake and spread of technology through many cultures makes it crucially important to carefully examine the issues. We find the "philosophy of technology" is a relatively young field, and at least two different approaches can be identified: the engineering and humanities approach. Some find that technology is already embedded in society to such an extent that we cannot isolate it and reflect on it apart from anything else: thus the field is already obsolete although the ramifications of technology are by no means over. We consider some of the "issues" of technology that impact society and warrant philosophical consideration. We also distinguish between technology's impact upon society and its impact upon individuals including (1) the "techno-phobia" that is bred by actual technological disasters, and the failures of technology, (2) the "self-sufficiency" that technology fuels, increasing people's autonomy, (3) the "spiritual degradation" created where people are reduced to "machines" in a "producer-consumer" society, and (4) the confusion that technology creates about personal identity.

Chapter 3, "21st Century Technologies," introduces and outlines four different 21st century technologies being (1) ICT — information and communication technology, the backbone of society, providing the infrastructure upon which other technologies can sit, (2) AI — artificial intelligence, with its endeavour to make "human-like" machines that are able to undertake intelligent action in the human world, (3) ubiquitous computing and ambient intelligence, promising a seamless environment of information and communication between the human and computer world, and (4) virtual AI, enhancing Internet ICT with intelligence and sophistication, merging with ubiquitous computing to make a world where the interface between the virtual and real are continually blurred. We aim to provide a snapshot of the state of the art in technologies, rather than talk about technology in the abstract. We also introduce the difference between "real AI" and "virtual AI," suggesting that the goals of much current day AI have shifted from those of the pioneer's. The aim to reproduce human behaviour in a machine, and understand how and what computation may achieve this, has been replaced by a new aim: that of supporting human intelligence and producing "smart" gadgets. This means that to some extent, the philosophy of AI has been given a backseat over practical engineering tasks that, in no way, resemble achieving human-like behaviour.

Chapter 4, "Future Directions and the Challenges," describes some of the challenges that face 21st century technologies, focusing upon the challenges of AI. The main challenges revolve around the necessity for machines to relate to the human world, to be contextualised within the world, to be "relational" and "social," with a human-machine interface that surpasses the current scope for interaction. In such a situated context, the "behaviour" of the machine needs to be controlled and carefully considered. It is important to point out some of these challenges, since a later consideration of the philosophy of AI will highlight some of the contributions that can be made to AI with a shift in its underlying philosophy. These challenges represent the current limitations of AI and the problems that require addressing; they motivate some of the future suggestions for "incarnating" computing, and the importance of physically realising a system within the world in order to achieve semantics. Interaction with the world is as vital as interaction with people, and as much a part of human interaction as face-to-face interactions are. Optimistic predications about the future capabilities of technology, and the speed of change, only underlie the fact that one of the biggest future challenges will be the philosophical and ethical challenge of where we are going with technology. In fact, we find that the future challenges are not just philosophical, but they are theological and religious.

Chapter 5, "The Techno-Religious Age," draws attention to the "religious quest" that is happening in the 21st century world. It points out some of the "similarities" of religion and technology. Both technology and religion are found to have transcendence as a common motivation. The Christian concept of "bodily resurrection" is the prime example of overcoming the ultimate human limitation, death. We also want to introduce and outline five of the major world religions: Christianity, Judaism, Islam, Buddhism, and Hinduism. We seek to observe the ways that they seek to transcend, and how technology has facilitated that transcendence. We particularly seek to draw out where unique elements of the religion intersect with Internet technology, for example, where pilgrimage is important, there are facilities for taking a "virtual tour"; where "image veneration" is important, there is scope for downloading them; where teaching and "knowledge for enlightenment" is vital, there is online learning; where community is important, there are electronic forums stimulating it. In many ways, we are in a techno-religious age, where technology and religion have united in the most human of quests for transcendence.

Chapter 6, "21st Century Christianity," describes Christianity in the 21st century. The background to the contemporary situation is traced through its origins in Christendom, which many see as a failed ideology. We consider some of the ways that Christianity has "failed" in the wars, violence, and persecutions it has caused, the oppression that distorted religion brings (e.g., in colonialism), and the moral failure of its members. Failures of Christianity in history have, by default, been failures of Christendom. The 21st century is witnessing the end of Christendom; there are changes occurring in Christianity. The changes are being noticed among that community which is distinctly the community of those who believe, the church. These changes include many new "expressions" of church outside the institutionalised Christianity of Christendom. One of the biggest innovations being a missional church that is within society. We want to point to the crisis that exists within the church today, and the general decline of participation in the organised church. This context provides the background to understanding the synthesis of technology and religion: a synthesis that is enabling new expressions of religion.

Chapter 7, "Church and the Internet," seeks to understand the different ways that the Internet is being used in entities that might call themselves "church." The examples mentioned range from Internet ventures sponsored by official mainline churches (e.g., I-Church) providing paid staff for pastoral oversight, to those set up by self-help organisations for the blind (e.g., EChurch-UK), to satirical efforts at making religion humorous (e.g., Church of Fools), and sites that appear "scam-like," designed for collecting funds and offering schemes to "get rich." We find that the two main usages of the Internet in Christianity are in (1) fostering "community" through discussion, exchange of opinion, and theological debate at many different levels, and (2) increasingly, the Internet is being used for evangelism. We investigate a typology for "Internet church." Bednell's typology for Internet church predicts six different types of church, based on whether they are founded around "information" or "communication," and then whether they support current institutions, bridge to current institution, or create new forms of institution. Our approach to a typology seeks a classification according to the technological features and ecclesiological functions that a Web site supports. We want to raise the question of whether the Internet church is a "valid expression," and if so, what features are required; if not, why.

Chapter 8, "Christian Community: Real and Virtual," considers the nexus of real and virtual Christian communities. We want to point out some unique characteristics of Christian communities in both the real and virtual worlds. In the real world, we find that, ideally, Christian communities are underpinned by a type of relationship that is unique. Secular communities are broader in type and do not necessarily have this bond underpinning. There is evidence that both secular and religious communities have largely broken down in Western cultures. Many have found that the computer and virtual communities that are emerging are actually assisting people to find community once again. One of the strengths of virtual communities is the "communication" and "interactive life" that underpins them. Interaction is vital in Christian communities, where the community exists for the sake of personal connectedness and building community itself (rather than any purpose such as education or game playing or other). Presence is an issue to consider in virtual communities. It is possible to physically meet and yet fail to "meet" in other ways, raising questions of whether a virtual community is even better than a physical gathering. Nevertheless, technology has a long way to go before adequately mediating physical presence. As technology progresses, it may be possible to tailor a virtual community to achieve the optimal level of social and physical presence.

Chapter 9, "The Theology of Technology," shifts perspective. Having seen the way that technology is influencing religious expression through virtual religion, we now consider the way that technology may be impacted by theology. We start off distinguishing the term "theology of technology" from "cybertheology," the vague notion that there is "theology" happening in the Internet, because we draw parallels between technological themes and religious themes or find "theological content" present on the Internet. The "theology of technology" is concerned with "conventional theology" being applied to technology. We examine six different patterns for the way that science and theology have been related, and consider how in AI, technology and theology are related in some special ways. One of the most obvious ways that conventional theology can be applied to technology is to provide ethical input into the moral use of technology. Within AI, we are faced with some unique questions of the "morality" of a scientific product itself. The "morality" of human action (and even the possibility of moral behaviour) is a theological question. The question of human morality is intimately related to the question of human identity. For many years, human identity was understood in terms of rational, logical thought. AI will benefit from broadening its conception of human identity, in particular, the insight from theology of "Imago Dei." From Descartes conclusion of "I think therefore I am," to Turing's infamous question "can a machine think?", the Western world has turned to logical thought as evidence of human identity. It is time to broaden the conception.

Chapter 10, "The Philosophy of AI," examines how the "theology of technology" can help inform the philosophical underpinnings of AI beyond the necessity for machine morality. We start with elucidating the idea of computation, from Turing machine computation as "step-by-step" algorithmic procedure, to Putnam's conceptions and "everything is computation," and Searle's "observer-related" computation. Much of AI operates with the assumption of computationalism: the idea that Turing's conception of computation offers an explanation for cognition. We consider some of the arguments for why cognitive functions are nonalgorithmic in Turing's sense. We also consider other "aspects" of human intelligence that are just as important as "thinking": aspects that are not well understood, including "emotional" intelligence and "relational/social" computing, even "consciousness" itself. The objective of this chapter is to outline the understanding of computation that dominates AI, as well as computer science and much of mathematics. This understanding of computation is essentially rule-based, expressed through formal systems such as the Post system, lambda calculus, and the Turing machine. However, for many people, the rule-based mathematical model is the undoing of computationalism, since formal systems have inherent limitations (in expressivity and deductions that can be made), but the human mind does not appear to be limited in the way that formal systems are. This chapter is necessary to provide the philosophical background to the implications that the "theology of technology" has for AI.

Chapter 11, "Principle-Based Engineering," discusses a new conception of computation. The conception is one of constraints rather than rules. The constraint-based approach "models" the constraints in operation in the system, and between the system and the environment. There are similarities with Putnam's idea that "everything is computation" because (1) computation must be "situated," and in a profound way, embedded and "incarnated" in its environment, but, there is also (2) a move away from the intuitive idea of "algorithm" as a step-by-step procedure, since a system is understood in terms of "constraints." We find some theological themes emerge in the importance of "incarnating" computation. There is also a theological theme in moving towards a constraint-based understanding of the universe, and away from an "evolutionary" comprehension, where the most general principles of the natural and human world are understood in terms of Darwin's evolutionary ideas. Principle-based engineering offers an alternative "general" mechanism over and above the artificial life school and emergent AI. In offering an alternative to the evolutionary paradigm, we can also return to the idea of "design" and "purpose" underlying intelligent systems, and the importance of considering other "general mechanisms" over and above evolution, that may just as well explain the universe and the presence of intelligent beings. We are keen to consider the theological underpinning of such "incarnated" computing, over evolutionary approaches.

Chapter 12, "Beyond Culture," concludes the examination of religion and technology. We have explored both how technology is impacting religion and, in the last few chapters, how theology impacts technology. We draw these strands together now in a consideration of the cultural impact that the nexus is having. This is the scenario of a society where technology and religion not only co-exist, but contribute mutual benefit to each other in their synergy. We start by describing the new global or "transcultural" culture that some people consider ICT technology is creating: a techno-culture that transcends particular traditional cultures. We propose the Five-Is of information, immediacy, interaction, intelligence and Internet as underpinning elements of computer-facilitated life in such a culture. We see such a transculture as a framework for a techno-religious age, a global "virtual worldview" that frames society and life in a technologically impacted, and impacting age. We also examine the consequences of not acknowledging the nexus of technology and religion, reiterating the importance of this nexus of technology and religion. Technology, like religion, represents humanity's striving to transcend. Yet religion and technology may both be regarded as "human constructions" within which it is probably impossible to transcend the human paradigm. In their respective ways, both technology and religion work together to reveal what it is to be human — in revealing the machine and in revealing the human. Both religion and technology can point humanity to the divine, the source and end of "faith."

Conclusion

Religion and Technology in the 21st Century: Faith in the E-World is a unique treatment of technology and religion. It will interest a variety of readers especially readers from:

- **Artificial intelligence:** The "synergy" that we have already outlined makes the text contribute uniquely to AI. Practically, it suggests a paradigm and philosophy of doing AI that is very important for the technical world;
- **Christian theology:** The "synergy" that we have outlined makes the text contribute uniquely to religion, particularly Christianity. Practically, it suggests a way of "doing religion" that is also important for the religious world. It raises the question of whether religion can facilitate faith, and the shape of a post-Christendom church that facilitates faith and not religion;
- **Cultural anthropology and philosophy of religion:** The text gives a rare examination of the "transcendence" offered

by five major world religions, and how technology facilitates that, assisting appreciation of how technology and religion integrate in a variety of societies. Practically, it helps comprehension of the extent of penetration of technologies into different religions, and how cultures are influenced by the synergy of technology and religion.

- **Philosophy of technology:** Those concerned about technology and its influences on humanity will be reminded of the pressing questions of the age, and encouraged to think afresh about the unique status of religion as a field impacted by technology, and the ways that technology may indeed help humanity, and not "lay waste" its nature. Practically, it offers justification for the continuation of technology, even if there were a choice to suppress it, tainting the justification of that continuation with the importance of "connecting" humanity with its "spiritual quest" and intrinsic identity and nature.

Religion and Technology in the 21st Century: Faith in the E-World will assist readers of various levels, especially those pursuing research in: (1) the impact of technology upon society, (2) the philosophy of AI, and (3) contemporary Christianity. It is a text that challenges established disciplinary boundaries, making it relevant to a wide audience.

Acknowledgments

The author would like to acknowledge the help of all involved in the collation and the review process of this book, without whose support the project could not have been satisfactorily completed.

Thanks go to all who provided constructive and comprehensive reviews and comments. The staff at Idea Group Inc. have also made significant contributions to this final publication, especially Kristin Roth, Michele Rossi, Jan Travers, and Mehdi Khosrow-Pour. Without their input, this work would not have been possible.

Finally, thanks to my husband David F. J. George for his support and love throughout this project.

Susan Ella George

University of Wales, Australia

University of South Australia, Australia

Chapter 1

Technology and Religion

"God is the second most sought after reality on the Internet."
Richard Jensen

"On a daily basis, more people use the Internet for spiritual purposes than for gambling, banking, finding a date, trading stocks, or buying and selling."
The Pew Internet & American Life Project

1.1 Introduction

This text examines technology and religion. We start by pausing to define technology. We find that the superficial definitions describe examples of technology. The deeper definitions seek to identify its nature and essence. Overall, technology is to be distinguished from science. Unlike science, technology is applied to daily life. Science seeks knowledge as an end in itself. Science can be considered to be "neutral," without any moral or ethical bias, while technology can never be neutral because it is applied. In technology, there are questions of what applications are made and what is done with the technological product.

We also consider why we are making a focus on technology, and not science. There is a long history of debate between science and religion, but not much has been said about technology and religion. The earliest reference to trades and crafts were the ancestors of technology. This sort of technology was dismissed by Christianity. This type of "technology" was found to be irrelevant to Christianity's ultimate concerns: those of salvation and resurrection. The indifference turned to an antagonism between science and religion. The disharmony peaked with the persecutions that were made against scientists by the church. The relationship turned to debate, and then each discipline went its separate ways. Some found common ground, but largely the controversy subsided. Many see science and religion as having common aims and motivations. Instead, it is technology that has risen to be the crucial point of contact with religion and secular society.

We move on to define what is meant by religion, also finding that this is not an easy topic to define. Definitions of religion may be broad enough to encompass anything that is ritualistic and social, or too narrow in that things we would naturally label religion are not captured. We may take various approaches to religion: seeing it as a social construction and as wish fulfillment, as alienation and a "human construction" that is defiance in the face of God. Definitions of religion may also offend sensibilities, suggesting that religion is the epitome of human idolatry, inhibiting God's self-revelation and undermining all that Christendom has "constructed" in church, society, theology, and doctrine. We find "virtual religion" is as hard to define, being essentially religion that is finding electronic expression. To that extent, it may simply repeat and copy conventional religion into the virtual world, or it may be "different."

Finally, we consider in more depth some of the issues that will be of interest in the nexus of religion and technology. We emphasise that it is the synergy of the two fields that is the most important aspect in this text: how each furthers the aims of the other; how the philosophy of technology is informed by the nexus as technology facilitates a spiritual quest, as technology reveals what it is to be human, and as technology is influenced by humanity, and not vice versa.

The objective of this chapter is to introduce and define the basic terms religion and technology. We also aim to motivate why the particular combination of religion and technology is of interest, and in fact, imperative to examine and reflect upon at the start of the 21st century. We also aim to outline the unique synergy that we propose is important in the nexus of the topics.

1.2 Defining Technology

Technology comes from the Greek word "tekhnologiā," meaning a systematic treatment of an art or craft (tekhnē-, skill + -logiā, -logy). It suggests craftsmanship. Here are some definitions of technology summarised from Answers.com (n.d.):

- "(a)The application of science, especially to industrial or commercial objectives. (b) The scientific method and material used to achieve a commercial or industrial objective" (Houghton Mifflin Company).
- "Applying a systematic technique, method or approach to solve a problem" (Computer Desktop Encyclopaedia).
- "(a) the practical application of science to commerce or industry. Synonym: engineering, (b) the discipline dealing with the art or science of applying scientific knowledge to practical problems. Synonyms: engineering, engineering science, applied science" (Wordnet).

Other definitions include:

- "the application of scientific advances to benefit humanity" (sln.fi.edu/franklin/glossary.html).
- "The creation of products and processes for the purpose of improving human chances for survival, comfort level, and quality of life" (www.geog.ouc.bc.ca/conted/online courses/enviroglos/t.html).
- "The practical application of knowledge, especially in a particular area such as engineering" (www.projectauditors.com/Dictionary/T.html).

High tech refers to "high technology," technology that is at the cutting edge and the most advanced currently available. It is abbreviated to "hi-tech." In terms of the innovations impacting the business world and society, Christensen (1997) distinguishes "disruptive" and "sustaining" technologies. A "disruptive technology" is a new technological innovation, product, or servicethat eventually overturns the existing dominant technology in the market. Disruptive technology is both radically different from the leading technology, and often initially performs worse than the leading technology. For example, automobiles were disruptive technology to cars and initially did not perform so well upon roads designed for horses, but the road system was updated in order to permit cars to function better. A "sustaining technology" refers to the successive incremental improvements to performance incorporated into existing product: for example, improving the performance of washing machines with ever more sophisticated wash programs, fuzzy logic controllers, mechanical balancing, and other innovations. These innovations do not revolutionise domestic laundry, but merely "improve" the product.

However, the distinction between "disruptive" and "sustaining" technologies is not always clear. Dvorak (2004) claims that there are no disruptive technologies: "There are inventions and new ideas, many of which fail while others succeed. That's it." To some extent, the distinction between these different types of cutting-edge technology is not as important, outside the economic realities of business, as the fact that some even find need to create vocabulary to talk about the increasingly rapid changes. In some ways, technology is synonymous with "change," and change that impacts the everyday life of society. That "change" is the bigger "disruption" than the technology itself.

Of the newest "virtual" technologies, the terms "post-technology" and "hyper-technology" have been coined, or "meta-technology" (Mitcham, 1995). This term captures the progressive development of a global electromedia infrastructure and its culture. Mitcham reminds us that today "we live in a new interrelating or interconnecting of the realms. Increasingly it is recognized that science depends on technology as much as technology has been reputed to depend on science. Economics implicates politics and vice versa, politics implicates religion and vice versa, art even implicates economics and vice versa" (Mitcham, 1995). This "inter-connecting of the realms" is part of meta-technology. He further sees that the best instance of this meta-technology is the World Wide Web. Mitcham says "What is being created is what might be called a virtual common culture in large part through technology, the most visible instance of which is currently the World Wide Web. It is this which, for want of a better word, I refer to as a meta-technology" (Mitcham, 1995). In his definitions, Mitcham moves beyond the "technical" into the sociophilosophical. Many would still classify the World Wide Web as an information and communication technology, albeit an "infra-structure" technology that does cut across every discipline.

Beyond these "superficial" definitions of technology, there have been many attempts in philosophy to define the essence of technology, to distinguish between modern and premodern technologies, to draw out the nature of technology, to form typologies of technology and other. For example, here is a sample of the range of views on technology, its nature and essence:

Martin Heidegger (1977) understood humanity and its relation to technology in terms of "standing reserves." We loose sight of our essence, as we become "users" of the world around us, including other humans.

Karl Marx (1977) wrote of technology and its effects on society. Marx raised the question of technological determinism-is it our society that determines the direction of our technology, or is it our technology that determines the direction of our society?

Langdon Winner (1986) felt that technologies are forms of life, and they can engender a world around them. There are two types of technologies for Winner, "non-inherently political technologies" and "inherently political technologies." The so-called non-inherently political technologies are those which carry no political implications when they are created and in use. Inherently political technologies are ones that were created with intentions to have political implications.

Florman (1986) believes in technology as a self-correcting process: each time we create a technology it has both positive and negative implications. We must accept technology for what it is, a self-correcting process, and take that into account whenever we use it.

Margaret Benston (1988) has written some material on technology as a language. She understands technology as a language for action and self-expression, but finds men control this language, and therefore this makes technology a "gendered language."

In seeking to define technology, it is important to distinguish technology from science. Aristotle made the most famous reflections on science and technology (Barnes, 1984). Aristotle drew four important distinctions that are frequently repeated still today, giving them a kind of common sense status:

1. Science (episteme) is about the unchangeable, while technology (techne) is about the changeable.
2. Theoretical science (theoretike) and poietical science (poietike) with regard to the objects' different principles of motion. The objects of techne or poietical science, have their principle of motion from without, that is, they are moved or generated by the technician's activity, according to his aims that may change from day to day.
3. Science starts from sensations of concrete things and aims at general knowledge, whereas technology goes one step further and applies general knowledge back to concrete things.
4. Scientists look for theoretical knowledge (theoria), that is, an activity having an end in itself; technicians produce new things (poiesis), and such an activity has always an end in something else. That is, the purpose of scientific activity is just that activity itself, whereas poietical activity is always good for something else.

Traditionally, technology has been seen as "flowing from" science. The idea is that science discovers the knowledge, and technology later applies it. The distinction between pure and applied research often hinges on whether there is an immediate application of the knowledge. While science has traditionally been regarded as "coming before" technology and enabling advances in technology, increasingly there is a reciprocal relationship. That is, through technology, science is enabled to advance. In this sense, technology must come first before the next scientific breakthrough can be made.

One undeniable distinction of technology is that it becomes part of everyday life. Science may remain in the research lab, but technology is found in the home, the workplace, the supermarket, the church, and the mosque. Technology cannot be separated from everyday life, and is becoming increasingly pervasive, "incarnating" itself in every walk of life. Technology is also often "hidden" and "unobtrusive," so that we may not observe the extent to which technology is permeating life. This gives technology a unique "invisible" dimension, which science does not have. It makes technology potentially quite "dangerous" since it is not always readily perceived. The "assumed benefit" that often accompanies technology, adds to the importance of considering the role that technology does play in society.

Finally, and in resonance with Aristotle's fourth distinction, technology cannot be "neutral." Science is cognitive in attitude and aiming to obtain "objective" knowledge. Technology is applied. It cannot escape the question of whether its use is moral and ethical or not. This is one of the biggest distinguishing aspects. The pursuit of knowledge without application is a different endeavour to that with application. Of course there is the general question of whether knowledge is used to make a weapon or produce medicine, and once a particular application has been selected, there are ethical questions of just how and where that product is used. While science may claim to be "neutral," technology never can.

1.3 Why Technology and Not Science?

Given these unique features of technology, there are clear reasons why technology, not science, is of more concern when its role in society is to be considered. However, in the context of religion, it has traditionally been science, not technology, that has been of interest. We pause to consider why a particular focus is being made in this text upon "technology," and not "science," given its dual interest in religion.

One reason that technology and religion has not been a long-debated topic is the relative recency of modern technology as a recognised "influence" in society. It is true that Augustine, in *The City of God,* presents an early reflection on religion and technology. He carefully describes many trades and crafts of the first millennium. He points out that we may find solace in them, but that they have absolutely no significance for Christianity's aim to be redeemed from the fall. In technology having "no significance" to Christianity, it has historically meant that more is said about "science and religion."

Science came into conflict with religion as early as the 17th century. At that time, Galileo (1632) was persecuted by the Roman Catholic Church for his view that the earth went round the sun. Galileo's views on science and religion (as seen from his Letter to the Grand Dutchess Christina) are very radical for his time. He suggests that physical sciences must be separated from theological studies. This is because the goals of the two disciplines are totally different: theology is concerned with salvation of the soul, while the sciences are concerned with understanding of nature. He believes that the clergy apply faith where there is none involved. Galileo suggested that it is a job of scientists to examine nature, and it is the business of theologists to make sure the Bible agrees with it, the reasoning being that nature is no less a manifestation of God than the Holy Bible itself.

Also, in the 17th century, Bacon delineated the principles of the inductive method. This method constituted a breakthrough in the approach to science. Bacon claims that a true science must be free of religious tenets. He described the different uses and abuses of religion. These can either further or impede the advancement of science. Perhaps most notable of them is the idea of differentiating true faith from superstition. The true faith is derived from the scriptures and applied only to the matters of salvation. Superstition is a dangerous mixture of philosophy and religion. It is applied to matters where there is no faith involved, such as politics and natural sciences. Bacon suggests that religion is not a means of establishing physical truths, because it does not rely on practical experimentation. He also suggests that since the Bible was written centuries ago, it lacks the information scientists established from natural experiments. This means using it to explain the natural phenomena is not appropriate.

The message of scientists from the 17th century onwards has been that science must be free of religious and ethical constraints. This is necessary in order for humans to master nature. Not surprisingly, this view created antagonism between science and religion. The antagonism was particularly significant given the church-state alliance that was Christendom. In this ideology, the state religion was Christianity. This religion was imposed upon the entire Roman Empire in the fourth century; lead by what became the Roman

Catholic Church. In the 16th century, the Protestants broke away from the Catholics in the Magisterial Reformation. However, the political alliance between religious bodies and governments still existed, and the church had much authority to implement controls over the populace of Europe, and in many cases its rulers. In that climate, where religion was married to politics, many scientists were persecuted for their "antireligious" views. Scientists were regarded as subversive to the state. The political situation also created tensions between Protestants and Catholics and other religious people. Many were killed for their religious views.

In this situation of state persecution, America was founded. It was to be a society that would demonstrate religious "tolerance" among the religious and between science and religion. The American constitution took effect in 1789. The various forms of Christianity would flourish and science would be released from its constraining quarters. At that point in history, technology was not an issue for the religious to consider. To a certain extent, the separation of church and state in America did achieve these aims. Europe also continued to emerge from Christendom influences with the French Revolution. This was a notable landmark, making France a highly secular society. The church-state alliance was weakened, persecutions for scientific pursuits were gradually eliminated, and the mood fostered for intellectualism and scholasticism. This brought the masses to react against religion and the church in the Revolution. The antireligious climate continued.

In the 19th century, there was a stunning example of science gaining widespread respect. The ideas of Charles Darwin gained a marked following among the masses, despite being at odds with the teachings of Christianity. Darwin introduced his ideas in two separate treatises. The first outlined the basic principles of a theory called evolution (1859); the second applyed them to humankind (1871). In his later work, *The Descent of Man,* he explained how humans shared a common ancestor with apes. This "common ancestor" extends to all creation, and is perhaps the most stunning tenet of evolution: humans and oak trees, whales and spiders are all related, coming from the same source. It was not a cosmological theory, also explaining this "original source." Darwin's ideas, nevertheless, rapidly gained popularity.

The popularity of Darwin's work reflects an increasing "admiration" for "intellectualism" and "scholasticism" within society, as much as it does "scientific truth" reigning over religion. Even though Darwin's theory was concerned with processes and not with origins, it has been the focus of much 20th century "debate" between science and religion in the realm of "creation." Some religious fundamentalist attempted to curtail the teaching of evolution in schools, and only brought shame and scorn upon the "religious perspective," leading to the eventual "triumph" of evolutionary ideas as more "scientific." Religious creation accounts were considered "incredible," while evolution is presented as more "credible."

Darwin's work may also mark a widespread antireligious reaction to the political control and persecutions of the church in Christendom. Religious interest certainly dwindled into the 20th century. The population masses were brought to react against religion and the church. The rationalism accompanying science led many to find "faith" wanting in the light of "reason." The antagonism between religion and science was reversed, and it became the scientific secular world that came to shun the religious, although not with such horrific persecutions and crimes as the religiously inclined had inflicted upon the secular world.

After the antagonism between science and religion reached a peak, there were attempts later in the 20th century to integrate science and religion. Many considered that they were not necessarily disciplines bound to be at loggerheads in a confrontation of "faith" and "reason." Many suggested that science and religion were, in fact, related. *The Daily Telegraph*, London, May 26, 1999 reports "Science and religion (are) no longer seen as incompatible." Rather, science and religion are both searching for truth, asking different questions on the route.

Richard Bube (1995) discusses seven different fundamental patterns he finds in relating science and Christian theology. He presents the "complementary insights" pattern, noting that science and theology tell us different kinds of things about the same things. Each provides valid insights into the nature of reality from different perspectives. It demands that both scientific and religious perspectives be brought to bear on the same reality, and is slightly different to the observation that science asks "how" and religion asks "why." Attempts to integrate science and religion and show they have the same mutual essence are also found. Many see that they share mutual goals and have common themes.

While antagonists existed on both sides, a certain "co-existence" has been found. Only the most militant of rationalists continued to argue their points on both sides, for or against science or religion. In the wake of ever declining religious adherence and interest in organised religion, the battle may well have been won. The masses had come to accept that "science" was not so alien. Remaining religious adherents were by then entrenched in a society where suddenly the fruits of science–technology–had already overtaken it.

Thus, it is at the start of the 21st century that we choose to focus on "technology and religion" and not "science and religion." It is a situation where the church has lost a lot of its Christendom power; where science gains more popularity than organised religion; where technology is already entrenched in society; and where Augustine's conclusion that technology has "absolutely no significance for Christianity's central aim of redemption" is long overdue for revision. Because of the pervasiveness of technology in the everyday lives of people across the world, technology cannot be ignored and deemed irrelevant to any area of life. Because of the new technologies and ways that it is being applied, it most certainly cannot be deemed irrelevant to the "redemptive" aim of Christianity. There are many ways that technology itself is bringing the Christian message to the world. There are ways it is being a vehicle through which salvation is being found. In technology, we have not an adversary to religion, but a tool: albeit a tool that philosophers of technology may consider to "lay waste" our nature. Technology and religion promise particularly interesting topics to consider in historical light of the "science and religion" debate. In technology, both science and religion have met.

Paul Davies (1983) finds that the increase in science and technology has actually been fuelling the "spiritual" quest of humanity in various ways. With others, he considers that people are no less "spiritual" in a technological society, and are even looking to technology itself for "comfort" in an uncertain world; people are paying only lip service to rational thought and science; science is becoming a sort of superstition, and the basic human spiritual quest is unchanged. Combined with unrealised promises of technology and the shift to ever-greater degrees of moderninity and post-moderninity, technology may unwittingly be fuelling a shift from the "scientific" to the "religious" once again. However, people are not turning to the conventional religion and organised

Christianity of Christendom that has in so many ways betrayed them. They are turning to new technological religious expressions that have the "comfort" and "assurance" of science underpinning them, where religion has failed them.

In particular, we find information and communication technologies (ICT) as a technology that is crucial to investigate at this juncture of history. It is a technology that is permeating society, and spreading rapidly throughout the Western and developing world. ICT is impinging upon almost every facet of life in both direct and indirect ways. ICT is merging with intelligent technologies to deliver even more advanced communications. It is merging with medical science and agriculture, engineering, and all manner of disciplines as the evolution becomes ever more rapid with technologies merging with technologies. Some make predictions of a "technological singularity," where technology just changes so rapidly that humanity cannot keep up with it. Vinge (1993) traces the concept of technical singularity to von Neuman. The idea is that intelligent machines will advance themselves through automatic programming, without the need for human intervention. This will create a world that changes ever more quickly, combined with a world where machines and people are ever more closely integrated.

So, a focus is being made upon technology and religion because the historical debate between science and religion has shifted to new ground. Technology's impact upon every facet of life, its rapid spread and development, its invisibility, and other characteristics make it important to consider in its own right. The fact that ICT is being used as a tool to spread religious messages and foster religious communities means that the most ancient challenge, that "technology has nothing to do with Christianity's aims," is defunct. It impacts upon every facet of human life–including religion–and cannot be ignored. In the 21st century, we consider that the most interesting points of contact are not between science and religion, but between technology and religion.

1.4 Defining Religion

Religion does not prove an easy topic to define. Definitions of religion are often too narrow, and exclude many of the belief systems that most people will agree are religious: or they are too vague and ambiguous, leading one to conclude that just about any and everything is actually a religion. Definitions of religion are rarely neutral, and favour the institutions with which one is in sympathy while penalising those to which one is hostile. Mc Grath (2001) distinguishes between two fundamentally different approaches that may be adopted when attempting to give an account of religion. The "detached" approach seeks to give account of religions from the standpoint of philosophy or social sciences, often aiming not to suggest a monotheistic, moral system such as Christianity. The "committed" approach seeks to give an account of the origins and functions of religions from a Christian perspective.

McGrath (2001) also provides some pointers to the question of what is religion at http://www.blackwellpublishing.com/mcgrath/textbook/chap1Q_A/chap0017a.asp, where five approaches can be identified. These approaches usefully categorise the general "stance" taken on religion and its role:

- **Religion as a corruption of an intrinsic religion of nature:** This concept of religion is directly traceable to the Enlightenment and its confidence in human rationality. Religion was a "husk" to be broken through to find a more original, deeper, universal, non-superstitious original.
- **Religion as an objectification or projection of human feeling:** This concept of religion stresses that what is central in religion is the subjective human experience. God is the projection of all human fears and hopes, in a similar way that Schleiermacher found religious feeling or piety to be an expression of divinity within. Feuerbach simply asks the question, "Why must it be divinity within and not merely human nature itself'?"
- **Religion as a product of socioeconomic alienation:** McGrath finds that "The extension by Marx on Feuerbach is Marx's placement of religion as a human impulse or projection into a material context, the result of socioeconomic realities on human psyche and culture." God is merely the "reflection" of alienated human beings. However, the alienation within human life is due to material socioeconomic forces, not metaphysical forces.

- **Religion as a wish fulfilment; as a ritual within society:** Sigmund Freud's assessment of religion as wish fulfillment is similar to Feuerbach, in that Freud is keen to emphasize the existential aspect of religion, as the expression of human fear and longing, but relocates it to human development.
- **Religion as human invention or idolatry:** Barth and Bonhoeffer, following the Apostle Paul (Romans 1:18-25), stated that religion is a purely human construction understood as the attempt by humanity to find God on its terms-the making, in short, of an idol.

McGrath's analysis of the approaches to religion usefully categorise the different perspectives on religion, or about what it is and what has created it, but they do not answer what may be considered a religion. Smart (1992) notes that some of the more successful attempts at a definition identify a set of markers, such as practical and ritual, experiential and emotional, narrative and mythical, doctrinal and philosophical, ethical and legal, social and institutional, and the material. The more markers present, the more "religiouslike" the belief system is. Erickson (1998) also notes, religion has proved a hard topic to define. However, he does see certain common features, including a belief in something higher than the individual human person (and this may be a personal god or a whole collection of supernatural beings, a "force" or even humanity itself). Typically, there is a distinction between sacred and secular, extending to persons, objects, places, and practises, and some relationship with the higher object.

One important element of religion is its communal and social expression. This aspect is often used to distinguish religion from spirituality: used to refer to the more devotional aspects of faith and interior individual "mystical" experiences (McGrath, 2001). The communal and social expression entails inclusion in a social community, with accompanying "rights" and "responsibilities," personal fulfillment through that community, as well as spiritual and emotional benefits from that community. Also, national religions usually have to do with the common bonds of a shared language, culture, ethnic background, or a shared history. In this respect, with "national religions," there is no distinction between the "religious" group and the wider community-they are one. In contrast, "universal religions" have divorced themselves from a specific society to such an extent that they have become "portable," and are often oriented towards converting people of other faiths to be part of their "community." To some extent, the communal and social elements of religion make religion fulfil a "social" need, the broad ritual actions of a community and need have no reference to the divine or supernatural.

If religion is hard to define, the term "virtual religion" also poses a problem. "Virtual" is derived from the Latin word vertus, meaning truth: that which is "virtual" looks like reality, but is not completely real. Thus, the term "virtual" is often applied to the e-world of computer-mediated communication, a world that is essentially intangible "information" and "interactions." The term "virtual religion" may conjure up the idea that a "virtual religion" is something "approximating" religion. While it may be this, it is also that "religion" that is finding electronic expression. Virtual religion is religion that occurs in the virtual world.

It is probably necessary to distinguish virtual religion from the "divinising of technology," and ways that technology comes to fulfil a religious role in society. Strong (1991) has the view that technology itself has become a religion, or a modern day "god" of society. Technology itself becomes an object of desire, as we seek maximum availability of a technology and see it as progress when the availability of technological goods is increased. Materialism strives for more commodities, and the being is enslaved to that which would free it: in the religious sense that Christians find one is enslaved to that which is not God. In a similar vein, Paul Summit (1993) cites Fore's (1987) observations that television technology is fulfilling the function that religious institutions once fulfilled. He finds ". . . in many ways television is beginning to replace the institution that historically has performed the functions we have understood as religious. Television, rather than the churches, is becoming the place where people find a worldview which reflects what to them is of ultimate value, and which justifies their behaviour and way of life." Summit sees that "media in general and not just television that is replacing the church as center of what we understand as religious." Thus, there is certainly evidence that technology is fulfilling a religious role in society.

Barths' observations on religion as a human construction is to be distinguished from the approach to religion that might seek to explain it in terms of the science of humanity: anthropology or sociology or psychology. What is objected to in the "human construction" is the human attempt to construct a system of beliefs that restrict God's freedom to self-reveal. In reference to Christianity, they rejected the sense that human institutions could be conflated with God in a direct manner. This was important in the context of German nationalism and the anti-Semitic degeneration of German Christianity. Barth sees the phenomenon of religion at work as much in Christianity as in other "religions." Religion is often not a God-revealed principle, so much as human idea.

At this point, we pause to consider what is meant by "faith." "Faith" is often contrasted with "reason," as if faith were unreasonable. However, faith and reason are essential aspects of all human activities, including science, technology, and Christian theology. Science, technology, and theology make assumptions (faith) and draw conclusions from them (reason). The belief that the universe is rationally comprehensible is an assumption of science. Faith, in this assumption, not only motivates scientists to do research, but actually makes it possible and effective. Thus, we can find similarities between "faith" and "reason" that do not necessarily set them in opposition. If "faith" and "reason" are unfairly set in opposition; then "faith" and "belief" are often unfairly confused. Thus, it is necessary to make a distinction between "faith" and "belief."

Faith is not identical to belief. Belief is more general, essentially being mental ascent to certain "propositions" held to be true. As we alluded earlier, scientists can have belief, for example, that water boils at 100C (at least at zero altitude). Repeated observation of a given event may provide evidence to support the belief, until it is eventually given status as a "fact," that is "repeatable" and hence "true" in absolute terms, at least until demonstrated to the contrary, or qualified to be "true" under certain conditions. This same mental ascent can be found in the various world religions, which as we shall see, all have different "beliefs" or "teachings"/doctrines. Giving mental ascent to teaching is "belief." "Faith" has a narrower meaning.

Theologically, "faith" is defined in two ways, being (1) mental ascent to a body of doctrine and also (2) an attitude, a lifestyle and a relational expression of "trust" between personal entities. Thus, it is possible for a Christian to express "faith" in God in relational terms, rather than merely through mental ascent to certain propositions that may be held about the nature of the divine. The relational definition of faith may require mental ascent to certain propositions (such as the existence of the divine), but it is not the totality of faith. To a large extent, "religion" has perpetuated the definition of faith that produces mental ascent to certain propositions. In cases where these propositions are particularly dubious and untenable, erroneous or unprovable, a mockery is made of the "faith" of Christianity. Ultimately, this "relational" faith is a divine gift; it cannot be taught, or caught, studied or mustered up by willpower. This is a basic theological point about "faith" that points to the transcendence of God. God alone can break into the human paradigm and bestow "faith"; human construction achieves nothing.

1.5 Why Technology and Religion?

In this section, we pause to consider the question of why religion and technology are being considered. We are certainly not the first ones to consider this nexus, but do so from a unique perspective, one that considers both (1) the way that religion is being influenced, and (2) how technology may benefit from a broader basis. That is, we bring out the synergy of how each can assist and benefit the other. Figure 1 illustrates this unique synergy of technology and religion, which this text explores.

Most work in the field considers the influence of technology upon religion from a sociological perspective. It is interested in the way that the Internet is changing religious expression through the rise of virtual religion; it is interested in the way that different cultures may be appropriating technology for religious expression in their religious context; and it is interested in the rising phenomena of virtual Christianity within the West. Sometimes there is a distinctly Christian interest in religion and technology, where the focus is analysis of contemporary society, and how religious bodies may appropriate technology for their purposes. While we do consider this sociological aspect, we do not confine ourselves to it. For we are also interested in the way that this utilisation of technology in religion intersects with more philosophical questions: from a religious perspective, whether the use of technology is merely a different expression of religion, or whether virtual communities constitute something entirely differ-

Figure 1. Technology meets religion in the 21st century

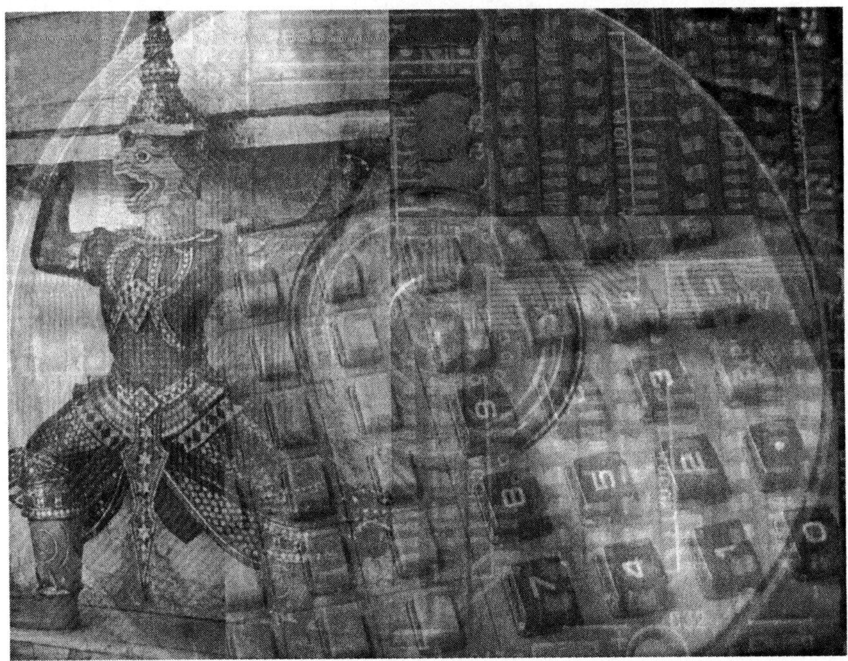

ent in nature; from a technological perspective, there is the pressing question of how technology is benefiting humanity and not "laying waste its nature" in ever increasing automation, and so forth. The way that technology has been used as a tool in a spiritual quest is part of the answer to this "technological determinism" question.

Perhaps most uniquely, this text is interested in how technology itself may benefit from a broader basis. There are some examples in the debate between science and religion where the intersection of theological themes with scientific themes has been explored. Some of the most recent work draws parallels between technical principles and theological principles, although this does not specifically benefit technology: it merely helps contextualise theological themes in the contemporary technical world. Also, answers to the ethical questions surrounding application technology have drawn upon theological and religious knowledge; this provides some benefit to the philosophy of technology, but the actual daily practice, in technical realms, is not affected. This is where this text starts to make some quite novel headway examining intelligent technologies. In the endeavour to achieve "human-like behaviour," some fundamental questions of a theological nature are encountered, such as the distinguishing aspect of human morality in behaviour, the corruption and restoration of this moral nature. There are questions that intersect with the philosophy of AI, such as the nature of human identity; whether "computation" could ever produce that identity, and its corresponding behaviour; whether and how that human identity needs to be "situated" or can be "abstracted," as many AI endeavours hope.

In the following points, we summarise some of the reasons why the nexus of religion and technology is important to explore:

- **The "science and religion" debate:** To some extent the topic combination is part of the debate between science and religion. In daily life, it is technology, rather than science, that has greater immediate impact upon people. If science and religion is considered an important topic, in many ways technology and religion is even more so, because of the immediacy and pervasiveness of technology.
- **The common underlying themes:** There are common themes underlying both religion and technology, the main one being the idea of transcending human limitation. Both religion and technology maybe considered "human constructions" in this goal of transcendence. Huang (2005) reports how Fuchs believes "they have common goals: improving society and transcending human frailty." Understanding the driving forces of the two fields puts philosophical perspective upon the fields.
- **Sociologically:** There is sociological interest in the impact that technology has upon the expression of religion within society. From the earliest times in human history, there have been important attempts by philosophers and theologians to explain and examine social life. Today, sociologists are also concerned with these themes.
- **Cultural anthropology:** Anthropology is also interested in the cultural change that technology is bringing to the world. There is the question of whether technology is changing the world's religiosity; making people more or less religious, and

influencing a component of humanity that, from the most ancient of times, has been integral to the species.

- **Religion:** The nexus of the disciplines is of interest to religion itself: to comprehend the phenomena of virtual religion, and the ways that technology may help further religion's goals.
- **The philosophy of technology:** The question of how technology may benefit humanity without laying waste its nature may find answer in the "spiritual quest" that it is facilitating; technology assisted religion serves humanity, as a special case tool.
- **The historical origins of a technological society and its future:** Historically, the emergence of a technological society from Christendom represents an interesting start to the technology-religion nexus. Originally, the dominant societal force was religion; after a period of persecution, science rose to the forefront; toward the end of the 20th century, many found a synthesis in science and religion. The 21st century may witness further synthesis in a techno-religious age.

As already indicated, the novel perspective that this text brings particularly includes how technology may benefit from a broader basis. In technology itself, theological themes inform intelligent technologies and the attempts to mimic human action and being. In the philosophy of AI, there are many unanswered questions surrounding the nature of "computation" and just how a machine could implement that "computation" from which human behaviour and identity emerge. Taking theological themes such as "creation in the image of God" to explain the intrinsic nature of identity, and "incarnation" to point to the importance of the physical in humanity, assist with foundational assumptions of AI. In this application of theology, the basis of technology is broadened. AI already draws upon diverse fields to its benefit: from mathematics to psychology, philosophy to linguistics. Thus, intelligent technologies will particularly benefit from a broader perspective, recognising that the theological is also a component of this unique human realm, and the philosophy surrounding it.

References

Answers.com. (n.d.). *The definition of technology*. Houghton Mifflin Company. Retrieved from http://www.answers.com/technology

Barnes, J. (Ed.) (1984). *Aristoteles: The complete works of Aristotle*. Princeton, NJ: Princeton University Press.

Benston, M. (1988). Women's voices/Men's voices: Technology as language. In C. Kramarae (Ed.), *Technology and women's voices: Keeping in touch*. New York: Routledge and Kegan Paul.

Bube, R. H. (1995) *Putting it all together: Seven patterns for relating science and the Christian faith*. University Press of America.

Christensen, C. M. (1997). *The innovator's dilemma*. Cambridge, MA: Harvard Business School Press.

Darwin, C. (1859). *On the origin of species by means of natural selection*. London: John Murray.

Darwin, C. (1871). *The descent of man and selection in relation to sex* (2nd ed. revised & augmented). London: John Murray.

Davies, P. (1983). *God and the new physics*. Penguin.

Dvorak, J. C. (2004). The myth of disruptive technology. *PC Mag.com*. Retrieved from http://www.pcmag.com/article2/0,1759,1628049,00.asp

Erickson, M. (1998). *Christian theology* (2nd ed.). Baker Books.

Florman, S. (1986). Technology and the tragic view. In A. H. Teich (Ed.), *Technology and the future* (4th ed.). New York: St Martin's Press.

Fore, W. (1987). *Television and religion: The shaping of faith, values, and culture*. Minneapolis, MN: Augsburg Publishing House.

Galilei, G. (1967). Dialogue concerning the two chief world systems (S. Drake, Trans.). University of California Press. (Original work published 1632).

Heidegger, M. (1977). *The question concerning technology and other essays* (W. Lovitt, Trans.). New York: Harper and Row.

Huang. (2005).

Marx, K. (1977). Preface to a critique of political economy. In D. McLellan (Ed.), *Karl Marx selected writing*. New York: Oxford University Press.

McGrath, A. (2001). *Christian theology: An introduction*. Blackwell.

Mitcham, C. (1995, Fall). Notes toward a philosophy of metatechnology. In D. Baird (Ed.), *Society for philosophy and technology 1*(1-2). Retrieved from http://scholar.lib.vt.edu/ejournals/SPT/v1_n1n2/mitcham.html

Smart, N. (1992). *The world's religions*. Cambridge University Press.

Strong, D. (1991). The promise of technology versus God's promise in Job. *Theology Today, 48*(2). Retrieved from http://theologytoday.ptsem.edu/jul1991/v48-2-article4.htm

Summitt, P. (1993). *Future technology as religion*. Retrieved from http://www.summittnewmedia.com/Paul/nonfiction/Religion.htm

Vinge, V. (1993, Winter). The coming technological singularity. *Whole Earth Review*. Retrieved from http://www.ugcs.caltech.edu/~phoenix/vinge/vinge-sing.html

Winner, L. (1986). *The whale and the reactor: A search for limits in an age of high technology*. Chicago, IL: The University of Chicago Press.

Chapter 2

The Philosophy of Technology

"Technology is a gift of God. After the gift of life it is perhaps the greatest of God's gifts. It is the mother of civilizations, of arts and of sciences."

Freema Dyson

"The world is very different now. For man holds in his mortal hands the power to abolish all forms of human poverty, and all forms of human life."

John F. Kennedy

2.1 Introduction

We start by outlining some of the problems concerning technology and society that have led people to reflect upon it. One of the most poignant questions is that of "technological determinism" and the extent to which technology is "under control" vs. the extent to which it controls society. The speed of change, the assumption that technology is beneficial, the uptake and geographical spread of technology across cultures, and the extent to which technology creates a never-ending cycle of increased complexity are just some of the "issues" that require examination in the question of technology's impact upon society.

We continue to look at some of the approaches and solutions to these questions of "technology." We find the "philosophy of technology" as a relatively young field that has emerged in recent years that does seek to reflect upon technology. The engineering and humanities approach to the philosophy of technology can be identified, with some of the earliest contributions coming from Heidegger. Other more pragmatic approaches can be found, together with those that question whether the field has already ended. Technology is embedded in society to such an extent that we cannot isolate it and reflect on it, apart from anything else. It is as if there is a return to the pre-modern condition where there was not a necessity for a separate philosophy of technology.

Finally, we consider some "issues" of technology that impact individuals. In general, the "technological determinism" question is concerned with technology's impact upon society, and the "philosophy of technology" is concerned with approaches to understanding the situation at the "macro," or societal level. In this section, we look at some of the ways in which technology impacts individuals. Of course, society is made of individuals, but we find the exercise raises some very different questions when concerns are framed in a less "collective" manner; when technology's influences on the identity of individual people are at stake. We find some have spoken of the positive influence of technology upon "self" as well as "issues" that we see as more problematic, including (1) the "techno-phobia" that is bred by actual technological disasters, and the failures of technology, (2) the "self-sufficiency" that technology fuels, increasing people's autonomy, (3) the "spiritual degradation" created where people are reduced to "machines" in "producer-consumer" society, and (4) the confusion that technology creates about personal identity.

The objective of this chapter is to raise some of the issues that have emerged with recent developments in technology. We want to bring out the technological determinism question, and some of the concerns about "technology and society" that the philosophy of technology has raised and started to address. We also want to contrast these concerns about technology and society with concerns about technology impinging and influencing individual people. Of course, society and individuals cannot be separated, but there is a need to consider "personal identity" and "technology" as well as the broader questions of technology and society. Philosophically, when "essential being" is located within the world, technology, or any other aspects of the world, becomes a dangerous threat to human identity. When such "identity" is located in that which transcends the world, perhaps in God's image, there is the possibility for coexistence with technology without threat to essential identity.

2.2 What is the Problem: Technological Determinism

Perhaps the key question concerning technology is the extent to which it is "under control." Technological determinism is the question of "Who's shaping who?" Is technology shaping society, or society shaping technology? Thomas P. Hughes, in Technological momentum (Smith & Marx, 1994), argues that it is not black and white. "A technological system can be both a cause and an effect; it can shape or be shaped by society. As they grow larger and more complex, systems tend to be more shaping of society and less shaped by it." Thus, it is a sliding scale according to age and embeddedness of the technology. Once a technological system has human values assigned to it, and the physical underpinnings of those values are in place, it becomes increasingly hard to affect change in that system. While technologies may initially be social products, susceptible to democratic controls, they rapidly become more "autonomous."

Another perspective on technological determinisim is that provided by Andrew Feenberg. Feenberg has identified that in recent years, technology studies have benefited greatly from the adoption of a historicist approach, as derived from the work of Thomas Kuhn in the history of science. Feenberg explains: "Instead of regarding technological progress as a deterministic sequence of developments, we have learned to see it as a contingent process that could lead in many different directions." (http://www-rohan.sdsu.edu/faculty/feenberg/method1.html). Kuhn's most renowned work is *The Structure of Scientific Revolutions*. Kuhn argued that science is not a steady, cumulative acquisition of knowledge. Instead, science is "a series of peaceful interludes punctuated by intellectually violent revolutions."

After such revolutions, "one conceptual worldview is replaced by another." Kuhn was responsible for popularizing the term paradigm, which he described as essentially a collection of beliefs shared by scientists, a set of agreements about how problems are to be understood. It appears Feenberg is suggesting that technology progresses like science, in a series of paradigm shifts.

The extent to which technology shapes society is not unrelated to the speed with which change occurs and is adopted. Unwitting, cultural choices occur as technology is used. For example, a bridge linking two villages across a river is more than just a bridge aiding communication. The social, economic, and transport networks are altered, as well as the whole landscape of the individual villages, creating something new. The bridge has not just impacted "transport," but a whole realm of other human concerns. Or the existence of a time-keeping mechanism, such as a clock, goes far beyond gears and mainsprings. Dutch (2004) explains the subtle shaping influence, as a society with accurate time-keeping devices emerged to be very different to one without such a measured sense of time. As that technology becomes entrenched within society, it becomes harder and harder to change, and we may not realise the influences that it is having. Thus, technology has some very subtle influences on society that we may not notice, and which is adopted with ever increasing speed.

Technology is often assumed to be beneficial. Advertising and other promotion ensures that people are persuaded of its benefit. Consumers are unlikely to be in the best position to evaluate the technology when advertising promotes a need and convinces people the technology will benefit them. For the technically minded, being reflective about technology is often too "philosophical." Simply achieving "objectivity" about technology is very difficulty. But there are many problems with this naïve assumption that it will "improve life." Even apparently uncontroversial "benefits," such as better preventative medicine for health care, may solve the immediate question of health, but have repercussions in other areas that are more negative. For example, improvements in preventative medicine may lead to greater "isolation" as people stay healthier and need less "help." This may affect social networks, even ultimately human compassion in caring for those who are sick.

In one of the earliest examples of technology, the wool and cotton mills in England between 1811 and 1817, an anti-technology movement spread rapidly through England. Dubbed the Luddites, after Ned Ludd, an English worker who had supposedly destroyed weaving machinery in the late 1700s, the movement advocated destroying the labor-saving machines created by the industrial revolution. In particular, they attacked wool and cotton mills. While the movement had an underlying economic motivation, the term Luddite has come to mean one who opposes technology and technologic advances. The anti-technology movement of the Luddites stands in interesting contrast to the anti-technology movement of today. Today many feel "trapped on machine treadmills" of the very type that the initial industrial revolution replaced.

Technology also leads some to see society as trapped on machine treadmills. Sometimes we continue to apply technology solutions to problems that technology created, instead of looking at root causes. Thus, we become dependent on new machines to solve the mess left by the old, and ever add to the technological complexity of society and our lives. For example, too much of the rich food and a life of physical ease means we need new anti-obesity technologies, or vitamins to enhance the "natural" diet that many in the West are missing. Florman (1986) believes in technology as a self-correcting process. Each time we create a technology it has both positive and negative implications, but the next time we create technology it is to correct the negative aspects of the previous one, and so on in a continuous cycle. In a technologically determined society, machines demand machines, and we no longer have much say in determining direction, only forecasting coming apocalypses and exciting new software revisions.

Related to this assumed benefit is the fact that the technological has become almost synonymous with Western lifestyle and culture. The association can unnecessarily override the underlying political or religious context and change the society in ways that it need not, and which may not be beneficial. While Western society may have infrastructure for health and education, agriculture and manufacturing and other, it is breaking down at its heart in family life. Relationships are failing, children are turning to crime, and in many places society is crumbling. In contrast, simpler communities, in societies without technology, are still living as close-knit villages, where relationships are primary and everyone is part of an extended family.

Dreyfus and Spinosa (1977) identified the key question for our generation, as one of reflection on technology: its role in humanity, and how we relate to it. Yet this "philosophical" questioning is sometimes the last consideration. To some extent, even when some recognition is given that a technology has to be evaluated, there is the problem that people will not necessarily agree on the "values." This is a general product of what some have called the post-modern condition. Values depend upon a worldview, and that will colour whether a particular technology is meritorious. For example, if "productivity" or "efficiency" or "ease" or "pleasure" are valued in the worldview, then naturally, technology that furthers these aims will be favoured. A worldview that values "freedom" may not appreciate a "big brother" surveillance system, while a society that values "security" may see such infringements as necessary and desirable for safety. The extent to which technology supports these "desirable" aspects of society is the extent to which the technology is beneficial. Thus, worldview makes it hard to make a "neutral" assessment of technology, even if the task is recognised as necessary.

Gordon L. Ziniewicz presents three unhelpful views about technology in the context of social change. These are that (1) Technology is a good thing. It liberates human beings and brings about prosperity (utopia); (2) Technology is a bad thing. It is an autonomous force that threatens individuality, freedom, and the environment and (3) Technology is not as important as the first two groups think. History has shown that people can and have adapted to changes in technology. He finds that all three of these views are oversimplifications that fail to grasp how technology causes social change and how it affects the future.

Noble (1999) demonstrates that modern man's enchantment with things technological was inspired by, and grounded in religious expectations and the quest for transcendence and salvation. The two early impulses behind the urge to advance in science, he claims, are the conviction that apocalypse is imminent, and the belief that increasing human knowledge helps recover what was lost in Eden. Noble suggests that the relationship between religion and technology has perhaps outlived its usefulness. Whereas it once aimed to promote human well-being, it has ultimately become a threat to our survival.

These are just some of the issues of concern when we pause to take a reflective look at technology and its impact upon society: the under-developed philosophy of the area and the lack of acceptance of more reflective thought, the fact that technology is running away with us, that it is being uncritically adopted, and pervasive in society, that its immediate "benefits" are not countered with consideration of its negative influences, that its uptake is frequently associated with other unnecessary cultural hangovers from the Western culture, that technology can leave people "trapped" in a never-ending cycle of increased complexity with more technology applied to solve problems that technology actually creates. Against this backdrop of the need to "reflect" about technology, we pause to consider some of the approaches and solutions in a philosophy of technology.

2.3 Approaches to "The Technological Problem"

The philosophy of technology is a relatively young field. To a large extent, it is still emerging and remains on the margins of modern technology. The questions to ask, the issues and the approaches to take are not always clear. The sub-themes and areas of concern are still taking shape. Some philosophers have made obscure and sometimes impenetrable contributions that have not helped the field. The technically minded often do not accept the need for such a pursuit. Here we simply note that the philosophy of technology is a relatively young field: at least some of the most interesting questions have been raised in relatively recent years, with the rapid speed of progress contributing to the discussions of the field. Durbin (1998) surveyed the advances in the philosophy of technology from the 1960s to the turn of the century, and found that "real though limited progress has been made."

The field as we know it today, perhaps began with Martin Heidegger's essay The question concerning technology (1977). The essay contains an analysis of the true nature of technology, and his critique of modern technology. He distinguishes modern technology from more primitive technology (that does not tend to treat nature as standing-reserve), and is primarily interested in how we can have a free relationship to modern technology. As long as we perceive "technology as an instrument, we remain held fast in the will to master it." Heidegger claims that technology is relentlessly overtaking us, and believes that humanity's goal is to find a way of living with technology that does not allow it to "warp, confuse, and lay waste our nature." Heidegger puts it that "Only a god can save us" from the juggernaut of progress (Heidegger, 1977). His political views veered towards German national socialism as a better "control" of technology than democracy (1976), but this political spin to much of his work has hindered its reception. Nevertheless, we cannot consider the question of "what is technology" without reference to his work.

Heidegger (1968) is also concerned to point out that the scientist is locked into a particular perspective from which it is hard to remove himself. He recognises that the scientist views the world from a particular "subject-object" perspective in which he or she is entrapped. Through this, they are unable to conceive an alternative way of thinking. Tied to the technological way of thinking, the scientist, and by extension most of the contemporary world, lacks the ability to think outside of this mode of thought. Heidegger argues that the power of subject-object analysis is such that the technological model of thinking is enshrined throughout the world, and dominates all thought. We must learn to step beyond the contemporary technological worldview. This requirement is a demanding one when technology is ever increasing in invisibility and pervasiveness.

Carl Mitcham (1995) provides a useful categorisation of approaches to the philosophy of technology in the "engineering" approach and the "humanities" approach. He locates Heidegger's contributions in the humanities approach that has come to be associated with a negative criticism, in contrast to the engineering philosophy that is more positive about technology. The approaches to the philosophy may be summarised as follows

- **Engineering philosophy of technology** (e.g., Mitcham): Uses technological thought and action as a model for understanding even non-technological thought and action; puts non-technological experience in technological terms.
- **Humanities philosophy of technology** (e.g., Mumford, Heidegger, and Ellul): Regards technological thought and action as only one aspect of human thought and action; delimits the technological within a larger framework (lifeworld or culture).

Mitcham finds that "engineering" philosophers of technology have succeeded by getting engineers to think about their work and distinguishing technology from science as a field to be examined, but has failed as an approach in not having a grand scheme comparable to that of the humanities criticisms of technology. In some ways, engineering philosophy gives uncritical praise of modern technology, and fails to deal with its problems. In contrast, the "humanities" philosophy of technology can be unnecessarily obscure and impenetrable, even making criticism of the very possibility of such a philosophy, and generally warning of the "disastrous" influences of it.

Within this framework where technology is isolated from either an engineering or humanities perspective, there are various questions and issues to focus upon: (1) We may simply reflect upon technology and ask what it is, what is its nature, how is it technology, and so on. (2) We may take a more pragmatic approach and examine technology's failures and disappointments, seeking a way forward to stop a tragedy, or understand a disaster. (3) We may take an anthropomorphic approach and use technology as a vehicle with which to understand humanity, perhaps examining religiosity or some other aspect which technology impacts. (4) We may take a sociological approach and try and see how technology fits within society. (5) We may take a philosophical approach that examines the underlying worldview within which technology succeeds. There are a bewildering array of questions that may be asked of technology in its "philosophy," and approaches that may be taken.

Durbin (1998) believes that a social action approach to the philosophy of technology is necessary, as proposed in the very first volume of *Research in Philosophy and Technology* (1978), following the lead of American pragmatist philosophers (George Herbert Mead and John Dewey). This pragmatic approach is summarised by Bijker, Wiebe, and Law (1992) in "*Shaping Technology/Building Society*, where they emphasise the need to understand particularly the "technological disasters." They are looking for a practical solution to make sense of (technological) horrors, "...and more important, do something about them . . . what we urgently need is a tool kit."

A less pragmatic approach to the philosophy of technology is taken by Dreyfus and Spinosa (1997), who ask how can we relate ourselves to technology in a way that not only resists our devastation, but that also gives it a positive role in our lives. They marked this question as the key question for our generation. The need for evaluating and assessing the impact of technology on the social, ethical, political, and cultural dimensions of our world is highlighted in this approach.

Such a negative view of technology, per se, is countered by Feenberg (1991). He finds the real questions are not concerned with technology or progress per se, but the variety of possible technologies and paths of progress among which we must choose. In this way, he differs to those who find a more general "threat" in technology. The nature of the evaluation would be vastly different in a comparison of technologies vs. whether technology is even to be used.

Simpson's thesis is that technology removes "meaning" from the world. He finds that "(T)he growing hegemony of the temporality of making (techne), at the expense of temporalities of doing (praxis), stands as a threat to the continued presence of meaningful differences in our lives and to there being meaning in a life as a whole." For example, consider the task of house painting. There is the "meaning perspective," where the fact that the painting takes a week is not necessarily experienced as a negative factor. The length of time may even be a positive factor in deepening communal feelings and commitments. There is also the "means-end" or "values" perspective, where the goal of painting the house is paramount. Any time taken to paint it is a waste of time. Thus a "paint-bomb" technology that painted the house in seconds would be optimal. This is the classic humanities philosophy of technology critique of the modern technological project. The "meaning" of the activity is removed through the technology and the switch from meaning perspective to the goal. Simpson believes that the "efficiency" of technology constitutes a threat to meaning in life. This classic humanist view fails to take account of the new development of meta-technology in which we are "located," and in which time can still meaningfully be spent.

Another problem with the philosophy of technology is that others see that, as a field, it may already be over! Economic historian Karl Polanyi and the critical theory of Jürgen Habermas have placed the philosophy of technology in a broad, three-phase historical framework. The historic phases are:

1. **Pre-modern technology or technics:** In this phase there was no need for a separate philosophy of technology because technics is embedded in a lifeworld or culture that can be examined by general philosophy.
2. **Modern technology or autonomous technology:** In this phase there was a decontextualizing. Technology was disembodied from society, made an abstract resource, in which its instrumentality was studied, separate from culture.
3. **Meta-technology:** In this phase there was a recontextualization of technology. It is not quite the same as "technology within culture," but forms a new culture of its own, a global or "transcultural culture." A new techno-culture transcends traditional particular cultures. One might ask the extent to which this techno-culture dissolves and embraces other cultural aspects (see Pacey).

We are in the midst of a virtual recontextualization or re-embedding that, although it is in no way a return to the pre-modern contextualization or interlinking of science, religion, art, and so forth is nevertheless a stepping beyond the specific autonomies of modernity. Mitcham (1995) sees that the philosophy of technology can be seen as an epoch-specific event that is "coming to an end; it is petering out in a kind of exhaustion or displacement. If this is true, then the philosophy of technology may well be in the process of being replaced — not with a philosophy of meta-technology but by philosophy in a general sense that reincorporates into itself reflection on the meta-technical condition of the post-modern techno-lifeworld".

Mitcham (1995) suggests, "The last twenty years in the philosophy of technology has been an attempt to think technology as something we do. The next twenty years must be an attempt to think meta-technology as something we are part of." It is as if the "rapid pace" of technological change spoken of at the field's inception, has indeed run away; technology has now penetrated society and is not something we can reflect on in isolation as if it were a separate component of life. Particularly through the "meta-technology" of information and communication technology, it is as if there is a return to the pre-modern condition, where there was not a necessity for a separate philosophy of technology; the "technology" was contextually entangled in the life and major institutions of society. Only during the modern phase, where decontextualisation isolated separate philosophies of religion, art, and so forth, did "technology" emerge as a facet of society requiring reflection.

The very act of isolating technology as a field of study is an example of decontextualising. There is an attempt to remove technology from all other aspects of the world to which it might be linked. The world is turned into a series of unlinked resources. This disembedding has occurred in economics, science, technology, religion, art, and other disciplines. The pursuits are methodologically separated, turning the world into a series of unlinked resources. However, with technology so embedded in society, we can no longer isolate it from our culture.

2.4 Technology and Identity

In this section, we examine the impact of technology upon an individual's identity. In general, the "technological determinism" question is concerned with technology's impact upon society, and the "philosophy of technology" is (generally) concerned with approaches to understanding the situation at the societal level. In this section, we look at some of the ways that technology impacts individuals and their identity, and frame our concerns in a less "collective" manner. First, we examine some of the more optimistic perceptions that have been made about technology's impact upon identity. We find more negative "issues" include (1) the "techno-phobia" that is bred by actual technological disasters and the failures of technology, (2) the "self-sufficiency" that technology fuels, increasing people's autonomy, (3) the "spiritual degradation" that is created where people are reduced to "machines" in a "producer-consumer" society, and (4) the confusion that technology creates about personal identity.

There are two main perspectives about the self in current Western philosophical literature: individualism, based on the liberal rights-based conception of the self, and communitarianism, based on the conservative conception of the self in society. Joanne

Baldine (1997) summarises that "whether it is better, in an ethical sense, or more useful, in a practical sense, to see ourselves as separated individuals rather than as connected selves depends somewhat upon where we find ourselves situated in the first place." She points out that "Powerful individual persons in communitarian cultures will argue that communitarian values are more truly human; whereas individuals submerged in low status positions in communitarian cultures look toward individualistic cultures with hope of liberation. Likewise, powerful individuals in individualistic cultures praise individual striving and achievement, whereas individuals submerged in low status positions look toward kinder, gentler, communitarian values to help them survive."

We also distinguish the self-concept from identity. It is possible that the self-concept is wrong, and different to actual identity. For example, a person may have a negative self-image, creating a self-concept where they are worthless. Their perception of identity may be very different to the reality, although they just cannot perceive it. Alternatively, a person may have an elevated conception of their self and their importance. People in power and authority may believe themselves to be indispensable and infallible, not just overestimating their sense of importance, but having delusionary perceptions of themselves. For example, religious organisations are a context where people in authority even attach supernatural support to the imperative of their control and domination. Their self-concept is different to their actual identity. Having made these distinctions, we examine the role of technology in identity and self-conceptions.

Barbara Molony (2005) examines technology and identity, asking whether rapidly accelerating technology is eroding our sense of who we are. She finds that "as individuals, we have, throughout the long course of human history, found our identity in the relationships we have with those close to us in our families and communities; today, we must include the Internet as a space in which we create our identities." Since technology has changed rapidly, we must ask what is it now that constructs our identity? She cites Staudenmaier as finding "Identity, then, is something we cannot simply take for granted but must create in the new Internet context. Perhaps our identities are less bound to ourselves in this new age; perhaps they are to be found, as they were among humans of the past, in our communities." The potential outcomes for our identities in the information age can be both positive and negative. The Internet can make us more global in our view of ourselves, overcoming fundamentalisms of religion or ethnicity or ideology, but, ironically, it can also be used to support narrow-mindedness. There is cautious optimism that people will be able to craft new identities through the Internet that, paradoxically, help us forge old-fashioned connectedness in a seemingly disconnected, modernizing world.

Gordon L. Ziniewicz examined individual man in a technological age (http://www.fred.net/tzaka/mesthene.html), finding that the impact of technology on the individual has both positive and negative sides. He identifies the negative influences as being loss of individuality with pressure on the individual to conform or adjust, and decline in personal privacy with sophisticated eavesdropping and surveillance devices. The positive influences are the enhanced possibilities of developing individual potential with education, communication, and other.

Joanne Baldine (1997) considers whether human identity is an artefact and, in some sense, artificial. She asks, "Is the self merely a product of our own reflective creation, of technological advance, of history, or a by-product of the latest cultural trends?" Most technologically developed societies promote a highly individualistic conception of self. The assumption is that it is either a necessary condition for, or a necessary by-product of, living in a highly technological country. Japan provides a counter example that is both highly technological and self-consciously traditional. It is certainly a mistake to promote individualism as a means of achieving technological or economic development. Baldine does find that self is an artefact, and "even if cultural convergence means a subversion of the self, then a new self will likely adapt and construct a new identity." In general, such perceptions of technology and its influence on identity and self, find technology playing a positive role. We find some particular problems, or failures of technology, as it relates to the individual and their self-concept, if not their identity.

Firstly, we examine the "techno-phobia" that technology produces in individuals. Techno-phobia is the fear of modern technology. Techno-phobia is the opposite of techno-philia, which refers to enthusiasm for new technologies and technological innovations. Technology can instil a very real "fear" in people. Many different evidences of "techno-phobia" are found in society. Examples range from the fear of learning to use a computer, to choosing to withdraw money at a bank, rather than using an ATM. The widespread turning to "natural products" and "simple living" has been cited as an example of people turning from technology. Techno-phobia has also been used to explain the increased interest among Western people in Eastern and New Age religions. The Closer to Truth forum discusses how the contemporary world is also witnessing an increased interest in more organised, fundamental and extreme religions in Islamic fundamentalists (The Kuhn Foundation, 2003).

While it may seem that techno-phobia perhaps influences just a small section of people in society, popular literature, film and books, television plays, and other "entertainment" reveal that the phenomenon is more widespread; in fact "fear" of technology is one of the driving themes of many plots. Shelley's *Frankenstein* (1818) is a fictional story with one interpretation as a cautionary tale to convey just this warning: that technology could eventually destroy us. Chris Baldick (1990) describes the modern Frankenstein myth as a skeleton story requiring only two basic principles: (1) Frankenstein makes a living creature. (2) The creature turns against him and runs amok. Some have found profound religious motives in the story, although the clearest message is the "fear" that "failed technology" can produce, and the great fascination and widespread popularity in such a theme.

The actual "technological disasters" that have occurred only reinforce techno-phobia. Works such as *Inviting Disasters: Lessons from the Edge of Technology* (Chiles, 2002) discuss major accidents, from space exploration to aircraft and chemical processing plants, seeking to determine why they happen, and offering new insights into the increasingly frequent serious and tragic machine disasters that haunt our lives. The list is endless: failed planes, trains, ships, bridges, dams, factories; the shocking break up of the Challenger; the disintegration of the giant drilling rig Ocean Ranger. Chiles offers an informed analysis of the unfortunate chain of events that brought them about. And by grouping like incidents to show how fatal "system fractures" eventually developed through a combination of human error and mechanical malfunction, he also suggests how we might sidestep such tragedies in the future.

Johnson and Nissenbaum (1995) explore the Therac-25 computer-controlled radiation treatment: a shocking example of a malfunction disaster that resulted in loss of life for people who were receiving computer-controlled radiation treatment for cancer. They distinguish "backward-looking" responsibility from "forward-looking" responsibility, finding that "backward-looking" responsibility asks questions in wake of a harmful event and seeks to discover who is to blame for the harm and who should be punished. Whereas "forward-looking" responsibility addresses the particular responsibilities in advance: it defines guidelines for creating quality products, measures the quality of the product, and defines the method of evaluation, the limitations and scope of operation in advance of harmful incidents.

Techno-stress is directly related to techno-phobia, as Michelle Weil and Larry Rosen's (1997) book *TechnoStress* explains how the growing dependence on technology affects us negatively. They suggest that we count on our machines to do so much that when something goes wrong with our technology, we are thrown into a tailspin. They also demonstrate how widespread the possibilities of techno-stress are. If human lives are not negatively impacted by techno-phobia, they are certainly impacted by techno-stress.

Buber's (1958) book, "*I and Thou*, discusses the "real" destructive power of the IT-world, finding it to be its effect on man's psychology. In such a society, Buber tells us, man feels oppressed by causality. Man feels that he is a cog caught in the inexorable machine of various causal systems; biological, social, historical, cultural, and psychological. It seems to him that he has no freedom, but rather that his entire life is determined by the powerful laws of these various systems. Buber finds a close association of the relation to God with the relation to one's fellowman in the context of the IT-world. If Buber finds that technology is influencing human psychology.

Secondly, the "self-sufficiency" that technology fuels is increasing people's autonomy and changing their self-concept. There are ways that this self-sufficiency may be beneficial. However, with appropriate technology, the human can control many facets of the world, removing both the need for other people. Technology may move people from having a sense of being a member of a gregarious community to autonomous individuals. The earliest peoples advanced because they cooperated in hunting and formed tribal communities that worked together. However, technology breeds a sense of empowerment and self-sufficiency, to some extent promoting an "individualism" that works against this intrinsic "gregariousness" of humanity. With appropriate technology, the human can control many facets of the world, removing both the need for other people and for "god."

Borgmann (1993) sees that technology introduces a waning recognition of any substantial spiritual existence: that is, technology is simply breeding a sense of empowerment and self-sufficiency. It is as if technology destroys that "spiritual" component of humanity that would look beyond itself. In contrast, Carson (2002) sees that technology may be turning people to a "spiritual quest," as the overwhelming invasion of technology into every aspect of life continues largely unabated in the Western world. Strong (1991) sees that technology itself takes the place of a "god." There are elements of truth in each of these observations: without doubt, technology is influencing that sense of "spiritual" identity within people.

Thirdly, technology is often criticised as "degrading humanity," reducing people to "machines," whether in the context of a "productive" automated society, or the more abstract sense, where human intellect is reduced to an algorithm. In this area, the most general criticisms of technology have been made. Many of them revolve around the way a technological society is condemned to authoritarian management, mindless work, and equally mindless consumption. Heidegger (1977) again reminds us that the world and ourselves are being transformed into "standing reserves," raw materials waiting to be used up in the process. People are reduced to mere objects: the "techno-cratic" outlook that is single-mindedly insistent on an unambiguous view of progress, leading to greater progress and efficiency.

Robert Scharff (2002), in his anthology of the philosophy of technology, examines human beings as toolmakers vs. tool users. Some see the problem as technical rationality and human values contending for the soul of modern man, with degradation of labor, education, the environment, and anti-democratic values that govern technological development. In such a situation, reforms, such as a simplified lifestyle or spiritual renewal, make no fundamental progress in a society that sacrifices millions of individuals to production. Weizenbaum (1976) also urged consideration of the ethical use of technology, and the "degrading" influence of suggesting that people are simply "machine.".

Finally, it is at this juncture of what technology is doing to the "identity" of society's individuals, that "religion and technology" raises some interesting perplexities, even paradoxes. As we have seen, on the one hand technology is fuelling a sense of self-empowerment and self-reliance, diminishing the dependence upon other people or "god." But this self-reliance also turns people towards technology with increasing strength, until it does become a "god" that people are lost without. We have also seen that techno-phobia may be turning people back to simple lifestyles, and also reviving primitive religious beliefs through mysticism and other, yet there is a widespread techno-philia and continued uptake of technology. And there is the way that being part of a technological society, where the real possibility of being no different to a "machine" exists, impacts identity. There are many interesting questions raised about what technology is doing to individual identity.

In philosophy, the essence of your existence is known as dasein (German for "being there"). We each have our own dasein. Dasein is your essential identity, but stripped of all the worldly characteristics that we normally associate with who we are. It is essentially the skeleton of your identity on which all the details of your identity can be hung. Dasein applies to self-conscious human beings. Heidegger was one to relate technology to dasein. By using the expression dasein, Heidegger called attention to the fact that a human being cannot be taken into account except as being an existent in the middle of a world amongst other things (Warnock, 1970), that dasein is "to be there" and "there" is the world. To be human is to be fixed, embedded, and immersed in the physical, literal, tangible day-to-day world (Steiner 1978). Heidegger contrasted the differences between authentic and inauthentic lives. He did so through the agencies of fear set against anxiety, "speech" contrasted with "talk," genuine wonder opposed to mere novelty.

To some extent, dasein is an attempt to locate that "identity" that is "real," as opposed to that "self-concept" that is a psychological phenomenon. For Heidegger, human beings are never directly in the world except by way of being in some particular circumstance; it is dasein that is being-in-the-world. Differentiating between "essential identity" and "identity in the world," is apparently not possible philosophically. Thus, a world that is technological will have profound implications on human identity. Only when identity is located outside the world, perhaps in some transcendent divinity, might there be a possibility of retaining that "essential identity" while submersed in the technological "world."

As we shall see in the context of "artificial identity," both the Jewish and Christian traditions, the biblical concept of the "image of God" (Imago Dei) has been foundational for understanding the nature of personhood. The term image of God is applied uniquely to humans, and has its roots in Genesis 1:27, where God created people in His own image. People have been understood to bear the image of God, among other things, in their moral, spiritual, intellectual, and creative natures. Locating "identity" in this "divine image" makes it possible to have a dasein that is not within the world. Whether we are concerned about a "technological society" that is "running away" with humanity, or the influences of technology on individual people, it is theology that provides the answer to how we can coexist with technology, without it "warping and laying waste" our nature.

2.5 References

Baldick, C. (1990). *In Frankenstein's shadow: Myth, monstrosity, and nineteenth-century writing.* Oxford University Press.

Baldine, J. (1997). Is human identity an artefact? How some conceptions of the Asian and Western self fare during technological and legal development. *Society for Philosophy and Technology, winter* (2). Retrieved from http://scholar.lib.vt.edu/ejournals/SPT/v3_n2html/BALDINE.html

Bijker, W., & Law, J. (1992). *Shaping technology/Building society.* Cambridge, MA: MIT Press.

Borgmann, A. (1993). *Crossing the postmodern divide.* The University of Chicago Press.

Buber, M. (1958). *I and thou* (R. G. Smith, Trans.). New York: Charles Scribner's Sons.

Carson, J. (2002). *Technology and humanity.* Retrieved from http://www.applelust.com/alust/oped/All_Mac_Considered/Archives/carson_humanity.shtml

Dreyfus, H. L., & Spinosa, C. (1997). *Highway bridges and feasts: Heidegger and Borgmann on how to affirm technology.* Retrieved from http://www.focusing.org/dreyfus.html

Durbin, P. T. (1998). Advances in philosophy of technology? Comparative perspectives. *Techné: Journal of the Society for Philosophy and Technology, 4.*

Dutch. (2004). *The emergence of Western technology.* Retrieved from http://www.uwgb.edu/dutchs/westech.htm

Feenberg, A. (1991). *Critical theory of technology.* New York: Oxford University Press.

Florman, S. (1986). Technology and the tragic view. In A. H. Teich (Ed.), *Technology and the future* (4th ed.) New York: St Martin's Press.

Heidegger. (1968).

Heidegger. (1976, May 31). *Der Spiegel.*

Heidegger, M. (1977). *The question concerning technology and other essays* (W. Lovitt, Trans.). New York: Harper and Row.

Johnson, D., & Nissenbaum, H. (1995). *Computers, ethics and social values.* Englewood Cliffs, NJ: Prentice-Hall.

The Kuhn Foundation. (2003). *Can religion withstand technology? Closer to truth.* Retrieved from http://www.pbs.org/kcet/closertotruth/explore/show_14.html

Mitcham, C. (1995). Notes toward a philosophy of metatechnology. In D. Baird (Ed.), *Society for Philosophy and Technology 1*(1-2). Retrieved from http://scholar.lib.vt.edu/ejournals/SPT/v1_n1n2/mitcham.html

Molony, B. (2005). Technology and identity: Is rapidly accelerating technology eroding our sense of who we are? Retrieved from *STS Nexus* http://sts.scu.edu/nexus/Issue1-2/05_Molony.asp

Noble, D. (1999). *The religion of technology: The divinity of man and the spirit of invention.* Penguin.

Pacey.

Rosen, J. (2000). *The Talmud and the Internet.* Barnes and Noble.

Scharff, R. C. (2002). *Philosophy of technology The technological condition: An anthology.* University of New Hampshire.

Shelley, M. (1818). *Frankenstein.* Oxford University Press.

Steiner. (1978).

Strong, D. (1991). The promise of technology vs. God's promise in Job. *Theology Today, 48*(2). Retrieved from http://theologytoday.ptsem.edu/jul1991/v48-2-article4.htm

Warnock. (1978).

Weil & Rosen. (1997). *TechnoStress.*

Weizenbaum, J. (1976). *Computer power and human reason.* San Francisco: W. H. Freeman.

Ziniewicz, G. L. *Individual man in a technological age.* Retrieved from http://www.fred.net/tzaka/mesthene.html

Chapter 3

21st Century Technologies

"AI is more than a movie."

Bill Gates

"Any sufficiently advanced technology is indistinguishable from magic."

Arthur C. Clarke

3.1 Introduction

In this chapter, we introduce and outline four different 21st century technologies. The most important 21st century technology is ICT-information and communication technology. In many ways, it has come to be the backbone of society, and provides the infrastructure upon which other technologies can sit. It is extremely pervasive, rapidly increasing, and undoubtedly important. The future of ICT will see ever-increasing speed, reliability, interconnectivity and sophistication approaching that of the capabilities cyberspace offer.

A closely following 21st century technology is AI — artificial intelligence — with its endeavour to make "human-like" machines that are able to undertake intelligent action in the human world. AI has had some successes, although when the achievements are compared to the initial ambitious goals, the realities of what have been achieved are sometimes disappointing. At the start of the 21st century, AI is very much a part of daily life, with a tendency to embed intelligence within existing gadgets. The future of AI will see ever-increasing sophistication in the range of intelligent behaviour that machines can demonstrate.

Ubiquitous computing and ambient intelligence will embed many small and highly specialised devices within our everyday environment in such a way that they operate seamlessly and become transparent to the person using them. Ambient intelligence is sometimes described as the convergence of many different streams of computing, aiming to deliver "rich" environments that anticipate humanity's every need. It will build upon ICT technologies, wireless Internet, and AI technologies. Both these possibilities will clearly be important components of future technology.

Finally, we introduce the idea of virtual AI as technology that (1) augments the natural physical world in ubiquitous computing environments, and (2) enhances the artificial virtual world through computer-facilitated life. We distinguish it from "real AI" as that AI which is pursued in isolation from ICT and Internet technologies, and which has largely dominated the 20th century non-virtual world. To some extent, the aims of "real AI" are slightly different from the aims of "virtual AI." Real AI asked about reproducing human behaviour in a range of areas; virtual AI is more concerned with embedding intelligence in gadgets, supporting human action and human intelligence.

The objective of this chapter is to introduce and outline four different 21st century technologies, revealing them as (1) ICT — information and communication technology — the backbone of society providing the infrastructure upon which other technologies can sit, (2) AI — artificial intelligence — with its endeavour to make "human-like" machines that are able to undertake intelligent action in the human world, (3) ubiquitous computing and ambient intelligence — promising a seamless environment of information and communication between the human and computer world, and (4) virtual AI — enhancing Internet ICT with intelligence and sophistication, merging with ubiquitous computing to make a world where the interface between the virtual and real are continually blurred. We aim to provide a snapshot of the state of the art in technologies, rather than talk about technology in the abstract.

3.2 Information and Communication Technologies

Information and communication technologies are chiefly implemented by the Internet. ICT is perhaps the most revolutionary innovation that the 21st century enjoys, because it has impacted the daily life of so many people from across the globe. On a day-to-day basis, they influence more people than the impressive technologies that have enabled space travel, or even medical miracles that have brought cures to rare diseases. ICT facilitates human communication in a prolific way, even though this communication is predominantly text based. Day-to-day Internet exchanges contrast greatly with the more futuristic concept of "cyberspace" (a term coined by a science fiction writer suggesting far more sophisticated possibilities than yet delivered), yet even as a text-based human communication method, its importance, pervasiveness, and uptake is unique.

ICT is also distinguished by its rapid history of development. Hobbes (2004) presents a timeline of Internet development, starting with the ARPA-sponsored study on "cooperative network of time-sharing computers." Originating as a packet-switching network proposal for computers to share resources, one of the earliest technical research questions was how there could be multiple independent networks of rather arbitrary design all connected together in "open architecture networking." The underlying protocol that was developed was called transmission control protocol/Internet protocol (TCP/IP). Crucial in today's definition of Internet is the global nature of the information system, and the logical linking of computers that have a globally unique address; doing this via the Internet protocol (IP) or its subsequent extensions/follow-ons. Internet technology has not ceased to evolve, with mobile computing devices and "wireless Internet" now setting the agenda for future developments in business, personal, educational applications, and more. Increasingly, intelligent applications, wireless communication, virtual reality interfaces, and other developments will only continue to enrich and expand the Internet paradigm in its role of supporting a social network of human relationships.

From the start, the Internet has been associated with "information sharing," although as we have noted, there has been a subtle shift in emphasis from "computer-computer" to "person-person" communication. Even in the early days, electronic mail provided a significant application on top of the basic services. Leiner, Cerf, clark, Kahn, Kleinrock, Lynch, Postel, Roberts, and Wolff (2004) reported in the original Internet era, that electronic mail has probably had the most significant impact. E-mail provided a new model of how people could communicate with each other, and changed the nature of collaboration, first in the building of the Internet itself. Later the same was true for much of society. Leiner et al. (2004) is clear that the Internet has not ceased to evolve. The availability of pervasive networking, along with powerful affordable computing and communications in portable form (i.e., laptop computers, two-way pagers, PDAs, cellular phones) is making possible a new paradigm of nomadic computing and communications. Leiner sees that "the most pressing question for the future of the Internet is not how the technology will change, but how the process of change and evolution itself will be managed."

Science fiction writer William Gibson coined the term "cyberspace" to refer to the notional "information-space" loaded with visual cues and navigable with brain-computer interfaces. In 1991, serious efforts to construct virtual reality interfaces modelled explicitly on Gibsonian cyberspace were already under way, using more conventional devices such as glove sensors and binocular television headsets. True cyberspace technology is loaded with science fiction-inspired standards. Occasionally, the Internet as a whole is considered a crude cyberspace, although when the Internet entered public awareness, its mundane and everyday text interfaces did not meet the standards of "interactivity" with which true cyberspace was loaded.

The "Web," or W3, is a key application of the Internet (one that can often be confused with the Internet itself). The World Wide Web is part of the Internet, but the Internet is much more than the World Wide Web. It is a distributed information system originally created by researchers in 1989 at CERN (Conseil Européenne pour la Recherche Nucleaire), the European Laboratory for Particle Physics, in Geneva, Switzerland. A tool was needed to enable collaboration between physicists and other researchers in the high-energy physics community. Three new technologies were incorporated into the proposal: (1) Hypertext Markup Language (HTML) used to write the Web documents, (2) hypertext transfer protocol (HTTP) to transmit the pages, and (3) a Web browser client software program to receive and interpret data and display results. The availability of the World Wide Web system was publicly announced in August 1991. By the end of 1992, there were over 50 Web servers in the world. Many of these earliest Web servers were located at universities or other research centers. By June 1999, there were more than 720,000 public information servers. In April of 2001, there were over 24 million servers. The Web has geographically penetrated the world as a key information resource, and one that also supports human interactions and creates "virtual communities."

The Internet also aids communication for blind people. Screen readers, such as Jaws, produce voice output to replace to visual display of text on Web pages. Hardware and software produce synthesized voice output, as well as for keystrokes entered on the keyboard. Talking browsers use the same technology as screen reading software, but the reading functions are limited to Internet use. Careful design of Web pages can also facilitate this automated communication. Clearly, technology provides the potential to connect people who might otherwise not be connected; it facilitates exchange of information and communication in an unprecedented way.

The future of ICT is bound to improve communications in terms of speed, accessibility, reliability, and other. ICT is likely to merge with other technologies to produce more and more sophisticated forums for exchange and information, approaching the capabilities that the "cyberspace" image sometimes entails.

3.3 Artificial Intelligence

Today, most people probably know of artificial intelligence as it was popularised by the Warner Brothers (2001) film *Artificial Intelligence,* released in 2001. The plot revolves around highly advanced robotic mecha that are endowed with emotions but are not "real people." A boy mecha becomes lost and alone and searches to become "real" so that he can regain the love of his human mother. The search takes the boy mecha beyond the time when humans even exist, and just when the possibility of a reunion seems hopeless, there is the chance to relive just one single day with his mother in a surreal recreation facilitated by visitors to earth. At that point, the film either appears profound and meaningful, or to have dragged on with no plot. Nevertheless, it popularised the field of AI, and some of the endeavours that have been made to endow machines with human-like abilities, starting with intelligence.

McCarthy, in the 1956 Dartmouth Summer School, coined the term AI. This school was organised by McCarthy, Minsky, Rochester and Shannon (1955). They initiated a 2-month study that was based on the conjecture that every aspect of learning or any other feature of human intelligence can, in principle, be so precisely described that a machine can be made to simulate it. Over half a century later, the field is still a long way from achieving some of the original goals. Today, the American Association for Artificial Intelligence defines AI as "the scientific understanding of the mechanisms underlying thought and intelligent behavior and their embodiment in machines." (http://www.aaai.org/). John McCarthy likes to retain the distinction between doing-AI and doing it in a biologically observable way. Today, AI often aims to simulate "insect intelligence" rather than full-blown human intelligence. There are three main paradigms of AI: symbolic, sub-symbolic and artificial life.

A common distinction in AI practitioners is made between "neats" and "scruffies." The "neats" tend to try to build systems that "reason" in some way identifiably similar to the way humans report themselves as doing, while "scruffies" profess not to care whether an algorithm resembles human reasoning in the least, as long as it works. More importantly, neats tend to believe that logic is paramount, while scruffies favour looser, more ad hoc methods driven by empirical knowledge. Robert C. Moore (1995) distinguishes three uses of logic in AI: as a tool of analysis, as a basis for knowledge representation, and as a programming language. In representation, classical logic via propositional and predicates calculus has played an important role, as well as non-monotonic and modal logics for reasoning in light of "changing truth" and possible worlds. The most influential figure in logical AI is John McCarthy. The motivation for using logic is that even if the eventual implementations do not directly and simply use logical reasoning techniques like theorem proving, a logical formalization helps us to understand the reasoning problem itself. The claim is that without an understanding of what are the reasoning problems, it will not be possible to implement their solutions.

The symbolic school of AI was built upon the "physical system hypothesis" (Newell & Simon, 1976) that human intelligence is essentially the ability to process symbols, and that this symbol-processing power can, in principle, be replicated on a computer. A central part of symbolic AI has to do with the issue of knowledge representation in artificial systems. Brachman and Levesque (1985) provide a good overview of various issues in early knowledge representation covering both network based implementations (conceptual graphs, scripts, and other) and formal languages such as logic, including both the representational and computational properties for the formalisms. Symbolic AI has had some impressive successes with systems mimicking human expertise (expert systems) in a variety of fields that constitute narrow, but deep, knowledge domains. However, despite the successes and achievements that symbolic AI has made, there are many limitations. Areas that rely on procedural or implicit knowledge, such as sensory/motor processes, are much more difficult to handle within the symbolic AI framework. There is the ongoing question of how tacit knowledge can be represented and used. Addis (1989) makes a discussion of the role of knowledge representation in light of such knowledge. The very basis of the symbolic AI paradigm is the "representation" of knowledge and the world, and this has been found to be its limiting factor. The issues of "representation" are deep and perhaps unresolvable ones. By and large, AI has left these problems to sub-symbolic AI methods.

Sub-symbolic approaches do not rely upon explicit representation of knowledge. The sub-symbolic school was biologically inspired from the human physiological system and the neural network found in the brain. Sub-symbolic AI involves modelling intelligence not with variables that represent particular pieces of knowledge. Instead, they simulate small areas of the brain, with variables representing brain cells. These cells are "connected" inside the program so that they can pass their signals from one brain cell to another. These connections can be strong or weak, so that a large part of the signal is passed on or only a small part: hence, the term artificial neural network. The original attempt to model the brain in this way was made by McCulloch and Pitts (1943), where researchers first looked at representing the logical operations within the human brain in terms of neurone networks. Rosenblatt's (1958) Perceptron followed. This modelled the human visual system, and actually taking light stimuli from the world in the form of geometric shapes. Minsky and Pappert (1969) put an end to much work until the 1980s, where increased computer power and a theoretical breakthrough caused interest to resume with self-organising feature maps (Kohonen 1982) and adaptive resonance networks (Carpenter, Grossberg, & Mehanian, 1989).

The artificial life or Alife approach to AI emphasises the importance of emergent computing and evolutionary methods. Artificial life attempts to model living biological systems through algorithms. It offers a synthetic perspective, beginning with simple rules and concepts, and combines them to see what complex phenomena are produced. Steven Levy's (1992) book on artificial life provides an introduction to the field, beginning with a review of the field's history, from the early suggestions made by John von Neumann and John Conway's *Game of life* (Gardner, 1970) all the way to current efforts. Levy also discusses the suggestion of several researchers that predict Alife creatures will eventually inherit the earth, replacing us humans as the next step in evolution as a sensational conclusion. Artificial life is both simulated in computer programs, and physically realised through robots (Steels & Brooks, 1995) physically situated in a real world context, navigating through that context.

Related to the evolutionary computing approach are the natural physical world complex systems that computers are often used to mimic, such the fractal patterns of the Mandelbrot set, chaotic weather patterns, and the emergence of flight patterns in a flock of birds. Waldrop (1992) outlines the emerging interest in complexity theory. The science of complexity studies how single elements, such as a species or a stock, spontaneously organize into complicated structures like ecosystems and economies: stars become galaxies, and snowflakes avalanches, almost as if these systems were obeying a hidden yearning for order. Complex systems and their modelling is a priority research area due to the computational complexity of many computer implementations that seek to model them, for example, traffic simulations that require dedicated hardware in order to undertake microlevel modelling of the system in real time traffic control (McArthur, Cameron, While, & Wylie, 1994).

The agent-based approach cannot be ignored within artificial intelligence. We briefly consider it here, since we find some parallels between agent-based AI, artificial life and the paradigm of AI that goes beyond "algorithmic" boundaries. When many agents "operate" together, they fit naturally into the artificial life school. The idea of an agent is a computer program that helps maximise computing "experiences," just as human "agents" are those with expertise entrusted to go out and act on your behalf. Franklin and Graesser (1996) propose a formal definition of an autonomous agent that clearly distinguishes a software agent from just any program. They also investigate a "natural kinds" taxonomy of autonomous agents, and discuss possibilities for further classification, together with sub-agents and multi-agent systems.

Franklin and Graesser (1996) report the various definitions of agents and the properties that they emphasise. One definition of agent emphasises its autonomy: "the term agent is used to represent two orthogonal concepts. The first is the agent's ability for autonomous execution. The second is the agent's ability to perform domain oriented reasoning" (http://www.crystaliz.com/logicware/mubot.html). Russell and Norvig (1995) were interested in software agents embodying AI techniques and defined an agent as "anything that can be viewed as perceiving its environment through sensors and acting upon that environment through effectors." Maes (1995) emphasises both the autonomy of the agent and their solving a goal: "Autonomous agents are computational systems that inhabit some complex dynamic environment, sense and act autonomously in this environment, and by doing so realize a set of goals or tasks for which they are designed." Smith, Cypher, and Spohrer (1994) add the quality of persistence to an agent. Hayes-Roth (1995) adds the requirement of "reasoning" to agency, stating "Intelligent agents continuously perform three functions: perception of dynamic conditions in the environment; action to affect conditions in the environment; and reasoning to interpret perceptions, solve problems, draw inferences, and determine actions." IBM's intelligent agent strategy white paper, views an intelligent agent as acting for another, with authority granted by the other (http://activist.gpl.ibm.com:81/WhitePaper/ptc2.htm).

Wooldridge and Jennings (1995) define agent as " ... a hardware or (more usually) software-based computer system that enjoys the following properties: autonomy: agents operate without the direct intervention of humans or others, and have some kind of control over their actions and internal state; social ability: agents interact with other agents (and possibly humans) via some kind of agent-communication language; reactivity: agents perceive their environment, (which may be the physical world, a user via a graphical user interface, a collection of other agents, the Internet, or perhaps all of these combined), and respond in a timely fashion to changes that occur in it; pro-activeness: agents do not simply act in response to their environment, they are able to exhibit goal-directed behaviour by taking the initiative."

AI has had some successes, although when the achievement is compared to the initial ambitious goals, the realities of what have been achieved are sometimes disappointing. There was much initial hype that reality has modified to more realistic goals and expectations, and now solutions that are entering industry, business, and other as routine technology. The definition and practice of AI presents the difficulty of a shifting target: once a particular "intelligent" behaviour is achieved, the aim alters and a new goal is attempted. Present day research and projects also include those that are driven by the consumer marker: domestic gadgets, autonomous vehicles, and architectural tools for designer living spaces. There is also important research occurring in speech recognition and synthesis, with intent to integrate a "verbal" version of the Web as an information resource, facilitating more "natural" human interaction with intelligent machines.

At the start of the 21st century, AI is very much part of daily life. Tim Menzies (2003) states that although in the 21st century, AI is not necessarily amazing and is often routine; it is certainly "no longer a bleeding-edge technology — hyped by its proponents and mistrusted by the mainstream." AI has penetrated the everyday life of many people, often through "smarter" versions of existing technology. This infiltration of technology is particularly subtle, since there is an incremental development, and not a dramatic introduction of a "super robot" or other science fiction like revolutionary technology. When AI is combined with ICT technologies, in virtual AI, there is an important combination of technologies.

3.4 Ubiquitous Computing and Ambient Intelligence

Marc Weiser invented the term "ubiqutious computing." The goal of ubiquitous computing is to move computers away from the central focus of the user's attention (and into cupboards, behind walls, etc.), where they are used subconsciously, to enhance existing tools or communications. Ubiquitous computing should eliminate many of the "interface" issues that can plague current ICT technology. Weiser (1996) sees ubiquitous computing as the future of computer technology. He says "The first wave of computing, from 1940 to about 1980, was dominated by many people serving one computer. The second wave, still peaking, has one person and one computer in uneasy symbiosis, staring at each other across the desktop without really inhabiting each other's worlds. The third wave, just beginning, has many computers serving each person everywhere in the world. I call this last wave 'ubiquitous computing'." The main aim of ubiquitous computing is to embed many small and highly specialised devices within our everyday environment in such a way that they operate seamlessly, and become transparent to the person using them. The three main aims of ubiquitous computing products are to be everywhere (e.g., by being portable), to be small, and to be aware (of its environment, of its user, etc.). To make true ubiquitous computing possible, research needs to be done to develop the required techniques, hardware, and software. This research will include several research areas including low-power devices, low cost, and high mobility.

Ubiquitous computing is closely related to "calm technology." Calm technology is concerned with making technology truly assist a user, give them a sense of control (perhaps despite a range of devices and gadgets that may become overwhelming, even when "hidden" in cupboards and in domestic appliances). Calm technology envisages a world where computers do not cause stress, but enhance our lives and make many tasks easier: they do not distract, but remain unobtrusive, assisting with a task, not being the focus on the task. The greatest strength of calm technology, therefore, lies in the fact that computers are made to conform to their users, and not the other way around. Information is presented in the manner that a user decides, and is easily accessible. The user does not feel distracted or slowed down by using this calm technology. Weiser and Brown (1995) inform us that "Designs that encalm and inform meet two human needs not usually met together. Information technology is more often the enemy of calm: pagers, cellphones, news services, the World Wide Web, e-mail, TV, and radio bombard us frenetically." Calm technology with ubiquitous computing is set to make an interesting future for AI and ICT technologies in augmenting the real world.

Nigel Shadbolt (2003) explains a related concept of "ambient intelligence." Ambient intelligence explains how your fridge can infer your shopping list and call your mobile phone as you pass the supermarket, because your diary informed it that you have invited friends over for dinner, and their meal preferences do not match what is in the fridge, and the GPS in your mobile phone realises you are approaching a supermarket where it has determined that the crucial ingredients are on special. Ambient intelligence is the convergence of many different streams of computing aiming to deliver "rich" environments that anticipate humanity's every need. Shadbolt (2003) reports there are various streams coming together to achieve these environments: "The first is ubiquitous or pervasive computing. Its major contribution is the development of various ad hoc networking capabilities that exploit highly portable or else numerous, very-low-cost computing devices. The second key area is intelligent systems research, which provides learning algorithms and pattern matchers, speech recognition and language translators, and gesture classification and situation assessment. A third element is context awareness; research on this problem lets us track and position objects of all types and represent objects' interactions with their environments. Finally, an appreciation of the social interactions of objects in environments is essential." The real challenge for ambient intelligence is the perennial problem of a power source. How do you keep the myriad devices and the ever-present ubiquitous and pervasive infrastructure powered up?

Scanlon (2004), in Shrobe's computerized office, is just one of dozens of pervasive-computing technologies being developed as part of Project Oxygen, which began in 2000. The researchers are concerned with workspaces that adjust themselves according to their inhabitants' habits. One development is an intelligent conference room that helps people run more efficient meetings. The latest version of the room can, when prompted by spoken commands, show agenda items on a wall display, transcribe and save participants' comments, or find pertinent video clips from previous meetings. The end result is expected to be a collection of technologies embedded in workplaces and homes, working together seamlessly-and often behind the scenes-to help us go about our daily lives. Today, the group is working to couple intelligent spaces with a software platform that will allow people in different locations to share and display data with whatever gadgets happen to be handy: perhaps cell phones, or a projector in a meeting room. The project is not trying to develop standalone technologies in networking, speech, vision, or anything else, but seeks the integration of these technologies

In their article, "Basic concepts in wearable computers and augmented reality," Barfield and Caudell (2001) project that in the future "(the networked) computers (on our body) will monitor our physiological state, perform the duties of a secretary and butler in managing our everyday life, and protect us from physical harm." When extending the body and creating new connections to the environment, body (nets) blur the boundaries between internal and external, between self and others. The individuals'body and cognitive abilities are extended, their boundaries no longer determined by skin, or even by the body's proxemics, but by the artefacts that are part of his/her network, and respond to his/her presence. The emphasis is on anticipation, preemptive action. The body (net) knows the individual as well (or better) than he/she knows him/herself. It acts on the individual's behalf without the need for conscious input. The possibilities for control and loss of privacy, although not explicitly mentioned, are certainly a possibility. Among the more subtle effects we could imagine, for instance, the creation of invisible entities — spaces or activities — that are not modelled into the body (net) and thus become intangible.

Virtual AI enhancing the real world will naturally incorporate wireless Internet into the scope of its operations. Alesso and Smith (2001), in *The Intelligent Wireless Web,* explore the synergy and convergence among five key technologies, proposing to see to what extent AI can be incorporated into the Web. They aim to integrate both AI and wireless technology into the Web, finding an integration of speech recognition, mobile wireless devices, network integration, and software to be crucial in supporting wireless intelligent applications. They provide a general overview of artificial intelligence and how it might be applied to Web protocols. From the author's standpoint, the Web currently does not really express intelligence since it does not adapt: a necessary requirement for learning. The authors also find that the semantic Web holds much promise for building an intelligent Web. Particularly interesting is the discussion of the need for self-organization in order for the Web to be considered intelligent. The property of self-organization will also be the most problematic to implement, due to the extreme distrust that some now feel against software that has not been validated by a human. The challenges of an intelligent wireless Web are considerable, not only from a technical standpoint in the creation of intelligent applications, but also because of legacy issues.

3.5 Virtual AI

In this section, we seek to introduce the concept of "virtual AI" and how it is distinct from "real AI." We are not the first to note the convergence of AI and ICT technologies, but we coin the term "virtual AI" to describe the phenomena. We seek to retain the two-pronged nature of virtual AI as that intersection of AI and ICT that both (1) augments the natural physical world in ubiquitous computing environments and (2) enhances the artificial virtual world through computer-facilitated life. The future of both AI and ICT lies in integration and synthesis, producing more and more sophisticated environments for human communication through the Internet (enhancing the virtual world), while providing a seamless intelligent computing environment (enhancing the real world).

First we define "real AI" as that AI that is pursued in isolation from ICT and Internet technologies, and that has largely dominated the 20th century non-virtual. It is real AI because it occurs in the "real world." It is an AI that focuses upon independent intelligent machines that do not share information or "interact" and that are typically dedicated to perform a specific, independent, intelligent function in the real world. Real AI includes all the methods and problems, issues and solutions that we discussed earlier: from the knowledge representation of symbolic AI, to the emergence of artificial life; from the modelling of human biological processes, to the philosophical questions of whether symbol manipulation underlies human "intelligence."

In contrast, virtual AI is the intersection of AI and ICT technologies. Virtual AI is that AI which both enhances the real world through ambient intelligence, and enhances interaction in the virtual world. Virtual AI is applied to contexts that are Internet-based, reliant upon sharing information, remotely controlling devices, facilitating human to human interaction in "virtual life" and human-machine interaction, sharing and distributing information, through wireless "networked" environments. Virtual AI may not be as concerned about the underlying philosophy of AI, since its aim is "intelligent environments" and as such, is different to the aims of the pioneers of "real AI."

William Halal (2004) speaks of a convergence of communication and computer technologies. He says "Information and communication technologies are rapidly converging to create machines that understand us, do what we tell them to, and even anticipate our needs. ... two relentless supertrends are moving this scenario toward near-term reality. Scientific advances are making it possible for people to talk to smart computers, while more enterprises are exploiting the commercial potential of the Internet. ... advances in speech recognition, artificial intelligence, powerful computers, virtual environments, and flat wall monitors are producing a 'conversational' human-machine interface. These powerful trends will drive the next generation of information technology into the mainstream by about 2010 in the synthesis of computer intelligence and the Internet."

We seek to retain the two-pronged nature of virtual AI as that intersection of AI and ICT that both (1) augments the natural physical world in ubiquitous computing environments and (2) enhances the artificial virtual world through computer-facilitated life. In so doing, we see virtual AI as closing the gap between "real" and "virtual," "artificial" and "natural." We also recognise that virtual AI intersects with a number of related fields, including pervasive computing and ambient intelligence, wireless Internet, virtual reality and wearable computers. It integrates them into a new paradigm that "blurs" the distinction between virtual and real worlds. The crux of the "merging of worlds" is found in the more natural communication that is facilitated between people and machines, mediated through the Internet. Virtual AI does not in any sense imply that it is not "AI," nor does it reduce to a sub-problem of AI, such as natural language processing or speech synthesis. Virtual AI is a discipline in its own right.

Virtual AI is more than distributed AI. Distributed AI is "the study, construction, and application of Multiagent Systems, that is, systems in which several interacting, intelligent agents pursue some set of goals or perform some set of tasks" (Wooldridge, 1999). Of course, as we have seen, there is no universal definition on what constitutes an agent. Multi-agent systems require additional considerations, for example, communication mechanisms, environmental and world knowledge maintenance, as well as communication, and societal issues such as which agent is assigned to a particular task. These additional requirements ensure that the design of a multi-agent system is much more complex than that of a single agent system. Distributed AI systems can also encounter problems because of the need to share resources. Through agents pursuing their own goals, there is the inadvertent risk of an agent destroying those resources. These and related research questions of "resource" sharing, "interaction" and "communication" drive the research agenda in distributed AI. Clearly, there will be distributed AI in virtual worlds and virtual AI will entail some of the questions of distributed AI, but virtual AI is more than just multi-agent systems.

Virtual AI will encompass many of the standard issues of real AI. In fact, one of the most direct ways that the problems and methods of AI will intersect with Virtual AI is through the semantic Web. The fundamental notion is that everything on the Web will be "indexed" for automated retrieval because of the resource description framework. The semantic Web is one attempt to integrate "semantics" into the information stored on the Web. Providing a semantic structure to the information that is stored, and expressing this in a universally agreed formal representation is essentially a knowledge representation problem. The scope of the task is vast when the range of different types of knowledge is considered (procedural to declarative), and the extent of the taxonomy that will be necessary in order to capture the different concepts that might be encountered. However, even a limited semantic structure to the information on the Web will facilitate more sophisticated usage of the information, and not only give structure to that which is to be stored, but enable sophisticated query, retrieval, exchange, and reasoning, especially by automatic agents that are able to "interpret" the semantic structure, making automatic use of the information possible in a more appropriate way than the hypertext-based framework.

Virtual AI will also draw upon agent-technology in order to facilitate virtual life. A good overview of agent technologies is provided at http://www.aaai.org/AITopics/html/agents.html. One particular intelligent software agent, known as the "bot," is designed to facilitate virtual life by processing data to bring back relevant answers. The word is short for robot of course, which is derived from the Czech word "robota" meaning work. The term bot is interchangeable with agent, indicating that the software can be sent out to find information and report back. There are various types of bots: search bots, shopping bots, metasearch bots, Newsgroup search bots, stock bots, tracking bots, artificial life bots, Web monitoring bots, news bots, personal assistant bots, file sharing bots, download managers, surf game bots, and many others (See for example http://www.botspot.com/). Bots have great potential in data mining, the process of finding patterns in enormous amounts of data. Automated and autonomous software in the form of "bots" eliminates information overload, increases productivity, and enables a sharp competitive advantage.

Virtual AI will naturally have to integrate with the research on "virtual reality" and user interfaces as more sophisticated ways for people "interacting" through ICT are developed. Jaron Lanier initially coined the term "virtual reality." It is used in a variety of ways and often in a confusing and misleading manner. Originally, the term referred to "immersive virtual reality," where a person becomes fully immersed in an artificial, 3-dimensional world that is completely generated by a computer. The head-mounted display (HMD) was the first device providing its wearer with an immersive experience. An HMD houses two miniature display screens and an optical system that presents a stereo view of a virtual world. A motion tracker continuously measures the position and orientation of the user's head and allows the image-generating computer to adjust the scene representation to the current view. As a result, the viewer can look around and walk through the surrounding virtual environment. Beier (2004) explains the unique characteristics of immersive virtual reality, summarizing them as follows: (1) head-referenced viewing for navigation in 3-D space, (2) stereoscopic viewing enhancing depth and the sense of space, (3) full scale virtual world, (4) realistic interactions with virtual objects via data glove, (5) the illusion of being fully immersed in an artificial world can be enhanced by auditory, haptic, and other non-visual technologies, and (6) networked applications allow for shared virtual environments.

Beier (2004) continues to explain, "Today, the term 'virtual reality' is also used for applications that are not fully immersive. The boundaries are becoming blurred, but all variations of VR will be important in the future. This includes mouse-controlled navigation through a three-dimensional environment on a graphics monitor, stereo viewing from the monitor via stereo glasses, stereo projection systems, and others." There are also a number of technologies related to virtual reality including "augmented reality" which allows the viewing of real environments with superimposed virtual objects. There are also "telepresence systems" in medicine, and robotics that immerse a viewer in a real world that is captured by video cameras at a distant location, and allow for the remote manipulation of real objects via robot arms and manipulators. It is assumed that VR will reshape the interface between people and information technology by offering new ways for the communication of information, the visualization of processes, and the creative expression of ideas.

In virtual AI, issues of "interface" and "human-like" communication will also be vital. Many computer-business leaders have focused on "interface" issues as crucial in the 21st century. Halal (2004) reports that "a few years ago, Microsoft chairman Bill Gates claimed, 'The future lies with computers that talk, see, listen, and learn.'. Robert McClure of IDC stated recently, 'What the graphical user interface was in the 1990s, the natural user interface will be in this decade.' Sony President, Kunitake Ando expects the PC of 2005 to be a more personalized, intelligent system, acting as a 'teacher, agent, and guide.' Ian Pearson at British Telecom sees a resumption of Internet growth in 2005 and 2006, driven by 'better interface technology ... and artificial intelligence.' And computer scientist Ray Kurzweil forecasts, 'It will be routine to meet in full-immersion virtual reality for business meetings and casual conversations in five to seven years.'" Halal believes that "these powerful trends will drive the next generation of information technology into the mainstream by about 2010. Rather than forcing us to hunch over a keyboard, this Intelligent Internet should allow people everywhere to converse naturally and comfortably with life-sized, virtual people while shopping, working, learning, and conducting most social relationships."

One of the limitations of Internet communication is the difficulty of expressing emotion. Emotion is an important component behind a verbal utterance, and can communicate meaning that is not explicitly contained within an utterance. It is not surprising that people often seek to encode such information in the text-based exchanges that predominate on the Internet, and that a coded convention has developed to express these "hidden" emotions that are to be conveyed with the text message. Smilies are small graphical images that are sometimes used to replace the textual symbols in order to convey emotion. Through a technology called "avatars," we are already seeing an enhancement of communication exceeding these simple smilies and text symbols.

An avatar is a 3-D representation that is able to express a range of actions, emotions, and gestures as a person chats in a 3-D multiuser environment. Avatars can effectively "embody" real people in a virtual world. They have been used by companies in the context of computer-based learning, where they add an almost human touch that reinforces the message, and are cheaper and more efficient than human trainers, delivering a more consistent message. The word "avatar" comes from a concept in the Hindu religion, where an avatar is an incarnation of a deity; hence, it suggests an embodiment or manifestation. The Sanskrit word avatara means "the descent of God" or simply "incarnation." Virtual AI will naturally enhance the "communication possibilities" further endowing "avatars" with more impressive natural language understanding, speech synthesis, and other "human-like" behaviours.

Virtual AI will augment the real world through ubiquitous computing, providing a seamless intelligent environment for living through wireless Internet and other technologies. We see the integration of technologies as crucial in facilitating the "rich" environments of pervasive or ubiquitous computing, sometimes known as "ambient intelligence." The crux of the "merging of worlds" is found in the more natural communication that is facilitated between people and machines. Virtual AI is more than distributed AI. Virtual AI will encompass many of the issues of real AI including that of knowledge representation in the semantic Web being proposed to augment Web hypertext. Virtual AI will also draw upon agent technology in order to facilitate virtual life. Virtual AI will draw upon the research on virtual reality and user interfaces, since issues of "interface" and "human-like" communication will be vital. Avatars are just one intelligent software agent-based approach to "embodying" a human-like entity in the virtual world and enhancing "interaction" between person and machine.

In summary, we define virtual AI to be that intersection of AI and ICT technologies leading to an Internet-based AI distinct from real AI. In virtual AI, information is shared and distributed, computing is ubiquitous, and "intelligence" is sharing information, remotely controlling devices, facilitating "virtual life" and enhancing communication within the virtual environment, both between people and machines and between machines and people. There is a two-pronged nature of virtual AI that both (1) augments the natural physical world in intelligent ubiquitous computing environments and (2) enhances the artificial virtual world through computer-facilitated life, especially enhanced communication. An environment of seamless communication with machines is the crux of merging the "real" and "virtual" worlds we inhabit. Virtual AI will encompass many of the issues of real AI including that of (a) knowledge representation — as the semantic Web is developed to "overlay" Internet hypertext and facilitate more sophisticated query and retrieval, (b) agent technology — in intelligent software "bots" and avatars that will deliver information in more human-like ways and perform other tasks to support virtual life, and (c) natural language processing and speech synthesis — in the avatars and interactive components that will greatly exceed text-based attempts at communication, where limitations in expressing even the simplest of human emotions abound.

3.6 References

Addis, T. R. (1989, June). The science of knowledge: A research programme for knowledge engineering. In *Proceedings of the Third European Workshop on Knowledge Acquisition for Knowledge-Based Systems (EKAW' 89)*, Paris.

Alesso, H. P., & Smith, C. F. (2001). *The intelligent wireless Web*. Addison-Wesley Professional.

Barfield, W., & Caudell, T. (2001). Basic concepts in wearable computers and augmented reality. In *Fundamentals of wearable computers and augmented reality*. Mahwah, NJ: Lawrence Erlbaum Associates.

Beier, K. P. (2004). *Virtual reality: A short introduction*. Retrieved from http://www-vrl.umich.edu/intro/

Brachman, R., & Levesque, H. (1985) (Eds.). *Readings in knowledge representation*. Los Altos: Morgan Kaufman.

Carpenter, G. A., Grossberg, S., & Mehanian, C. (1989). Invariant recognition of cluttered scenes by a self- organizing ART architecture: CORT-X boundary segmentation. *Neural Networks, 2,* 169-181.

Franklin, S., & Graesser, A. (1996). Is it an agent, or just a program? A taxonomy for autonomous agents. In *Proceedings of the Third International Workshop on Agent Theories, Architectures, and Languages.* Springer-Verlag. Retrieved from http://www.msci.memphis.edu/%7Efranklin/AgentProg.html

Gardner, M. (1970). Mathematical games: The fantastic combinations of John Conway's new solitaire game "life." *Scientific American, 223,* 120-123.

Halal, W. (2004). The intelligent Internet: The promise of smart computers and e-commerce. *The Futurist: The Intelligent Internet.*

Hayes-Roth. (1995), An architecture for adaptive intelligent systems. *Artificial Intelligence: Special Issue on Agents and Interactivity, 72,* 329-365.

Hobbes, R. (2004). *Hobbes' Internet Timeline v7.0.* Zakon Group LLC. Retrieved from http://www.zakon.org/robert/internet/timeline/

Kohonen, T. (1982). Self-organizing formation of topologically correct feature maps. *Biological Cybernetics, 43*(1),59-69.

Leiner, B. M., Vinton, G., Cerf, D. D., Clark, R. E., Kahn, L., Kleinrock, D. C., et al. (2003) *A brief history of the Internet.* Retrieved from http://www.isoc.org/internet/history/brief.shtml

Levy, S. (1992). *Artificial life: The quest for a new creation.* Pantheon.

Maes, P. (1995). Artificial life meets entertainment: Life like autonomous agents. *Communications of the ACM, 38*(11), 108-114.

McArthur, D., Cameron, G., While, M., & Wylie, B. (1994). *Paramics: Parallel microscopic traffic simulator.* Edinburgh: Kings Buildings Edinburgh.

McCarthy, J., Minsky, M. L., Rochester, N., & Shannon, C. E. (1955). *A proposal for the Dartmouth Summer Research Project on artificial intelligence, August 1956.* Stanford University. Retrieved from http://www-formal.stanford.edu/jmc/history/dartmouth/dartmouth.htm

McCulloch, W. S., & Pitts, W. H. (1943). A logical calculus of the ideas immanent in nervous activity. *Bulletin of Mathematical Biophysics, 5,*115-133.

Menzies, T. (2003, May/June). Twenty-first-century AI: Proud, not smug. *IEEE Intelligent Systems.*

Minsky, M. L., & Pappert, S. A. (1969). *Perceptrons.* MIT Press.

Minsky, M. (1980). *Telepresence.* Omni. NY: Omni Publications International Ltd.

Moore, R. C. (1995). *Logic and representation.* Cambridge, UK: Cambridge University Press.

Newell, A., & Simon, H. A. (1976). Computer science as empirical Inquiry: Symbols and search. *Communications of the ACM, 19*(3).

Rosenblatt, F. (1958). The perceptron: A probabilistic model for information storage and organization in the brain. *Psychological Review, 65*(6), pp. 386-408.

Russell, S. J., & Norvig, P. (1995). *Artificial intelligence: A modern approach.* Englewood Cliffs, NJ: Prentice Hall.

Scanlon, L. (2004). *Rethinking the computer.* Retrieved from http://www.technologyreview.com/articles/04/07/scanlon0704.asp

Shadbolt, N. (2003). Ambient intelligence. *IEEE Intelligent Systems.* Retrieved from http://csdl.computer.org/comp/mags/ex/2003/04/x4002.pdf

Smith, Cypher, & Spohrer. (1994). KidSim: Programming sgents without a programming language. *Communications of the ACM, 37*(7), 55-67.

Steels, L., & Brooks, R. (1995). (Eds.). *The artificial life route to artificial intelligence: Building embodied situated agents.* Lawrence Erlbaum Associates, Inc.

Waldrop, M. M. (1992). *Complexity: The emerging science at the edge of order and chaos.* Simon & Schuster.

Warner Brothers. (2001). *Artificial intelligence*. Retrieved from http://aimovie.warnerbros.com/

Weiser (1996).

Weiser, M., & Seely Brown, J. (1995). *Designing calm technology*. Xerox PARC, December 21. Retrieved from http://www.ubiq.com/hypertext/weiser/calmtech/calmtech.htm

Wooldridge. (1999).

Wooldridge, & Jennings. (1995). Agent theories, architectures, and languages: A survey. In Wooldridge & Jennings (Eds.), *Intelligent agents* (pp. 1-22). Berlin: Springer-Verlag.

Chapter 4

Future Directions and the Challenges

"Where a calculator on the ENIAC is equipped with 18,000 vacuum tubes and weighs 30 tons, computers in the future may have only 1,000 vaccuum tubes and perhaps weigh 1.5 tons."

Unknown, Popular Mechanics, March 1949

"If the automobile had followed the same development cycle as the computer, a Rolls-Royce would today cost $100, get a million miles per gallon, and explode once a year, killing everyone inside."

Robert X. Cringely

4.1 Introduction

In this chapter, we take a reflective look at these 21st century technologies, considering the future directions. Rather than specific projects or predictions about what AI might achieve, we consider the future in broader terms.

First, we examine the penetration of AI technologies into society, observing that much AI is embedded in existing products. These products are commonplace and accepted, and people are often unaware that AI has even been utilised in them. AI will improve processes and services and continue to enhance tasks and operations that must be done manually. We consider how this trend will continue in the future. As the machine gains "intelligence" to act in society, the need to "relate" to the human world increases.

We see "relational AI" as the main challenge and future direction for intelligent machines of the future. "Relational AI" is the great variety of issues surrounding "interaction" and "communication" with the human world. The challenge of interacting with people, maybe with natural language, maybe directly through speech, is one of the greatest challenges that a machine could face. It was identified as the "big challenge" at the start of the field in the Turing test, and this human-machine interface is still going to be a challenge for the future.

Finally, in terms of general direction, we see that "relational AI" will only intensify the need for, and possibility of, machine "incarnation" and "presence" in society, in its own right. This will open a variety of challenges: from autonomous robotic entities that are able to navigate a human world, to intelligent agents serving human purposes in the virtual world. It also opens up a range of issues associated with "machines in a human world," and just how they will "behave."

The objective of this chapter is to consider some of the future directions of the 21st century technologies, focusing upon AI. We aim to point out some of the challenges that the field faces; challenges which revolve around the necessity for machines to relate to the human world, to be contextualised within the world, to be "relational" and "social" with a human-machine interface that surpasses the current scope for interaction; where the "behaviour" of the machine needs to be controlled and considered. It is important to point out some of these challenges, since a later consideration of the philosophy of AI, will highlight some of the contributions that can be made to AI with its underlying philosophy.

4.2 The Penetration of AI Technologies in Society

In this section, we consider the penetration of 21st century technologies into society at the start of the 21st century. We find that AI is actually already very much a part of everyday life, although it may not be obvious. We consider perspectives of what today's AI is about and focus on some specific projects, including the computerised office as an example of "pervasive computing," domestic robotics, autonomous vehicles, interactive architecture tools, and speech recognition and synthesis as the means of facilitating more "natural" interaction with intelligent machines. The message is that AI has penetrated society, largely through existing products, with some prototype "new" inventions that are still essentially "enhancements" of existing tools. The future directions will be market driven, and products are going to have to face the "human communication" challenge.

At the start of the 21st century, AI is very much a part of everyday life, although we may not often notice AI. But it is present: in computer games, in the cruise control of cars, the servers that route e-mail, and many other facets of life. Companies in health care, finance, and retailing are using artificial intelligence systems to filter huge amounts of data and identify suspicious transactions. AI software helps engineers create better jet engines. In factories, it boosts productivity by monitoring equipment and signalling when preventive maintenance is needed. The Pentagon uses AI to coordinate its immense logistics operations. And in the pharmaceutical sector, it is used to gain new insights into the tremendous amount of data on the human genome. AI often helps people in every field make better use of information to work smarter, not harder. Tim Menzies (2003) states that in the 21st century, AI is not necessarily amazing, and is often routine, but it is certainly "no longer a bleeding-edge technology — hyped by its proponents and mistrusted by the mainstream." It is simply "with us."

We see a trend that AI is penetrating society as a technology embedded in other technologies. It is not offering a "new" technology, a revolutionary device, or a super-human robot to shake society: rather it is infiltrating slowly in existing products. As a society, the Japanese are especially advanced in the general uptake and utilisation of AI, especially in domestic gadgets for the consumer market. For example, the domestic scene is witnessing more and more "gadgets," each making just a small step of improvement from the last. There is not a revolutionary new device, but the "evolution" of an existing one, as, for example, has occurred with the washing machine. The washing machine has become more sophisticated and able to automatically and "intelligently" adjust the way it washes according to the amount of soiling it detects in the clothes, the weight of the load, and so on. An AI method known as fuzzy logic is often behind the "flexibility" that such a device demonstrates. The "takeover" of existing technologies is perhaps one of the subtlest infiltrations that "intelligent" technology could make into society, hiding as it does in an already established technology, simply making them smarter.

AI will also improve processes and services, and continue to enhance tasks and operations that must be done manually. For example, we may be used to the idea of commercial organisations providing a "service" to protect its customers from fraud, but instead of this being done "manually," AI will play an increasing role. AI is already used to detect credit card fraud, with neural networks examining the patterns of usage to detect anomalies where it is not possible or appropriate to use conventional statistics. And no doubt, intelligence will continue to be applied to fraud detection enhancing existing systems. AI is used in signature verification systems and other biometrics, and the "intelligence," with which a machine "recognises" people, will continue to improve. We have services that aim to optimise transport systems, scheduling, plant operation, medical diagnosis, and many other facets of life. These will all benefit from AI application, perhaps enabling the apparent "intelligence" to increase, or at least augment/synthesise the information that the human receives to undertake the task and improve their performance.

The 21st century is also seeing a growing commercial viability of "intelligent systems" as is illustrated in Figure 2. The figure shows a summary representation of Tim Menzies (2003) "hype-curve," based on the IEEE intelligent systems article, 21st century AI: Proud, not smug. It shows how the technology developed through its early historical days, promising much and delivering little to its routine use today where it is entering into a plateau of profitability. AI was initially highly "visible," but has become less "obvious" at the start of the 21st century. As with any other technology, as it

Figure 2. The AI hype cycle

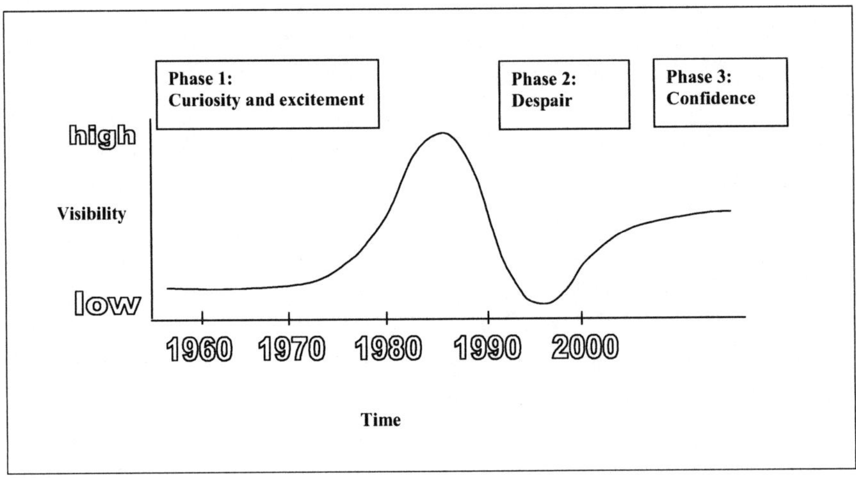

becomes "embedded" into use in society and daily life, it is absorbed without explicit awareness of the face that it is being used. Menzies further explains the "technology trigger" just before the mid-1980s, facilitating widespread inflated expectations that led to the "despair" phase and "AI winter" until in the later 1990s, Menzies reported a gradual rise of "enlightenment" to profitability in the 21st century

The AI "hype-cycle" represents one perspective of how AI has historically developed, although it omits a detailed picture of the very early days when there was much hype, and AI was perhaps as visible as it is reported in the mid-1980s peak of inflated expectations. The progress from the 1990s "despair" to the declaration of 21st century profitability is perhaps representing an overoptimistic version of AI embedded within society, as commonplace and profitable. Even if this is the general trend, the explanation as to why there has been this "improvement" from the overinflated expectations is not clear, nor why the current phase is one of "confidence." The absence of AI-related disciplines in core ACM computing curriculum for tertiary education is just one point in question that casts doubt on whether this "hype-curve" is a little overoptimistic; it may perceive AI is of greater importance, acceptance, and profitability than is in reality in existence. Perhaps time will enable the accuracy of this "historical perspective" to be better assessed. However, the message at the start of the 21st century is that AI is profitable; it is penetrating society in subtle ways, through existing products that it enhances.

However, while AI may most rapidly be penetrating society through existing products, there are also some "new" items filtering through. Many of them are still experimental and not widely available, but they exist. McKie and Smith (2004) remind us that robots are also finding their foot in everyday domestic life through vacuum cleaners and lawnmowers, and are optimistically set to become as common as TVs. The difficulties that have been encountered with robot movement, especially through making artificial limbs, have led to the embedding of intelligence within existing devices. Thus, we now have washing machines with chips attached, clever toasters, and intelligent fridges that will tell you when you are about to run out of milk. Baard (2004) reports on the autonomous lawnmowers "designed to give residential lawns that professionally manicured look, which only professional landscapers could offer in the past." The blades whirr at speeds up to 5,800 rpm with lights blinking steadily as the robotic mowers trim lawns right up to walkway edges and around flowerbeds and swimming pools. The latest Robomower, the RL1000, automatically navigates back to its docking station when it needs recharging.

For the most complex, sophisticated robot in operation, the top candidates must be the two automated surveyor vehicles, Spirit and Opportunity, that are now trundling across the surface of Mars. Akin is developing robots for use on the Hubble Space Telescope. The robots have considerable autonomy and have made remarkable discoveries, but they have real limitations. The two little rovers, each the size of a supermarket trolley, cost more than $600 million to build and launch, and have uncovered key evidence about past prevalence of water on the red planet since they landed last January. But it has been a very slow business, and takes Spirit or Opportunity a day to do what a human being can do in 45 seconds. McKie and Smith (2004) report "when Spirit or Opportunity comes to a rock or boulder, the robot has to stop and examine it carefully, slowly trundle round it, and then continue on its way. Each craft's computer brain estimates the distance it travels by counting numbers of revolutions of wheels. But these often slip in the sands of Mars, and the robots keep falling short of their programmed destinations. Now controllers are trying to reprogramme them to use visual cues."

From the U.S., McGray (2004) describes the robot car race organised by the Pentagon that offered $1 million for the team whose unmanned car could drive 142 miles across the desert from Barstow in California to Las Vegas in Nevada. The Pentagon wants a third of its trucks, tanks, and recon vehicles to operate on their own by 2015. But the contest proved to be a disaster. Only 13 of the 25 cars that were entered were able to start. The rest succumbed to various faults and accidents within seven miles of the starting flag, with the last surviving car falling into a ditch where it caught fire. The science of robot cars has a way to go, it would seem. Slow-moving exploratory robots are one thing. They stay out of trouble only because they creep. NASA's Spirit and Opportunity, roving around Mars, hit top speed at about a tenth of a mile per hour. Racing poses a different set of problems. Speed turns ordinary hills, rocks, and ditches into potentially fatal accident sites, and it strains visual sensors that, even while stationary, have all kinds of blind spots. The faster a robot moves, the less time its software has to make sense of the incomplete and contradictory data those sensors collect. And that means less time to pick a safe path, even using combinations of radar, ladar (a laser used to measure distance), stereovision, and GPS, while having to average more than 20 miles per hour to make use of the 10 hours of daylight available.

From China, "cybertecture" represents the future for design around the world, http://news.xinhuanet.com/english/2004-10/14/content_2090368.htm with "interactive architecture." Cybertecture environments are hybrids designed from the inside out, and using technology to give the space the intelligence needed to interact with its users. Cybertecture is aimed at enhancing and improving the quality of life by harnessing the power of technology, according to James Law, who has designed some of the world's most innovative cybertecture projects, including the world's first "morphable" house in cooperation with IBM in Denmark. Law's latest cybertecture project in China, Cybertecture Center of China Telecom located in Santou City of Guangdong Province, features cutting edge technology, including human presence detection devices, cybercharacter control and host, infrared location devices and ear sets, fiber optic projections, home automation devices, and animatronics presentations.

Perhaps most significant in the area of speech recognition and synthesis is the application that seeks to create a "verbal" information resource — Web-like in its capacity — permitting the users of mobile phones and other portable devices to access the Internet. The limited display options on handheld devices and the natural preference for people to communicate via speech rather than through typed text is further going to drive the future of natural language research, ensuring that it is very much a part of technology in the 21st century.

In the realm of speech recognition, IBM has a super human speech recognition program aiming to greatly improve accuracy; in the next decade, Microsoft's program is expected to reduce the error rate of speech recognition, making it match human capabilities. The MIT is planning to demonstrate their Project Oxygen, which features a voice-machine interface. Amtrak, Wells Fargo, Land's End, and many other organizations are replacing keypad-menu call centers with speech-recognition systems, because they improve customer service and recover investment in a year or two. General Motors' OnStar driver assistance system relies primarily on voice commands with live staff for backup; the number of subscribers has grown from 200,000 to 2 million, and is expected to increase by 1 million per year. The Lexus DVD navigation system responds to over 100 commands and guides the driver with voice and visual directions. BCC Corporation estimates total AI sales to grow from $12 billion in 2002 to $21 billion in 2007.

The message surely is that AI is here, it is embedding within existing products, and it is also spawning new products. As the penetration of AI and associated technologies continues in society, some fundamental differences between people and machines will have to be faced. One of these is the human ability to "relate" and "communicate" and "exchange information" and do so in a humanlike way; perhaps even through natural language. Achieving the "relational" machine is perhaps the current challenge of AI, and the biggest "limitation" that the field may face. There may be smarter and smarter domestic products, and as long as a switch or a button can control them they will be fine: or will they? Even in this context, the "technology" is required to "relate" and "communicate" with a human. It is with communication that the difficulties and limitations of AI and associated technologies become apparent.

In an attempt to understand the state of the art in today's AI, the MIT AI Laboratory met in 1997 with senior technical management and corporate strategists. They were interested in the future business impact of artificial intelligence technology. Development leaders from Microsoft, Netscape, General Electric, and Disney discussed numerous examples of AI-enabled products and product enhancements finding:

- Today's AI is about **new ways of connecting people** to computers, people to knowledge, people to the physical world, and people to people,
- Today's AI is enabled in part by **technical advances** and in part by **hardware and infrastructure advances**. The World Wide Web is here and truly gigantic high-resolution displays are coming.
- Today's AI invites **investment in systems** that:
    1. **Save money,** through applications such as resource allocation, fraud detection, database mining, and training.
    2. **Increase competitiveness** through applications that provide, for example, on-screen help and low-cost rationale capture.
    3. **Create new capabilities and new revenue streams** in areas such as medicine and information access.

If a component of today's AI is commercially driven, that will surely continue into the future. If today's AI is about "connecting people to computers, people to knowledge, people to the physical world, and people to people," tomorrow's AI will also have "connecting" and "interacting" as a crucial component. This crucial aspect of "interacting" or "communication" was observed as important right from the start of AI. That specific act of human-machine communication has never ceased to be an intrinsic problem and goal with which AI is concerned: and is going to be one of the most challenging problems of the future. The future of AI might even be reduced to that which is "interactive AI," or "relational AI," even "reality AI," representing the "incarnation" of the machine in the human world in a profound way.

4.3 The Relational Machine

The "relational machine" will be one of the biggest future projects in AI. Communication is, naturally, vitally important, whether between people in an ambient intelligence environment, or between people and machines, or even between computers. Communication was one of the original problems posed for the field in the Turing test, and will be one of the problems that remains with the field.

"Relational AI" will, at some juncture, have to face the challenge of human-machine communication. Such communication is not just the problem of natural language, whether it is through speech synthesis, voice recognition, textual comprehension, or other. The "embedded" social context of computing presents the most severe challenges of AI. Despite the great advances that are reported in natural language processing and speech recognition/synthesis, there are still fundamental problems that the field is encountering

Alan M. Turing introduced "the imitation game" in his 1950 article (Turing, 1950). He boldly began with the sentence: "I propose to consider the question 'Can machines think?' This should begin with definitions of the meaning of the terms 'machine' and 'think.'" The Turing test is meant to determine if a computer program has intelligence. Quoting Turing, the original imitation game can be described as follows: "The new form of the problem can be described in terms of a game which we call the 'imitation game.' It is played with three people, a man (A), a woman (B), and an interrogator (C), who may be of either sex. The interrogator stays in a room apart from the other two. The object of the game for the interrogator is to determine which of the other two is the man and which is the woman. He knows them by labels X and Y, and at the end of the game he says either 'X is A and Y is B' or 'X is B and Y is A.' The interrogator is allowed to put questions to A and B." (http://cogsci.ucsd.edu/~asaygin/tt/ttest.html). Essentially, the interrogator is connected to one person and one machine via a terminal: therefore, s/he cannot see his/her counterparts. The task is to find out which of the two candidates is the machine and which is the human, only by asking them questions. If the machine can "fool" the interrogator, it is intelligent.

The Turing test has most often been discussed in the context of the philosophy of AI where its adequacy as a test for determining intelligence was often questioned. The test is a behavioural test, where the "intelligence" of the machine is judged solely on the linguistic action it performs. Even if the responses were "appropriate" enough to convince a human participant that the machine was a person (and deceive the participant about its identity), there is the underlying question of whether this is really intelligence. The proponents of strong AI point out the impossibility of cognitive states in the machine, meaning that whatever behavioural aspects of humans might be reproduced, the essence in the cognitive states is still missing. The machine may appear to be intelligent, but it is not. This is certainly a valid point in terms of the test determining whether the machine is actually intelligent, and the test may be questioned on these grounds.

Additionally, the focus on language as an indicator of intelligence is a limitation of the test. The ability of a machine to make an appropriate response in a conversation says nothing about other "intelligences" such as planning, or problem solving, or creative ability, social intelligence, or other. It is interesting that natural language (often regarded as a uniquely human faculty distinct from any animal "language" because of the richness of its expression) was chosen for the test: but naturally, we may extrapolate the principles of this test to any field of human activity. We may, however, generalise the concept of the test and apply it to behaviour in many domains, and ask "whether a person can tell the difference between the behaviour of a person and machine." However, ultimately, we will encounter the same difficulty as we find in discerning the internal workings of another person when a certain behaviour is demonstrated. We cannot really tell whether another person "thinks" or "feels" or whatever.

The Turing test was taken very literally by Joseph Weizenbaum (1966), a scientist at the Massachusetts Institute of Technology, when he created a computer program called Eliza. The title of Weizenbaum's paper revealed his motivations: Eliza: A computer program for the study of natural language communication between man and machine. Eliza was a text-parsing engine that simulated a psychoanalysis session by answering input with related questions. Eliza actually had a set of stock phrases and some templates to match sentence patterns, and made responses according to this limited "knowledge" base. The program clearly had no intelligence, but was actually quite popular. Many humans used it even though it was limited in its ability, and after a while its "stock phrases" become apparent. Since then, there have been many attempts to have a machine communicate in an even more humanlike way, and do so in a far more sophisticated way than matching a template and selecting a response. AI awaits a convincing demonstration of machine natural language.

Today, the Loebner Prize supports a competition that is an extension of the language game of Turing. The Loebner Prize is based on a fund established by New York businessman Hugh G. Loebner. It is awarded annually for the computer program that best emulates natural human linguistic behaviour. During the contest, a panel of independent judges attempts to determine whether the responses on a computer terminal are being produced by a computer or a person. The designers of the best program each year win a cash award and a medal. If a program passes the test in all its particulars, then the entire fund will be paid to the program's designer and the fund abolished (http://www.loebner.net/Prizef/loebner-prize.html).

Barberi (1992) presents an enhanced version of the Turing test that is to be undertaken with computer-mediated communication. The underlying idea of the test is still the same, but the amount of interaction between judge and subject is increased greatly. The player bases his or her decision not only on written words, but also on spoken speech, nonverbal cues, and body movement. Like the original test, the judge has no way of telling if the subject is human or not until he interacts with it. Like the original test, the goal of the computer is to create a simulation of human action so realistic that not even other humans can tell the difference. The enhanced Turing test simply brings out the "human communication" that computer-facilitated communication, that is the Internet, is intended to facilitate. Many of the "rules" of face-to-face human communication are changed and altered, making it an environment where it is possible that a machine and person can communicate on more "equal footing." However, the horrendous complexities of "meaning" in natural language, even if partly resolved by the nonverbal elements that the enhanced test would incorporate, remain.

Tom Addis (2004) has been active in the field of "nonconventional" and socially sensitive computing, advocating that computers will never have the possibility of natural communication with people unless they become part of human society. Addis, writing on the challenges of nonconventional computing states "The proposal arises from the puzzle as to why, after sixty years of effort, millions of man hours and technology that boasts of silicon machines that do 1,000+ Gigaflops with a 1,000+ Terabytes of storage, have still not even addressed many of the important functions of a human brain; a device that looks like a bowl of porridge and consists of only 15 Gigacells working at about 50 cycles per second." Nonconventional computing recognises that the human is "situated." Addis finds that "lack of natural communication is evident by the common complaint of 'computer rage' and that the same paradigm shift that Wittgenstein took is thus long overdue for Computer Science."

The possibility of the "relational machine" is the biggest challenge for AI in the 21st century. Whether interacting in the virtual world, or the real world, the task is enormous, and has not yet been solved. Society awaits a machine that can support natural human communication between human and machine, and facilitate more natural exchanges in the Internet.

4.4 Mind Where You're Going

Finally, in terms of general direction, we see that "relational AI" will only intensify the need for, and possibility of, machine "incarnation" and "presence" in society in its own right. This will open a variety of challenges: from autonomous robotic entities that are able to navigate a human world, to intelligent agents serving human purposes in the virtual world. It also opens up a range of issues associated with "machines in a human world." Some see that the future developments of technology will not just be creating technological devices that are more "human." Rather there will be a "merge" of flesh and silicon augmenting the human body with technological devices and bionic implants. There is, and will be, a synthesis of technology and human flesh.

Optimistic predications about the future capabilities of technology and the speed of change only underlie the fact that one of the biggest future challenges will be the philosophical and ethical challenge of where we are going with technology.

First, in a very literal sense, the task of navigating in a human world is far from simple. The operation of walking is highly complex, and researchers have investigated "insect" intelligence for moving machines around. The difficulty of identifying and dealing with obstacles presents one challenge, the mechanics of operating artificial limbs presents another. Machine entities that have been constructed to operate and move in the physical world are vastly different in appearance from humans or even the insects and animals they may be imitating. The physical "movement" problem is so complex that we may wonder whether researchers may simply turn to another method of "navigating," — perhaps embedding intelligence into existing biological forms in order to overcome the physical difficulties of traversing the physical world. The area of "autonomy" is a highly challenging area. In a very literal sense, the machine has to "mind where it is going" so as not to harm itself or the physical world in which it is manifest.

We may think that the difficulties of physical incarnation can be overcome by restricting machine "intelligence" to the virtual world. In such an "abstracted environment," reality itself is virtual. We may think that in a virtual world the machine may have a better chance of being part of the human realm, not having to deal with the physical difficulties of incarnation. Just as humans "incarnate" to each other and have "presence" through computer-mediated communication, so may a machine. However, this "simplified environment" may eliminate some problems, but only introduces others. In some regards, the abstraction from the physical world only intensifies the problem of "context," a factor that is so vital to "meaning." To operate in the virtual world and exchange with other humans, a person needs a highly developed sense of "context," perhaps more so than the physical exchange that may occur when people are in the same room. In the virtual world, the human is denied a variety of "cues" that help meaning, and they have to draw upon sophisticated but often "tacit" knowledge. Operation in a virtual world may appear to eliminate problems, but actually creates others.

Perhaps one of the most challenging but common factors to incarnation in both the physical world and the virtual world is the challenge that some may call "mind" or "consciousness." The word "mind" comes with philosophical assumptions that we do not want to make here. We use it to capture the essence of having human aims and motives, being logical (and at times illogical), having memory and emotion, future goals, humour, and a whole variety of markers that would reveal "humanness" to another person. The idea of "mind," in fact, overlaps with the "relational machine," for it is in relating to a human that such a sophisticated "interface" is necessary. In stand-alone AI products or AI embedded in existing devices, we probably do not care about this "mind." It makes no difference whether a gadget "appears" human or not. But when we start considering "incarnational" and "relational" machines — in the physical or virtual world — we come across the need to capture something of the "human." And here is perhaps the greatest future and present challenge of AI.

If and when we ever attained the technology and methods that might achieve that "mind," there are of course the more "philosophical" questions about it. There are questions of teleology or purpose, the goals of that "mind," the intent and action stemming from that "mind," the "morality" of that mind, whether we could consider it "human," how we might ensure it "helped" and not "harmed" human life, whether it was predictable or gave the appearance of free will, and other issues. We are so far from achieving such a sophisticated "model" that such questions are safely within the realm of science fiction. But the questions cannot be ignored. There are also those who are less pessimistic about the possibilities of what technology will achieve in the realm of incarnational, relational AI.

For example, Sidney Perkowitz (2004) is a machine intelligence enthusiast who sees human robots developing human capabilities and more. This is the big issue in his book *Digital People: From Bionic Humans to Androids*. He defines intelligent robots as machines that react and adapt to their environment. Although the robots of today can move in human worlds, talk and interact, they are a long way from becoming self-aware, or really being truly humanlike in facial expression; voice recognition; and ability to walk, talk, and make decisions. Yet Perkowitz frames the robotic revolution, which is advancing in leaps and bounds, to be a technological notch in our evolution. He describes how a new generation of robots could serve as "the next level of humanity."

In contrast to creating machines that are more human, there are those who see technology as potentially augmenting the human body with technological devices. McKie (2002) describes the bridging of the human and technological, finding that human evolution is being shaped by technology: using genetic techniques, and bridging the gap with robotics. Loft (2004) believes that "sometime in the not-too-distant future, the worlds of people and robots will merge." Humans already are heading in artificial directions. As people live longer and medical technologies offer new kinds of replacement parts, people will become more and more hybrid — part flesh and bone, part wire and titanium. Eventually, these bionic parts will evolve beyond the mere mechanical functioning within the body's nerve network. This is the science of neurorobotics. The future of this technology "is the formation of direct connections between living organic systems and nonliving ones at the neural and brain levels." This angle of the identity "merge" will see people become more "techno" than flesh.

There is an undeniable and increasing merge of "flesh" and "silicon" in some extraordinary ways. Aside from false teeth and artificial limbs, there is the RFID (radio frequency identification device) chip. Granneman (2003) explains that RFID tags are essentially microchips, some are only 1/3 of a millimeter across, acting as transponders (transmitters/responders), always listening for a radio signal sent by transceivers or RFID readers. When a transponder receives a certain radio query, it responds by transmitting its unique ID code back to the transceiver. Most RFID tags are powered by the radio signal that wakes them up and requests an answer. Most uses of RFID are for tagging pets and swipe cards to operate gates, although the list of uses is endless, from surveillance to security in supermarkets. Some manufacturers are planning to tag just the packaging, but others will also tag their products. There is no law requiring a label indicating that an RFID chip is in a product. Some RFID chips are designed to withstand years of wearing, washing, and drying, and are microscopic. While they could be crushed, punctured, or microwaved, they would have to be found first!

However, these RFID chips are not just restricted to implantation in products. They could possibly create a kind of human "cyborg." The VeriChipTM from Applied Digital (http://www.adsx.com/content/index.htm) is designed for implantation in people. Only 11-mm long, it is designed to go under the skin, where it can be read from four feet away. They sell it as a great way to keep track of children, Alzheimer's patients in danger of wandering, and anyone else with a medical disability. Some patrons of a club in Barcelona used RFID as a means of paying for their drinks, and some Mexican law enforcement officials had the chips implanted as a means of fending off attempted kidnappings.

Kevin Warwick, University of Reading, UK, made one of the earliest examples of "flesh meets silicon." Warwick stunned the scientific community in 1998 by having an RFID silicon chip transponder surgically implanted into his arm. For Warwick, the chip made it possible to turn the light on and off when entering a room. He proved that it is indeed possible to link humans and machines, thereby directly harnessing machine intelligence. Warwick received a lot of criticism as he married humanity and technology in this way. More recently, Warwick (Best, 2004) has warned that viruses can infect humans as well as PCs, as "cyborgs" become more common than pure humans. If humans were networked, the implications of being hacked would be far more serious. With his own networking experiments, in which he used his body's connectivity to operate a mechanical arm in the U.S., Warwick did not publicise the IP address of his arm, in case someone hijacked it.

The merge of technology and flesh raises all manner of philosophical questions. Such technologies could potentially cause great harm to human life; even the survival of our species could be at risk. Seeking to understand the dangers, and working to prevent disasters, is an essential part of the future technological agenda. Optimistic predications about the future capabilities of technology and the speed of change only underlie the fact that one of the biggest future challenges will be the philosophical and ethical challenge of where we are going with technology. In fact, we find that the future challenges are not just philosophical, but they are theological and religious.

4.5 References

Addis, T., & Billinge, D. (2004). *Music to our ears: A required paradigm shift for computer science*. International Association for Computing and Philosophy, IACAP. University of Pavia. Retrieved from http://www.cs.york.ac.uk/nature/gc7/addis.pdf

Baard, M. (2004). Lawn mowing for lazybones, *Wired News*. Retrieved from http://www.wired.com/news/technology/0,1282,62853,00.html

Barberi, D. (1992) *The ultimate Turing test*. Retrieved from http://david.barberi.com/papers/ultimate.turing.test

Best, J. (2004). *Could future computer viruses infect humans*? Retrieved from http://networks.silicon.com/webwatch/0,39024667,39125887,00.htm

Granneman, S. (2003). *RFID chips are here*. Retrieved from http://www.theregister.co.uk/2003/06/27/rfid_chips_are_here/

Loft. (2004).

McGray, D. (2004). The great robot race. *Wired Magazine*. Retrieved from http://www.wired.com/wired/archive/12.03/robot.html

McKie, R. (2002, Feb. 03). Is human evolution finally over? *The Observer*. Retrieved from http://observer.guardian.co.uk/international/story/0,6903,644002,00.html

McKie, R., & Smith, D. (2004, July 18). Face of the future? *The Observer*. Retrieved from http://shopping.guardian.co.uk/gadgets/story/0,1587,1267100,00.html

Menzies, T. (2003). Twenty-first century AI: Proud, not smug. *IEEE Intelligent Systems*.

Perkowitz, S. (2004). *Digital people: From bionic humans to androids*. Joseph Henry Press.

Turing, A. (1950). Computing machinery and intelligence. *Mind, 59*(236), 433-460.

Weizenbaum, J. (1966). ELIZA-A computer program for the study of natural language communication between man and machine. *Communications of the ACM, 9*(1), 36-35.

Chapter 5

The Techno-Religious Age

"Computer science is no more about computers than astronomy is about telescopes."

E. W. Dijkstra

"Science without religion is lame, religion without science is blind."

Albert Einstein

5.1 Introduction

First, we consider the "spiritual search" that many have found to be foundational to humanity. Religion is foundational to humanity across the world. To some extent, sociology is a "secular panacea" for what classical philosophy called "The religious quest." The religious, and nonreligious quest is a search for meaning most commonly understood in religious contexts as a search for "god." In the last decade of the 20th century, a number of authors have recognized that technology is being used for a "spiritual quest." Increasingly, this is being expressed through the Internet and World Wide Web. The "search beyond Google" represents this human quest for meaning. Even though organised religion may be declining, the religious quest is not necessarily abating. Technology, along with some "alternative" religious expressions, is supporting the present day search.

Next we see how "transcendence" has been identified as a common theme of religion and technology. Technology, in its widest sense, is about transcendence, whether this is in medicine or agriculture. The extreme of technological transcendence is found in the transhumanist, who sees humanity to be in a transitional phase to be "completed" by technology. Most religions have a similar concept of "overcoming." The Christian concept of "resurrection" is the prime example of overcoming the ultimate human limitation, death, and religion seeking transcendence. If transcendence does unite the two disciplines, then it is also true that both religion and technology may be seen as "human constructions" — ultimate outworkings of the human striving to overcome. Putting religion and technology together creates a synthesis that we cannot ignore!

Next we look at five of the major world religions — Christianity, Judaism, Islam, Buddhism, and Hinduism — in order to see in what ways they hope to both find meaning and transcend. Christianity, Islam, and Judaism (Orthodox) share the vision of death being transcendence, enabling the person to be "with God." There is a sense that this is a "perfect state" entailing happiness and overcoming of human suffering, pain, and so forth, with Islam especially emphasising the "pleasures" of the world to come, including sensual pleasures. Buddhism and Hinduism find transcendence possible within this world. They also have the conception of "reincarnation," with Buddhism not necessarily having any sense of divine in which meaning is found. Zen Buddhism would locate this "meaning" within the individual.

Finally, we pause to find out where and how and whether these five major world religions have apprehended technology in their pursuit to find meaning and transcend. We make an emphasis on Internet and communication technology, since these are the main ways that technology has impacted religion. We seek where particular elements of the religion intersect with Internet technologies. For example, where pilgrimage is important, there are facilities for taking a "virtual tour"; where "image veneration" is important, there is scope for downloading them; where teaching and "knowledge for enlightenment" is vital, there is online learning; where community is important, there are electronic forums stimulating it; where "spreading the message" is vital, there are Web sites with apologetics.

The objective of this chapter is to point out the "religious quest" that is happening even in the 21st century world; to point out some of the "similarities" of religion and technology in the sense of transcendence, meaning, and "inevitable" human construction. We also want to introduce and outline five of the major world religions, providing some background for Christianity that will be discussed in more detail in subsequent chapters. Seeing the ways that different religions have apprehended Internet technology is then the final aim. We particularly seek to draw out where unique elements of the religion intersect with Internet technology, such as community and the virtual forums that stimulate it. In many ways, we are in a techno-religious age, where technology and religion have united in the most human of quests for transcendence.

5.2 The Search Beyond Google™

There is a search for meaning within humanity and each individual human that philosophers have long recognised. Common answers to the "meaning of life" include happiness, love, compassion, pleasure, reproduction, power, and knowledge. Traditionally, religion was the supplier of meaning, and the quest for meaning was found to be, at root, a quest for God. The prevalence of religion across every culture of the globe points to this "quest for meaning" and "God." The two points that anthropologists agree upon are (1) the unity of the human race and (2) the phenomenon of religious aspiration. Religion as a historical and psychological phenomenon is one common element across the world. Sociology and psychology confirm that various races are, in a basic sense, intellectually and emotionally the same. Demetrios J. Constantelos (1998) writes "the spiritual unity of humankind is proved by the existence of common or similar spiritual and religious experiences. It is also indicated by the essentially religious nature of the human being."

The human quest for meaning takes many forms. Stoker (1996) examines the religious and nonreligious quest for meaning, and aims to show how they are similar and how they differ. Both are intended to be the source of meaning for human questions of life and death. Javad (2004) explains how sociology, which is intended to rescue man from the valley of nonsense, has failed too. Modern social thought is concerned with the ultimate dimension of life in opposite to "death," that is, the meaninglessness of (this biological incidence) in relation to the meaningfulness (of the societal rationalization). Javad (2004) reports that "the quest of religion is what Socrates called the quest for the 'Examined Life.' He further argued that 'an unexamined life is not worth living.' If it is not worth living such a life, why should one bother to think about a system of thought, which does not offer any space for 'spiritual quest'? Sociology or what we have called the cosmogony of modern thinking has offered a 'secular panacea' for what Classical Philosophy called 'The Religious Quest,' that is 'sociology of religion.'"

The human quest for meaning takes many forms. Recently, Thomas Dunlap (2004) has written of environmentalism as a religious quest. Dunlap proposes that the environmental movement seeks to offer "material explanations. ... But looking beyond facts towards meaning." Environmentalism suggests that we should stand humble before Creation, even if there may not be a Creator, acknowledging our insignificance in a grand design. Dunlap sees environmentalism as countering rampant individualism and exploitation of nature. It seeks to use scientific facts in order to transform society, which is what makes it religious. Undoubtedly, there is a movement towards environmental concerns, as many people turn from the highly complex technological world to nature.

The decline in organised Christianity is also seeing people turn to "alternative" religions for the religious quest. The environmental and ecological concerns of environmentalism have already been noted as a new "religion." Neopaganism is also gaining popularity as the old gods and goddesses of pre-Christian polytheistic mythologies are reinvented and revived. People are also finding meaning in New Age philosophy: a collection of diverse movements that revolve around the central belief that humans are capable of shaping reality and establishing truth. Sometimes Eastern mysticism is imported to replace the vacuum left by conventional religion. There is also a resurgence of interest in atheism and secularism. Such "secular religion" includes those who are essentially passive with regards to belief and disbelief. Adherents tend to have their own personal philosophy and no stated affiliation with an organized religion: although some people do join "societies" and forums for fellowship purposes and mutual encouragement.

In the last decade of the 20th century, a number of authors have recognized that technology is being used for a "spiritual search." Increasingly, this is being expressed through the Internet and World Wide Web. Religious scholars, and seekers of enlightenment the world over, are starting to see the Internet as a dataline to the heavens: its seemingly limitless oceans of information perhaps persuading that the answers we all need, can be found somewhere online. The Net is more than just an information resource, however, also being a powerful communication tool, giving us new ways of interacting with the world.

Jensen (2004) has identified that God is the second most sought-after reality on the Internet (sex is the first!). He reports "This reminder of the human search for the divine is probably the most important thing we learn. People hunger for God. This reality surfaces in new forms in every generation." A similar observation was made by The Pew Internet and American Life Project (http://www.pewinternet.org/). They reported in late 2001 that one out of every four Internet users has sought religious or spiritual information at one point or another in their virtual travels, and on a daily basis, more people use the Internet for spiritual purposes than for gambling, banking, finding a date, trading stocks, or buying and selling at web auction sites like eBay, combined.

In their "search beyond Google," humans know that they need somehow to be plugged into something more important than the Internet, and are using the Internet-based virtual WWW communities in order to find those "answers." Nicky Gumbel (2003) articulates the basic human quest and search for God, finding seven basic questions. These are "Why does God allow suffering?" "What about other religions?" "What's wrong with sex before marriage?" "How does the New Age movement relate to Christianity?" "What is the Christian attitude toward homosexuality?" "Is there a conflict between science and Christianity?" and "Is the Trinity unbiblical, unbelievable, or even irrelevant?" These classical questions are often the stumbling block to people's participation in conventional organised religion. Even though organised religion may be declining, the religious quest is not necessarily abating, but technology is assisting it.

One context in which the religious quest is being pursued online is in countries and environments where real-world exploration may be suppressed. For example, within China, the climate has, for many years, sought to ensure the influences of religion are controlled. However, Reuters (2004) finds that the Chinese are very willing to use the Internet to discuss "spiritual matters": "the Chinese, meanwhile, are among the most active Net socializers. According to the study, Chinese Internet users say they rely on the medium to interact with others who share their political interests, hobbies and faith. 'It's more than in any other country and a significant figure for citizens of a nation in which religion is officially banned,' the study said of Chinese users' willingness to discuss religion online with others."

5.3 Mutual Transcendence

Noble (1977) finds that both religion and technology share one fundamental and underlying theme; that is their drive to transcend natural mortal life — nature, our bodies, humanity, and the world. Technology, in its widest sense, is about transcendence, whether this is in medicine or agriculture. Medicine promises to transcend sickness and postpone death through its application to disease and sickness. Improved fertilisers and genetically modified crops promise to produce bumper yields that will diminish famine. Computer and intelligent ICT technologies also aim to transcend. The prominence of computer-mediated communication is an example of transcending the distances between people, enabling interaction in online communities linking people from all over the world through the Internet. Intelligent machines are aiming to transcend human limitations of fatigue, or accuracy, or speed, or other through automatic sorting, machine readable postcodes, car number plates "read" by intelligent cameras, and a whole host of other applications. Science — through applied technology — assists and augments and promises to transcend natural limitations in just about every area of human life.

Religion is also frequently about "transcendence," typically with themes of "overcoming" and "transcending" this natural world. Most major world religions — with perhaps the exception of secularism — have the concept of "life after death"; whether this is "reincarnation" back to this world, or a "resurrection" to another. In this idea of "transcending" death, there is the ultimate expression of transcending human limitation, through transcending human mortality. The Christian concept of "bodily resurrection" is the ultimate example of overcoming the human limitation of death, with believers promised this "eternal life" not just for their "spirits" or their "souls," but for their whole, entire "person." That is, the complete identity of human beings may transcend this natural world.

The idea of transcendence may be behind the comparisons that have been made with technology as a religion that people follow as religiously as some people follow conventional religion. The technological gadgets and other devices fulfil a need within the individual — striving to consume or acquire or control or other — that conventional religion fulfils within its religious adherents. Also, the fascination with technology may represent the desire to seek something "greater" than one's self, as people look to the "miracles" of science in fear or sickness or some other predicament that only serves to underline human fragility. However, there is a vast difference between transcending the human condition and remaining human, and obliterating what it is to be human. Religion would enable the human to transcend and remain human, while technology makes no such promises.

In terms of actual desire to transcend the human condition, it is the transhumanist who most vividly represents the desire and drive to transcend through technology. The term "transhuman" goes back to the futurist FM-2030 (1989), who introduced it as shorthand for "transitional human," and saw it as an intermediary form between the human and the posthuman. Transhumanism includes the premise that the human species in its current form does not represent the end of our development but rather a comparatively early phase of its evolution. The transhumanist envisages a posthuman condition, where there is a "future being" whose basic capacities so radically exceed those of present humans as to be ambiguous and perhaps not human by our current standards. Many transhumanists wish to follow life paths that would, sooner or later, require growing into posthuman persons and reach transcendence: to intellectually surpass current human genius, as humans are above other primates; to be resistant to disease and impervious to aging; to have unlimited youth and vigor; to exercise control over their own desires, moods, and mental states; to be able to avoid feeling tired, hateful, or irritated about petty things; to have an increased capacity for pleasure, love, artistic appreciation, and serenity; to experience novel states of consciousness that current human brains cannot access.

The posthumanism FAQ claims it may be hard for us to imagine what a posthuman is like "Posthumans may have experiences and concerns that we cannot fathom, thoughts that cannot fit into the three-pound lumps of neural tissue that we use for thinking. Some posthumans may find it advantageous to jettison their bodies altogether and live as information patterns on vast super-fast computer networks. Their minds may be not only more powerful than ours but may also employ different cognitive architectures or include new sensory modalities that enable greater participation in their virtual reality settings. Posthuman minds might be able to share memories and experiences directly, greatly increasing the efficiency, quality, and modes in which posthumans could communicate with each other. The boundaries between posthuman minds may not be as sharply defined as those between humans. Posthumans might shape themselves and their environment in so many new and profound ways that speculations about the detailed features of posthumans and the posthuman world are likely to fail." The clear drive to "transcend" is undeniable in the ideas of the transhumanists and the posthuman condition they anticipate.

We could draw other similarities between technology and religion and find common ground. One of those is the way both may be regarded as "human construction." Hurd (2001) sees technology itself as a consequence of humanity: the act of creating and using "tools" for present and future use is part of what it is to be human. Also, while it may appear that humanity can transcend its own limitations through technology, there is no promise that this transcendence is either possible, or if it is possible, that it will not destroy humanity. There is a vast difference between transcending the human condition and remaining human, and obliterating what it is to be human.

Karl Barth (1969) also found religion to be a "human construction." For Barth, religion was an invention that represented an upward search for God on the part of humanity. Through rituals and the system of religious beliefs constructed, humanity "restricts" God's self-revelation. Barth wanted to distinguish between the "God discerned in Christ" and religion. While it may appear that humanity can transcend its own limitations through religion, Barth's observations make it questionable as to whether this transcendence is possible. In religion, the very striving for transcendence may inhibit perception of that revelation that has been made by the divine, although God may still graciously surpass that which has been made. Such a divine "intervention" may enable humanity to transcend their humanity, but remain human.

Both religion and technology are potentially devastating "juggernauts" that lay waste our nature; both are potentially "tools" that humanity uses to serve its own self-destructive purposes, and tools which humanity is "helpless" to transcend; both are "human constructions" that are "acts of defiance in the face of God" to the extent that they may stimulate a self-reliance and inhibit "encountering the transcendent"; both religion and technology are potentially the worst enemies of humanity. Putting them together may appear to be the ultimate act of self-destruction as a species. However, if human transcendence does ultimately need a "divine intervention" to be possible, and preserve what it is to be human, there is no reason why this "divine intervention" could not happen through the human construction of technology, rather than the "human construction" of religion. In fact, as mutual tool's of humanity, the phenomena of virtual religion is the inevitable combination.

5.4 World Religions

At the start of the 21st century, there are many, many religions in existence. Originally, only three religions were recognized: Christians, Jews, and pagans (i.e., everybody else). During the 1800s, comparative religion scholars increasingly recognized Judaism, Christianity, Islam, Hinduism, and Buddhism as the most significant "world religions." Even today, these are considered the "Big Five," and are the religions most likely to be covered in world religion books, and those we consider here. According to figures from Adherents.com (a collection of over 41,000 adherent statistics and religious geography citations for over 4,200 religions, churches, denominations, religious bodies, faith groups, etc.), the major two are Christianity and Islam.

In terms of doctrine, Christianity contains the belief that Jesus Christ is the Son of God, who came to earth as a man to restore the relationship between humans and God, which had gone wrong because of human sin. The Christian God is monotheistic and unique to all other religions is a God that "loves" in this dramatic way through restoring the relationship that humanity had broken. For an introduction to the basic tenets of Christianity, the "Alpha" course, by Nicky Gumbel (2003), provides an introduction that is used across the world. There are many variants of Christianity, with varying degrees of practise among adherents. The United States claims 44% of Americans attend church weekly, compared with 27% of people in Great Britain, 21% of the French, 4% of Swedes, and 3% of Japanese.

Christianity aims to provide an answer to the question of "meaning" by locating that in God. Theologian Carl F. H. Henry (1979) said: "the eternal and self-revealed Logos, incarnate in Jesus Christ, is the foundation of all meaning." Bruce Lockerbie (1986) puts it like this: "The divine nature manifesting itself in the physical form of Jesus of Nazareth is, " ... the focal point from which all being takes its meaning, the source of all coherence in the universe." In the Christian scriptures, the source of theology, the author Paul's sense of meaning and purpose was also found in Christ. Philippians 3:10–11 clarifies that "knowing Jesus surpasses all" and if it for transcendence "that I may know Him, and the power of His resurrection and the fellowship of His sufferings, being conformed to His death; in order that I may attain to the resurrection from the dead." Being united with Christ is at least one aspect of meaning that Christianity brings to human life. The purpose of life is found in "knowing Jesus," since it is through Jesus Christ that salvation is made possible and the human may be reunited with the Triune God — Father, Son, and Spirit-for eternity. Thus, in this meaning is found also the transcendence of this world that religion supposedly seeks.

Smart (1992) provides a survey of Islam, which began in its present form 1,400 years ago in Arabia in 722AD. In terms of doctrine, the main belief is in the God, called "Allah." Allah's last prophet was Muhammad, a man through whom God revealed his will. "Islam" means surrendering oneself to the will of God. A person surrenders to the will of Allah by living and thinking in the way Allah has instructed. Islam also provides a social and legal system, and governs things like family life, law and order, ethics, dress, and cleanliness. Every Muslim must perform the duties known as the Five Pillars of Islam: (1) faith or belief in the Oneness of God and the finality of the prophethood of Muhammad; (2) establishment of the daily prayers; (3) concern for and almsgiving to the needy; (4) self-purification through fasting; and (5) the pilgrimage to Makkah for those who are able. Islam is sometimes contrasted with Christianity as a "works" based religion, where the relationship with God must be restored by human effort, rather than through the love of God providing a solution, as Christians maintain through Jesus Christ. Islam now has around 1,200 million adherents. Islam has similar "political-religious" connections as were found in Christendom, with the Islamic state implementing various religious laws, and violation of religious laws also constitute civil violation. Changing religion is almost unheard of within Islam due to strict controls, ostracisation, and even death for changing belief.

In terms of meaning, Islam provides the answer in the holy book called the Qur'an, where it states: "I only created jinn and man to worship Me" (Qur'an, 51:56). Islam's view is that God (Allah) created man for one purpose only: this "worship." Worship entails the "obedience" to God that explains the "submission" that Islam is. The purpose and meaning of life is to obey, and it is through obedience that God's approval is won. This makes Islam what many Christians consider a "works-based" religion, where the purpose is "obedience," and the result of human effort brings reward. In terms of transcendence, Allah is totally unknowable. God is "Wholly Other," and essentially unknowable. He does not "reveal Himself" to human beings. Prophets bring his teaching. Humankind's present separation from God is due to God's transcendence. They believe God will raise all the dead, and on that day, God will reward every person according to his or her good or evil deeds. Thus, there is transcendence of the present human condition through death and good works.

In contrast to both Christianity and Islam, Hinduism is polytheistic, since there are many gods. It is the name given to a family of religions and cultures that began and still flourish in India. Hindus do not separate religion from other aspects of life. For Hindus in India, Hinduism is an inextricable part of their existence: a complete approach to life that involves social class, earning a living, family, politics, diet, and so forth., in addition to the things Westerners view as religious. Hinduism includes a very wide range of beliefs and practices; there is no founder, no creed, and no single source of authority. The things most often common to Hindus are a belief in gods who are aspects of a supreme God; belief that the soul repeatedly goes through a cycle of being born into a body, dying, and rebirth; belief in Karma, a force that determines the quality of each life, depending on how well one behaved in a past life. Most Hindus worship at home and have a shrine there, with no strong tradition of corporate congregational worship.

In terms of meaning, Hinduism is explicitly orientated towards the ultimate goal of individual liberation (nirvana). The sum of a person's actions in past lives constitutes their "karma." If enough has been accumulated through sufficient good actions through many lives, one may be freed from the continuous cycle or wheel, and released into "nirvana" or the ultimate bliss of union with God. Until that time, a soul is doomed to be incarnated repeatedly in order to gain knowledge, develop spiritual understanding, and increase in divinity. The aim of this life, therefore, is always the gaining of spiritual understanding. Humans cannot know the ultimate divine plans, but must fulfil their intended roles. "Samadhi" is that state of transcendence and pure experience of the divine that is possible in this world. It is attained through meditation and purity in thought, word, and deed.

Buddhism is a vast and complex religious and philosophical tradition which stretches back over 2,500 years (Hattaway, 2004). It was started by a young man who was troubled by the inevitability of suffering in human life. While meditating under the "tree of perfect knowledge" he reached enlightenment, and taught his followers about his new spiritual understanding. "Buddha" means "one who has woken up." A Buddha is someone who awakens to the knowledge of the world as it truly is, and so finds release from suffering in a state called "nirvana" over a cycle of reincarnations. A Buddha teaches out of sympathy and compassion for the suffering of beings, and for the benefit and welfare of all beings. There are many different "types" of Buddhism, with four main types of Buddhism being identified as follows:

- The oldest, called the **Theravada (Way of the Elders) tradition**, interprets Buddha as a great sage, but not a deity. It emphasizes meditation and ritual practices that help the individual become an arhat, an enlightened being.
- The **Mahayana (Greater Vehicle) tradition** refocused Buddhism to concentrate less on individual attainment of enlight-

enment and more on concern for humanity. It promotes the ideal of the bodhisattva (enlightened being), who shuns entering nirvana until all sentient beings can do so as well.

- **Zen Buddhism** encourages individuals to seek the Buddha nature within one's self, and to practice a disciplined form of sitting meditation in order to reach satori — spiritual enlightenment.
- **Tibetan Buddhism** holds the Dali Lama as the supreme ruler, and seeks to reach Nivarna within this lifetime rather than over a series of "reincarnations."

In terms of meaning and purpose of life, the significance and purpose of following the Buddha is to attain perfection. To follow the Buddha is to gain a clear and thorough understanding of this precarious human existence. Buddhism teaches doing good deeds, that there can be no peace when the mind is not at rest. The main tenets are to lead a moral life, to be mindful and aware of thoughts and actions, and to develop wisdom and understanding. The Noble Eight Fold Path is being moral (through what we say, do, and our livelihood), focussing the mind on being fully aware of our thoughts and actions, by developing compassion for others, and developing wisdom by understanding the Four Noble Truths, which are (1) life is suffering, (2) suffering is caused by craving and aversion, (3) suffering can be overcome and happiness can be attained, and (4) the Noble Eight Fold Path is the path which leads to the end of suffering. Buddhism explains a purpose to life, it explains apparent injustice and inequality and suffering around the world, and it provides a code of practice or way of life that leads to "true happiness": that is the goal of "nirvana" or transcendence.

Judaism is the oldest of the world's four great monotheistic religions. It is also the smallest, with only about 12 million followers around the world. The Holocaust of the 1930s and 1940s transformed Jewish demographics. If the Holocaust had not occurred, there would now be between 25 and 35 million Jews in the world. The essence of being Jewish is that one is part of a Jewish community, and lives one's life according to Jewish law and traditions. So, Judaism is a way of life inextricably entwined with a system of beliefs. The fundamental beliefs of Judaism are that there is a single, all-powerful God, who created the universe and everything in it, and God has a special relationship with the Jewish people, cemented by the covenant that God made with Moses on Mount Sinai, 3,500 years ago. In terms of meaning and purpose, Judaism's purpose is the Kingdom of God being established in the world. Moshe Tsvi Segal explains that "whoever thinks he understands and grasps Judaism without the centrality and ultimate importance of establishing the Temple, does not properly understand Judaism" (http://www.saveisrael.com/segal/segalmount.htm): the Temple Mount in Jerusalem being in the hands of a sovereign kingdom of Israel, to give expression to God's sovereignty over Israel.

In terms of transcendence, it is central to the Jewish experience. God is seen to be utterly distinct from and other than the world, subject to no laws or powers that transcend him. Yet He is involved with humankind in a special kind of relationship, a relationship symbolized by revelation and covenant. In the midst of a pagan universe, Abraham confronts this transcendence. Judaism is primarily focused on life here and now rather than on the afterlife. There is a great deal of room for personal opinion on where life is heading. The Orthodox Jew believes "there will be a physical resurrection. The righteous will exist forever with God in the 'World to Come.' The unrighteous will suffer, but disagreement exists over their ultimate destiny." Reform Judaism has no concept of personal life after death. It is said that a person lives on in his or her accomplishments, or in the minds of others.

A brief introduction to the five major world religions indicates that each of them does indeed address questions of meaning and purpose in life, the way to live, where life is going, and other related questions. Each major religion also carries with it some form of "transcendence" of the human condition. In Islam, Christianity, and Orthodox Judaism, this involves "meeting the divine." In Hinduism and Buddhism, this involves reaching a state of "nirvana," which can be found within an individual in this world. Each of these religions shares some common ground. Each of these religions also exists in a world that is technological and rapidly increasing in its technology. The question remains "What impact is technology having upon these religions?"

5.5 Technology for Religion

Brenda Brasher's (2001) book, *Give Me That Online Religion*, is one of the earliest sources that addresses the practical outworkings of "religion through technology." The book helps document and analyze the phenomenon of online religion. Brasher argues that online religion will be an integral part of our global future. Brasher presents the stories of three separate individuals, who are documented as they seek a spiritual goal via the Internet. One person sought more information about Jewish faith and ended up attending a virtual Seder and converted to Judaism. Another person sought a deeper faith and found it through interaction with the "Christ in the Desert" Web page. He followed his cyber visit, with a physical visit to the monastery in New Mexico, and physically became involved in off-line religion. The third person had a purely online experience as a neopagan who turned to the Internet for her various liturgical practices, rather than meet face to face. As Brasher says "cyberspace is a medium enabling a new generation of human spirituality to be actualized."

Genevive Bell (2004a, 2004b) observes that new technologies, "technologies of enlightenment," are delivering religious experiences in new mediums, and creating new possibilities and opportunities for spiritual and religious life. Intel's "Inside Asia" particularly focuses on religion and culture in Asia (http://www.intel.com/research/exploratory/papr/inside_asia_lessons.htm).

Their forum explains some anecdotes of how technology has impacted religious practice, including the following:

- "It is mid-afternoon in Malaysia. A devout Muslim stops his work, turns toward Mecca and says a prayer, as he is required to do five times a day. Although he is far from a mosque, he knows exactly where to position himself: his cell phone has an embedded compass that points him in the direction of Mecca."
- "The Chinese have a practice of burning paper items, typically paper money, during funeral ceremonies, to ensure the dead will have what they need for a good life in the next world. Today they also burn paper versions of cell phones, laptop computers, and flat-panel televisions."

It is particularly interesting that technology is facilitating a spiritual quest. Technology is functioning as a "tool," enabling humanity to pursue the "spiritual quest." It is providing new possibilities for religion and its expression. Far from decreasing that ancient "religious" inclination of humanity, technology is fuelling it. If religion is a "human construction," it is only natural that other "human constructions," such as technology, will come to play a role in what is "built." Hurd (2001) finds that technology is a natural consequence of a humanity developing tools to further its own quest.

Despite these recent investigations into "technologies of enlightenment," it is not clear exactly where and how different religions are utilising, or even avoiding technology. Certainly, each of the five major world religions discussed has information about their beliefs available in Web sites in virtual space. Thus, it is anticipated by them that people will "enquire" and "seek" after such detail, and use the Web. And clearly people conversant with the religions, many as obvious adherents, are engaged and using technology to produce the Web sites. A sample of the ways that these different religions are using technology is considered.

Considering Hinduism, *Asia Today* reports "Given the large percentage of Indians who are employed in high tech industries abroad, it is only logical that the internet should play a major role in the creation of a Hindu identity in diaspora Indian communities throughout the world" (http://www.asiasource.org/news/at_mp_02.cfm?newsid=39841). And the use of the Internet within Hinduism is certainly obvious. Before we consider some specific Hinduism Web sites, we pause to consider those aspects of Hinduism that are particularly interesting in light of the religious practices.

One interesting feature of Hindu devotion online is the transmission of the sacred image. This divine visual contact now occurs online through hundreds of "cyberdarshan" sites in which virtual images of deities are thought to convey the same sacred glance that temple figures and posters convey. New protocols about the treatment of such images have been created, with many Web sites suggesting that sacred images should only be downloaded for devotional purposes, are not to be printed out, and are to be approached with the same general respect as a sacred image in a temple or home shrine. Hindus generally agree that a temple in cyberspace is the next best thing to actually being at a temple in India.

India's sacred geography is also recreated in cyberspace, permitting devotees to go on a virtual pilgrimage. The Maha Kumbha Mela pilgrimage will be broadcast online courtesy of the Himilayan Institute, giving viewers in cyberspace the opportunity to join the hundreds of thousands pilgrims who gather in Allahabad to bathe in the Ganges.

There are a number of Web sites for Hindu material, for example:

- **http://www.hindu.org:** The goal of this Web site is to publish and connect all Hindu organizations, leaders, and resources, such as news, events, publications, Vedic sciences, art, music, and culture, on the Internet's World Wide Web. Most of the content of www.hindu.org consists of links to other Hindu or Hindu-related Web sites.
- **http://saranam.com:** This site allows worshippers to order a worship ceremony at the Indian temple of their choosing, for a small fee.
- **http://www.bhagavagita.org:** This site includes important Hindu scripture online, presented in Sanskrit and 14 other languages, including audio clips of the recitation of every verse.
- **http://www.hindugallery.com:** Mohan's Hindu Image Gallery offers hundreds of images of every major Hindu deity.

Considering Buddhism, Pannyavaro (2002) explains "The challenge that Buddhism faces today is not with the Dharma itself, the Buddha's teaching-as the timeless message embedded in the Four Noble Truths maintains its validity — but how to present this ancient teaching as a meaningful alternative to people who have been shaped by the values of the consumer society." He also observes "the World Wide Web, a very powerful communications network and learning environment," suggesting that it is appropriate for an e-learning environment to disseminate teachings. He wisely notes: "There is a temptation to merely dump data (facts) online rather than exploit the new ways of presenting information that the technology provides. Data and information do not necessarily translate into knowledge." The techniques of meditation, for example, can be explained and illustrated very well on the Net through streaming audio and video, with the student being guided by an online teacher.

Pannyavaro is also keen to emphasise that "The Internet should not be seen as just a new way to disseminate or repackage the Buddha's teachings but potentially as a base for an innovative online Dharma Community — a Cyber Sangha, that offers alternative social and spiritual values." The Internet, in its global interconnectivity, resonates with the interdependence and Buddhist understanding of core values and truth. "Its appreciation leads to the maturity that moves from an ego-self preoccupation to an interconnectivity that empathizes with all suffering life." Buddhism makes no effort to seek "converts": merely waits until questions are asked. It is a perfect environment for those seeking.

Some Buddhist Web sites include:

- **http://www.buddhanet.net:** This site claims to be the original Buddhist education and information network. It contains electronic books, audio, teaching, multi-media, photos, and more, aiming to facilitate a significant Buddhist presence in the ever-expanding realm of computer communications technology, applying this technology to helping make the Buddha's teachings freely available to all.
- **http://www.sacred-texts.com/bud/:** This site contains a freely available archive of electronic texts about religion, mythology, legends and folklore, and occult and esoteric topics. Texts are presented in English translation and, in some cases, in the original language.
- **http://Buddhism.org:** This is the most comprehensive directory service providing all the resources of Buddhism and Buddhists from around world.
- **http://www.dharmaweb.net/article.php?sid=102:** This Web site is a virtual Buddhist community available online. E-Sangha is an established discussion forum where Buddhists, and those who are interested in Buddhism, are able to meet on the Internet to discuss all matters relating to Buddhism.

Considering Islam, there are various ways that specific elements of the Islamic religion lend themselves to technological support. One example is the fatwa. The fatwa is an Islamic legal pronouncement, issued by a religious law specialist on a specific issue. A scholar capable of issuing fatwas is known as a Mufti.

Different Islamic clerics can issue contradictory fatwas. The effect depends upon whether or not this takes place in a nation where Islamic law (sharia) is the basis of civil law. In nations where Islamic law is not the basis of law, Muslims often must face two contradictory fatwas. In such cases, the fatwa deriving from leadership of their religious tradition would be honored. For example, Sunni Muslims would favor a Sunni fatwa over a Shiite one. Most fatwas are on mundane matters, although some pronounce death sentences. One use of the Internet has been for discussion regarding these fatwas.

Muslim women are a particular "issue" within Islam, at least from the Western perspective, where their "status" with respect to men is often questioned. Sabour and Vikør (1997) examine the Internet community and Muslim women. After examining over 200 newsgroup messages related in one way or another to issues concerning Muslim women, they find most messages relate to marriage: also circumcision, dating, veiling, feminism, mother's day, women in a mosque, women as state leaders, and so on. They see the Internet as a "new form of Western imperialism-it has even been called 'cybernetic colonialism.'"

Some traced the terrorist attacks in September 2001 to the use of the Internet to coordinate events. Deborah Wheeler (2001) writes "That the terrorists, acting in the name of Islam, used the Internet in part to coordinate their efforts makes the need for scrutiny in this context all the more pertinent, especially for those concerned with the social impact of the Internet, not to mention Islam. It is our job as scholars and educators to provide analysis that might remove misunderstanding and encourage ethical behavior because ... "

Once again there are a number of Web sites for Islamic material, for example:

- **http://www.islamonline.net:** Islam Online aims to create a unique, global Islamic site on the Internet that provides services to Muslims and non-Muslims, in several languages; to become a reference for everything that deals with Islam, its sciences, civilization, and nation; to have credibility in content, distinction in design, and a sharp and balanced vision of humanity and current events. There is a discussion board promoting a lively community.

- **http://www.islam101.com/dawah/course101.html:** This Web site is a beginner's short course on Islam
- **http://www.islam.tc/ask-imam/index.php:** This Web site is an online fatwa resource.
- **http://al-islam.faithweb.com/tv.htm:** This Web site makes it possible to watch prayers from Makkah and Medinah.

In 1996, David Fishman introduces the forum by Meir Bar-Ilan for "Who is Afraid of Computerized Judaism?" in *PC Media*. We are asked to consider "what kind of match can there be between a religion thousands of years old and a modern technology that is developing before our very eyes." One of the features of Judaism is its respect for the Torah — that portion of their holy scriptures that intersects with the Christian Old Testament in the bible. Judaism sees the "Imago Dei" of Genesis as being a mandate to create. Rabbi Chaim of Volozhin, Sefer Nefesh HaChaim, Sha'ar Alef says "When the Torah states: 'And God created man in His image, and in the image of God He created him' it teaches us that man was fashioned to be a creator, just as God is a creator." This mandate to manipulate the environment also comes with a sense of responsibility. Man is given a twofold mandate: while he is instructed "to subdue" the earth he must "rule over" the rest of creation. Our greatest challenge is applying the fruits of our God-given inquisitive nature in an ethical way.

Rabbi Cohen explains how "Palm Pilot helps me to be a better rabbi." He also finds that "Judaism would suggest a Divine influence that implanted in us the intelligence and the curiosity to seek out ways to make life better, to improve the world. Indeed, when we consider the possibility that with the computer, the Internet and cyberspace, we have the potential to open up the world to one another. We can now connect across the oceans and dividing barriers that have separated us throughout the ages, it is in some ways a kind of messianism, something so central to our faith." He goes on to compare the Talmud, the multi-volume post-Biblical literature, with the Web, explaining how Jonathan Rosen (2000) makes a metaphorical connection between Judaism and computer technology in "The Talmud and the Internet."

Figure 3 illustrates the meeting of Judaism and technology in the devotion that technology can facilitate. Some Web sites devoted to Judaism include:

Figure 3. Technology facilitates Devotion in Judaism

- **http://www.jewfaq.org/:** Judaism 101 is an online encyclopedia of Judaism, covering Jewish beliefs, people, places, things, language, scripture, holidays, practices, and customs, mainly from the Orthodox viewpoint.
- **http://shamash.org/:** Shamash strives to be the highest quality central point of Jewish information and discussion on the Internet. Their mission is to provide state-of-the-art Internet tools to Jewish organizations and individuals who maintain discussion forums for the benefit of the Jewish community.
- **http://www.ou.org:** Orthodox Union is the largest and most dynamic Jewish movement of its kind in the world.
- **http://www.jewishfamily.com/:** This Web site strives to help families apply Judaism and Jewish values to their everyday lives, and to be a source of user-friendly, family-oriented information and entertainment. They hope to provide a Jewish link to families who may not feel comfortable in traditional Jewish organizations.

- **http://www.askmoses.com/qa_list.html?h=118:** This forum provides the opportunity to ask a question. After searching the knowledgebase, there is the chance to chat with a live Scholar.

Finally, Christianity has appropriated the Internet, as we shall examine in more detail. One of the main thrusts of Christianity that make the Internet a most appropriate partner is the "evangelistic" nature of the religion. That is, unlike some religions such as Buddhism, there is a definite thrust towards "spreading the message" and evangelism. Just as Christians were charged to "go out into all the world" at the inception of the religion in the first century Roman Empire, so the Internet is considered by many to be a "Roman Road" in which Christians are charged to venture in the 21st century.

One of the main uses of the Internet in Christianity is in including apologetic literature, Christian materials, study aids, worship resources, and other supports to the teaching of the religion. Unlike some religions such as Hinduism, the sense of corporate worship and community is important, and the Internet is being used to foster virtual communities. Some of these communities call themselves "Internet church," as we shall examine, and foster not only discussion, but actual devotion and worship.

In terms of worship, Protestant Christianity has some unique aspects. Some religions have images that are considered sacred, even to hold special powers. The images are used not only to facilitate worship, but are worshipped. An electronic representation of this image would be important in such a religion. However, in Christianity, the elements of "online" worship are vastly different. Roman Catholic and Orthodox Christianity do support the use of images called "icons," although it is keen to emphasise that these are not to be worshipped. Thus, religious Christian images serve a very different purpose on the Internet compared to that which images from other religions may serve.

Once again, various Christian Web sites exist including:

- **http://www.christianityonline.co.uk/:** The Web site aims to help Christians wanting to find resources on the Internet. It also wants to help churches/charities to get themselves onto the Internet.

- **http://www.bible.com/:** Bible.com helps you know and love God, while spreading the truth of the Bible to others, through the cutting edge of the Internet. This ministry touches people all over the world.
- **http://www.churchbaby.info:** This Web site is dedicated to collating information about children/youth and church, provides a discussion forum for exchange, and promotes a reflective look at contemporary ecclesiology, especially promoting intergenerational/family based life.

In many ways, we are in a techno-religious age, where technology and religion have united in the most human of quests for transcendence and meaning. We will explore more aspects of this techno-religious age in the final chapter, where the marriage of religion and technology is considered in the context of the emerging "worldview" that technology has created: a worldview fashioned out of a post-modern society; a worldview in which the e-world is a very real part, and in which traditional Western "Christian values" are challenged for the "construction" they are.

5.6 References

Barth, K. (1969). *Church dogmatics*. T. & T. Clark Publishers, Ltd.

Bell, G. (2004a). *Technologies of enlightenment? Religion and ubiquitous computing at Intel and beyond*. Retrieved February 15, 2004, from http://www.sbs.ox.ac.uk/downloads/scitechseminar20040310.pdf

Bell, G. (2004b). *Getting to God: Technology, religion and the new enlightenment*. Retrieved from http://blogger.iftf.org/Future/000510.html

Brasher, B. (2001). *Give me that online religion*. Retrieved from John Wiley and Sons.

Constantelos, D. J. (1998). *Understanding the Greek Orthodox Church: Its faith, history and practice*. Brookline, MA: Hellenic College Press.

Dunlap, T. R. (2004).. *Faith in nature: Environmentalism as religious quest*. Seattle, WA: University of Washington Press.

FM-2030. (1989). *Are you a transhuman*? New York: Warner Books.

Gumbel, N. (2003). *Alpha questions of life*. Hodder & Stoughton Religious.

Hattaway, P. (2004). *Peoples of the Buddhist world: A Christian prayer guide*. Singapore: Piquant Editions.

Henry, C. F. H. (1979). *God, revelation and authority* (vol. III). Waco, TX: Word.

Hurd, M. (2001). Technology vs. humanity. *Capitalism Magazine*. Retrieved from http://www.capmag.com/article.asp?ID=152

Javad, S. (2004). What is sociology? A classical review: The ontology of modern cosmogony. *The Examined Life Online Philosophy Journal, 04*(15).

Jensen, R. (2004). *Internet-shaped preaching How the Internet may impact the art and practice of preaching.* Retrieved from http://www.elca.org/lp/ishaped.html

Lockerbie, D. B. (1986). *The cosmic center: The supremacy of Christ in a secular wasteland.* Portland, OR: Multnomah.

Noble, D. F. (1977). *America by design: Science, technology and the rise of corporate capitalism.* New York: Alfred A. Knopf.

Pannyavaro (2002). *E-learning Buddhism on the Internet.* Retrieved from http://www.buddhanet.net/gds-speech.htm

Reuters (2004). *New study shatters Internet "geek" image.*http://www.cnn.com/2004/TECH/internet/01/14/geek.study.reut

Rosen, J. (2000). *The Talmud and the Internet.* Barnes and Noble.

Sabour, & Vikør. (1997). *Ethnic encounter and culture change.* Bergen; London.

Smart, N. (1992). *The world's religions.* Cambridge University Press.

Stoker, W. (1996). *Is the quest for meaning the quest for God? The religious ascription of meaning in relation to the secular ascription of meaning: A theological study.* Amsterdam; Atlanta.

Wheeler, D. (2001). Islam, technology and community: September 11th and its global meaning. *Interface, The Journal of Education, Community and Values.* Retrieved from http://bcis.pacificu.edu/journal/2001/10/wheeler.php

Chapter 6

21st Century Christianity

"We have just enough religion to make us hate, but not enough to make us love one another."

Jonathan Swift

"If God would but reform the clergy, the people of England would soon be reformed."

J. I. Packer

6.1 Introduction

This chapter makes a focus on in the 21st century. We start with a focus on the ideology that was Christendom, tracing its origins, rise, and decline, in order to appreciate the present context. We find that Christendom represented a political alliance between church and state that, in many ways, compromised the church, and represented a secular invasion into it. The persecutions of the early church were abated, although the influences of the Roman Empire and imperial court remain to this day in church buildings, in the distinction of clergy from laity, in the passive nature of worship, and in many other ways. In accordance with those theologians who find religion to be a "human construction," Christianity in Christendom is, in many ways, the ultimate defiance, inhibiting both "faith" and God's self-revelation.

If there is dispute within the church as to whether Christendom was a "defiant construction" or not, there is no doubt within the secular world that Christianity has largely failed. We then move on to consider some of the general failures of Christianity within the context of the secular world. The main objections include (1) the wars, violence, and persecutions enacted in the name of Christian religion, (2) the oppression that distorted religion brings (e.g. in colonialism), (3) the moral depravity and failure of its adherents, sometimes especially its leadership, and (4) the intellectual objections against its metaphysical components, and the contradictory approaches to its teaching, with huge differences in theological interpretation of the claimed central "truths."

We move on to consider one of the most distinctive elements of Christianity, that is, the community of those who believe. The Christian community, unlike any other religious community, is one commissioned to be by the divine; it is of supernatural origin at Pentecost where the New Testament church was born. The question of what is the church is at once simple and complex. It is not a building, but may mean a local congregation or the worldwide community of those who believe in Christ; it sometimes refers to those who have already died and believers who will be. Distinguishing the essence of church from its expression is important. Churches today do not necessarily look like first-century churches. This may have a bearing on the role of technology in church. Community and witness are two distinguishing elements of the essence of church.

The objective of this chapter is to describe the context of Christianity in the 21st century by outlining its origins in Christendom, and examining the failures of Christianity, which by default have been failures within Christendom, the ways that Christianity has not enabled "transcendence" promised or sought by adherents. We also seek to consider the question of "what is the church," distinguishing between the "essence" and "expression" of church; and the tension between community and institution that has existed. We want to point to the crisis that exists within the church today, and the general decline of participation in the organised church. This context provides the background to understanding the synthesis of technology and religion that is enabling new expressions.

6.2 Christendom: The Ultimate Defiance?

Christianity emerged from Judaism in the time of the Roman Empire. It started off as a Jewish sect for those who saw Jesus Christ as the promised Messiah, and one who would lead the Jews to their destiny. The controversy over who Jesus was, lead Christianity to become a distinct religion from Judaism. The Jewish traditions such as circumcision became obsolete, "grace" replaced "law," and the religion broadened to include non-Jews, as well as Jews, in the "salvation" that was possible.

In becoming a separate religion, Christianity strayed from the toleration that the Roman Empire gave to Judaism. Christianity was seen as the source of riots and disturbances. In 64AD, Christians became the object of official persecution following the Great Fire of Rome. Emperor Nero accused the Christians and made them scapegoats for the tragedy. Persecutions were local and sporadic. Emperor Domitian (81-96 AD) developed new tortures and harassed philosophers and Jews. Septimus Severus (202-211 AD) persecuted the Christians and forbade conversion to Judaism and to Christianity. The Great Persecution of Diocletian (303-305 AD) was a particularly intense and horrific persecution, attempting to force Christians to pledge their allegiance to the Empire by the traditional means of taking part in the imperial cult. For 300 years, Christians were sporadically persecuted: socially, politically, economically, and physically.

Christians were misunderstood on many fronts. Their indifference to politics and public affairs, their abhorrence of heathen customs, were construed into "hatred of the human race." The "agape" or "love feast" was thought to be an orgy, rather than the celebration remembering the last supper of Christ with his disciples. The Christian refusal to pay tribute and worship Roman emperors was seen as subversive, potentially threatening to the Roman state, and hence illegal. Christians were blamed for a number of natural disasters because they wouldn't sacrifice to the gods.

Everything changed in 313 AD with the Edict of Milan. The edict moved from hostile neutrality to friendly neutrality toward Christians. The edict, in effect, made Christianity a lawful religion and granted freedom of worship to all Christians, although it did not, as is sometimes believed, make Christianity the official state religion. All government-sanctioned persecution ended, especially of Christianity. It gave to Christianity (and any other religion) a status of legitimacy alongside of paganism, and in effect, disestablished paganism as the official religion of the Roman Empire and its armies. The Edict was issued in the names of Constantine the Great (the Western tetrarch), and Licinius (the Eastern tetrarch). The edict came about after a military victory won by Constantine at Rome. Before the victory, Constantine reputedly had a vision of the Christian cross and heard the message "In this sign conquer." Subsequently, he had his army paint the cross on their shields before they marched on the enemy. Decisive victory was secured at Rome, and Constantine became emperor. In 324 AD, Constantine gained sole possession of the Empire, and ordered his rival Licinius executed for treason.

Constantine was convinced that Christianity was the means to assure continued military victory. From this point on, the Roman Empire was supposedly supporting the Church. It funded building of church buildings and the copying of Bibles, house churches give way to church buildings, the persecuted became persecutors (since the Empire persecuted nonorthodox Christians like the Arians and the Gnostics), Sunday was established as a day of worship, properties that had been confiscated from the Christians were returned, Roman gods were replaced by the Christian God, a distinction between the clergy and laity was made, worship became formalised in churches, clergy were given privileged positions, and many other changes were instigated that created Christendom. Christianity was not only regarded as some kind of "supernatural" insurance policy against invasion, but was one of the few remaining stabilising and civilising influences with potential to unify the Roman empire. Christians were admired for their sacrificial care of recent plague victims, even if their convictions still seemed strange.

The political organization of the Empire became the model for the Christian organization: that is, Christendom. The ideology of "christianitas" or Christendom, has dominated much of the Western world for over 1,000 years, as explained by Stuart Murray (2002). It is a church-state alliance that is epitomised in the first Ecumenical Council at Nicea, where Constantine called bishops from all over the Empire together in 325 AD and presided over it from his throne. Christendom became the community of Christians associated with Europe. The balance of power between the church and state has varied, with each being dominant at various times. There are examples from the fourth century onwards both of emperors presiding over church councils, and of emperors doing penance imposed by bishops. Sometimes, a balance of power has existed between them. Often there were power struggles. The medieval period saw many struggles between popes and emperors. The church often provided religious legitimation for state activities, and the state provided secular force to back up ecclesiastical decisions. Undeniably, the close partnership between the church and the state that Christendom represented set the church in the centre of society, in a unique and unquestioned place.

The close partnership between church and state meant the world became divided politically and religiously into "Christendom" and "heathendom." Despite this desire for unity, there was a schism between the Eastern and Western Roman empires resulting in the separation of the Eastern Orthodox Church from the then Roman Catholic West. Warfare was used to protect or extend Christendom. In the crusades, Christendom fought back against Islam, and while failing to repossess the lost territories, it strengthened the unity of Christendom (Vos, 1996). Throughout the history of Christendom, the church has been plagued by corruption, with various groups trying to reform the church. The particular horror that reformer Martin Luther spoke out about was the selling of "indulgences" in order to gain "salvation." The Reformation was an outcry against the way that the church was selling the forgiveness it proclaims that Jesus obtained by dying on a cross, and using these finances to construct St Peters in Rome. This Reformation led to a division between the Roman Catholic Church and the Protestant church and, eventually, a proliferation of various strands of Protestantism. Henry VIII headed the English Reformation, eventually leading to the Church of England ,and from within that, various strands emerged including Methodism and the Baptist church, while the German reformation continued the Lutheran Church.

Despite the Western world being "split" into Roman Catholic and Protestant, and the founding of America introducing a separation between church and state, in many places, the ideology of Christendom continued. The edict of Milan changed the world forever, placing Christianity as an ideology permeating society elevating the church to status of the state. The church often provided religious legitimation for state activities, and the state provided secular force to back up ecclesiastical decisions. Undeniably, the close partnership between the church and state that Christendom represented set the church in the centre of society, in a unique and unquestioned place. The "religious tolerance" of America may represent the recognition that Christendom fell short in many ways. The traditions of Roman imperialism were strong, and in many ways brought the Roman Empire into the church in an invasion that did more to destroy the church than any persecution.

Christendom also led many to question the possibility of truly being a Christian within Christendom. The way that religion and politics became confused in Christendom has led many to see the fourth-century edict of Milan not as a blessing to the church and the Christian religion but as the greatest curse it ever could have had: one that perverted the church, compromised its calling, and hindered its mission, achieving through infiltration what 300 years of persecution had failed to achieve. Christendom was not the triumph of the church over the empire, but the triumph of the empire over the church. Christendom perverted Christianity, defining "church" territorially, interpreting discipleship as good citizenship, with membership automatic upon birth. The possibility of "faith," at least Christian faith, within this Christendom context was virtually impossible.

Kierkegaard's (1850) central problem was "how to become a Christian in Christendom." Educational and cultural institutions tended to reproduce pseudoindividuals whose identity was determined by the institution. In contrast, Kierkegaard recognizes duties to a power higher than social norms. *Standford Encyclopedia of Philosophy* (McDonald, 2001) informs us "For Kierkegaard Christian faith is not a matter of regurgitating church dogma. It is a matter of individual subjective passion, which cannot be mediated by the clergy or by human artefacts. Faith is the most important task to be achieved by a human being, because only on the basis of faith does an individual have a chance to become a true self. This self is the life-work which God judges for eternity." It is essential that faith be constantly renewed by means of repeated avowals of faith. While Kierkegaard's existentialist thinking may be dubious, his identification of the "problem of Christendom" and the perpetuation of the social convention of religion was correct.

In a more contemporary comment, Bonhoeffer's "religiousless Christianity" understood the chasm between God and human culture, even church culture, to be so extreme that no common ground between them could be found. Christianity, then, should be "religion less" in that it should not heed the greater culture in order that it should be faithful to God's self-revelation in Christ. For a long time, the ideology of Christendom has "constrained" a certain form of religious expression. In Barth and Bonhoeffer, we may understand it in "defiant" terms as a human construction that restricts God's revelation. If Christendom were the ultimate defiance in the face of God, and the ultimate "human construction" that inhibited the expression and practice of Christianity, then the transition to a post-Christian, secular society in the 21st century may be good news.

There is certainly evidence that Christendom is slowly dissolving. It is expressed in the culture, music, and art of society. For example, the American music group REM, known for intellectual but murky lyrics, has produced popular albums such as "Losing My Religion" and "It's the End of the World as We Know It (And I Feel Fine)." It is expressed in the educational establishments. For example, Malcolm Muggeridge (1980) writes of a "war" against Christendom found on many fronts including the American public schools. It is expressed in churches, with a decline in adherence and participation. For example, the British and Australian churches once claimed support from 10 percent of the population, and in many places this is now less than 5 percent. It is expressed in politics, where government agencies are being set up to investigate the corruption of the church: for example, the Australian investigations into child abuse and sexual scandals perpetuated by ordained clergy.

While Christendom may be declining, its fall is unlikely to be sudden or total. It has a long history in Europe dominating, the Western world for over a thousand years with a pervasive nature. Even when the official relationship between church and state is completely dissolved, the Christendom mindset is likely to persist: in churches and, to some extent, also within society. A remnant may remain, considering themselves to be the "true church," perpetuating the establishment and institution of Christendom. Strongly institutional churches, such as the Roman Catholic Church, are likely to remain as they are, or change very slowly, due to the heavy value placed upon tradition and historical precedent. Even if Christendom was a "secular invasion" into the church, it was part of "history," and in some ways, will forever remain with the church.

6.3 Failures of Christianity

Religion, specifically Christianity, has been criticised on many different fronts. The main criticisms concern (1) the suffering, wars, and violence caused by organised religion, as adherents seek to promote or defend their ideas, (2) the oppression that distorted religion brings in everything from colonising primitive peoples, to the role of women and presence of children in church, (3) the moral depravity and failure of its adherents, sometimes especially leadership, (4) intellectual arguments against its metaphysical and nonscientific components, and huge contradictions against the claimed central truths.

First, Christianity, specifically Christendom, has failed in many people's eyes for the wars, violence, and suffering that it has caused. For many, the actual "wars" that have been fought in the name of Christianity, and Christendom are certain failures. Regina Schwartz (1997) finds that "monotheism" has brought "violent legacy" to Western societies. It has been said that organized religion has caused more suffering, wars, and violence than any other cause. Everything from the Northern Irish situation to the crusades has a "religious" element to them. Christendom has particularly given Christianity a bad name, as political advancement has been done under the guise of religion. Many view the crusades as the prime example of religious evil, although it is debatable whether the crusades were a political war or a religious cause.

Paul Coplan (2004) defends those who find religion has caused violence in finding it "is ironic that religion gets the blame for violence, but critics of religion are silent when a secular or atheistic faith — such as that of Stalin or Mao Tse-tung — wreaks utter destruction on millions upon millions of lives." In terms of the total people who have died as a result of war, Mao is number one, with an estimated 40 million deaths, and Stalin comes second, being responsible for 20 million. Thus, the two top sources of suffering and death were from a secular atheistic ideology —

Communism. Of course, some regard such ideologies as "religion," and the argument that religion has not caused great conflict falls apart. Hitler ranked third in terms of responsibility for the total number of deaths. Hitler may be regarded as a radical proponent of social Darwinism, although he may also be seen as a corrupter of Christianity. He gained the support of the German national church, and the initial discrimination was aimed at people of Jewish origin having leadership roles in the church. By sheer numbers, the slaughter of millions by these ideologies, dwarfs the specific religious skirmishes and wars that may have been found to have been fought in the name of Christianity.

We must ask "Is taking up the sword in the name of Jesus to promote Christianity consistent with what Jesus affirmed?" Those who advocate a "just war" find that Christianity actually speaks against personal retaliation or vengeance, not national. The ingredients of a "just war" include: just cause (self-defense), just intent (restoration of peace), last resort (when all else has failed), lawful declaration (from government), immunity of noncombatants (those not officially agents of the government should not be subject to violence), limited objectives (restoration of peace), limited means (only sufficient force to resist violence and restore peace).

Even if war is justified in some instances, Christianity must also explain the persecutions that were historically made. People have been burnt at the stake for matters of "faith." The church has encouraged terrorism and intolerance. People seeking to escape persecution in Europe founded America. Built into the American constitution is "freedom" and "tolerance." The country and its constitution was influenced by John Locke. The Pilgrim Fathers, puritans, and many other settlers were escaping oppression, and came to co-exist peacefully, accepting and agreeing to differ. It is astonishing that there has been so much aggression and hostility and persecution and death in the name of Christendom; that people have been tortured for being a protestant or catholic.

One contradiction for the secular world is that, assuming that killing and exploitation are wrong unconsciously appropriates Christian values. It raises a contradiction for the secular world that appropriates evolution and advancement through the survival of the fittest-why not let war and exploitation take its natural course? It is only a religious morality — specifically Christian morality — that suggests this is wrong. Some world religions contain the teaching that all things are one-including good and evil — and are questionable in their point of moral reference, but Christianity captures the sense of "natural justice" and provides a basis for pursuing justice and peace — and "forgiveness" — in a way that other religions do not. Secularists often end up side-stepping the logical implications of their own beliefs, and tack Christian values on to their anti-Christian base.

Secondly, the Christian church also has to explain the errors of violence and oppression made in missionary expansion, since these are seen as failures in the eyes of the secular world. Western colonialism, throughout much of the world, confused "religion" with "culture," and imposed values and other that were not intrinsically Christian or even religious. Everything from the wars against indigenous peoples of North America, to aboriginal assimilation in Australia, to imposing "Christian" names upon African converts, represents the worst of missionary expansion. The context of Christendom did little to disassociate true religion from Western culture, and aided the spread of racism and Western superiority. In *American Colonies*, Alan Taylor and Eric Foner (2003) explore the tragic encounter between Europeans and Native Americans that decimated the latter, primarily through inadvertent introduction of diseases, but also through warfare, slavery, and appropriation of their land, and destruction of the environment on which the Indians relied. The slavery that ensued from this oppression was atrocious, with many religiously inclined even supporting it, since the bible said nothing about abolishing slavery.

In terms of oppression, the 19th century Marx, and others, made damning evaluations of religion predicting its demise. Marx found that religion is seen as a tool of social control by the elected or ruling elites of a society. He regarded religion as "the sigh of the oppressed creature, the heart of a heartless world, and the soul of soulless conditions. It is the opium of the people." The abolition of religion as the illusory happiness of the people is the demand for their real happiness (Marx, 1844). Marx's insight is that the critique of religion is the premise of all criticism. Marx is advocating more than the blank denial of religion, suggesting that the historical understanding of its necessity and function in society leads to its dialectical negation when its function is completed. Marx thought it ought not to be at all, and proceeded to adumbrate a future society in which it would not and could not exist.

Part of the "oppressive power" of religion is the close ties that have been made between religion and politics. This is especially so in the ideology of Christendom that we shall describe. As mentioned previously, people have been burnt at the stake for their religious beliefs, and whole nations have been put to war over religion. While Christendom may have failed in many respects, the close ties between religion and politics is the real demise. It is largely recognised that Western society is in a post-Christian state. Europe and America, Australia and Canada, and other countries "influenced" by the powers of Christendom, are crumbling with religious decline. Statistics show that adherence to conventional organised expressions of religion is in decline, and in decline in "Christendom" and "Christendom-influenced" societies. Where any growth in Christianity is found, it is found in countries that have not married Christianity with state power. In Christendom-influenced countries, people are just not practising conventional religion. Religion under Christendom is failing in its own mission.

It is also necessary to remember that Christianity is not the only world religion that has been tied to politics. Andrew Sullivan (2001) regards fundamental Islam as another example of religion being tied to politics, stating "Its roots lie in an extreme and violent strain in Islam that emerged in the 18th century in opposition to what was seen by some Muslims as Ottoman decadence but has gained greater strength in the twentieth. For the past two decades, this form of Islamic fundamentalism has racked the Middle East. It has targeted almost every regime in the region and, as it failed to make progress, has extended its hostility into the West. From the fatwa against Salman Rushdie to the decade long campaign of bin Laden to the destruction of ancient Buddhist statues and the hideous persecution of women and homosexuals by the Taliban to the World Trade Center massacre, there is a single line. That line is a fundamentalist, religious one."

There are instances when it is the secular mindset that appears to have greater "morals" than those within Christianity. For example, the church has, for centuries, oppressed women: they have been prevented from taking leadership roles; they have been isolated from having "teaching authority" over other men; they have been prevented from having a priestly role; and in recent times, they are often the ones pushed out of churches into "ministries" that involve children. The exclusion of women from leadership, especially over men, has been justified from various places in Christian scriptures. Yet the general gist of Jesus' teaching was to affirm and reinstate women who were underdogs, even in Judaism. While the secular world may have taken feminism to the extreme, there are still many ways that the church could learn a moral example from the world. The recent fanaticism in churches for age-segregation, isolating children from families, and taking infants from worship (to sit in crèches and nursery's apart from their parents), could learn from the secular world. Since the rise of 18th-century Romanticism, secular society has come to value the child in many ways more than the church.

Thirdly, if Christendom can explain the wars and oppression, it still has moral failure within its ranks. The moral corruption within the church is abhorrent to many people, as the many emerging scandals of abuse demonstrate. (See, for example, NPR News, 2004). While the secular world is not immune from the same crimes that are perpetuated within the church, it is particularly vile when it does occur within a church. There has always been a tendency towards moral impurity in the church, despite theologians claiming a "holy" nature to the church. At the Council of Constantinople (381 AD), Ephesus (431 AD) and Chalcedon (451 AD), the church affirmed itself to be "one, holy, catholic, and apostolic." And these "marks" have become traditional descriptions of the church. However, theologians explain that the "holiness" of the church refers to its "calling" rather than its actuality: it does not mean free from sin, but as "separated from what is profane" and "dedicated to the service of God." Elwell (1988) explains that the "holiness" of the church makes no claim on present human perfection, but on Christ, who sanctifies and makes the church holy.

The Christian church has a lengthy history of "reform," as various groups and people within it have discerned the moral "impurity" of the church: from Luther's 95 theses speaking out against the "indulgences" of the Roman Catholic Church (1517) to the radical Anabaptist reformers (Weber, 2003) to the English Puritans and Dutch Pietists. For a good survey of church history and the various attempts to "purify" the church from its earliest days see Williston Walker (1997). Despite reforms, the moral purity cannot be guaranteed since the church is made of "sinners" whose perfection is not guaranteed in this world. In many ways, the secular world seeks honesty in the church, more than perfection. When it fails and sins and commits all manner of crimes, a simple acknowledgement that it has done so would go a long way to regaining respect among those who do not want anything to do with religion because of its moral failure.

Finally, the Christianity of Christendom has failed intellectually for many in the secular world. It is not just a case of the secular world having found that the best of the church's ethical and moral teaching does not need the metaphysical elements; nor that 18th-century rationalism swung people towards a "scientific" mindset, with 19th century Darwinians undermining Christianity creation, or the need for salvation from a fallen state; nor that humanity is stuck with questions of evil and suffering; nor that there are contradictions in the bible. One of the biggest failures of Christianity for the secular world is the contradictions that exist between Christians. It is often claimed that these "differences" between Christians are not over "core" values, however, increasingly they are. Scholars dissect the bible in different ways and come to different conclusions. Even those who are tolerant of the claimed "contradictions" within the bible are further confused, if not more so, by the scholars who cannot even agree upon what is sin and who shall be saved and how. Christianity is failing because there is a lack of consistent Biblical "truth."

The secular world also knows that those within the church have become intellectually lazy. People do not study doctrine, or theology, or history, and are susceptible to teachings that are heresies without realizing it. Many cults started because of a heretical teaching when it was offered to them. Christians do not subject their beliefs to any scrutiny. There are many different versions of "end times" teaching and what will happen, but not many would be able to explain where the doctrine of Trinity came from. In a society where education is valued so highly and knowledge and understanding recognised as power, it is a failure that the church keep itself so ignorant of the truth; that so many people rely upon a weekly talk, often a poor excuse for a sermon, for their teaching. Preaching may be in a dilemma, but so is the church for encouraging such passivity and ignorance among its adherents; for elevating the status of ordained clergy and making religious professionals whose job it is to "teach" people and simultaneously keep them from truly learning through what church has become.

6.4 What is Church?

In this section, we consider the question "what is church?" The English word "church" derives from the late-Greek word "kyriakon," meaning the Lord's house or a church building. The answer to "what is church" may appear simple enough: perhaps it is a building, perhaps a local congregation of people, perhaps a whole denomination, perhaps the entire collection of people who call themselves Christian across the world, perhaps it extends backward and forward in time to all who have salvation through Christ, perhaps it is manifest in every family, or perhaps where there are two or three believers, or something else. The theological field concerned with the study of "church" is "ecclesiology." Millard Erickson (1998) reminds us that the 20th century ecumenical movement has been a recent stimulus to ecclesiology. Basic agreement is required on what makes a church a church, whether it applies to a local congregation, to a denomination, to a federation of denominations, or other. There are various approaches to defining church. Ecclesiologists have explored various definitions of church, including that which defines it theologically, in relation to scriptures, church history, and doctrine.

The very first New Testament "church" was established in Jerusalem at Pentecost. This was an event that occurred shortly after Jesus was crucified. Followers of Jesus were hiding behind locked doors, in fear that they would suffer the same fate for their association with him, but at Pentecost, they experienced a miraculous transformation. There was a supernatural event that transformed the disciples from fearful people into bold witnesses. They went into the open and proclaimed the message of "resurrection" and Christ's triumph over, and salvation for, all people. Miraculously, those who did not speak the disciple's language could understand. These once fearful, now bold witnesses, also performed miracles of healing in their "witness to Christ." This "witness" and "proclamation" has been the essential work of the church ever since.

Initially, the church was composed of disciples who were a sect within Judaism. It was not long before the New Testament church separated from Judaism and Christianity emerged as its own religion. In the earliest days, "community" was at the heart of the church. The earliest communities were found in households: families, extended families, their servants, and their families. There were networks in society and no church buildings. People within the church would meet together for mutual encouragement and teaching; they would share a meal in remembrance of the meal Jesus shared hours before his death; they would initiate people into their community, and they would live "transformed lives" as they professed and bore witness to Christ. Very soon the church widened well beyond the cultural and national boundaries of Judaism, into the Greek and Roman world.

The gathering of such a community became known as "ekklesia," now translated "church." "Ekklesia" was a classical Greek word used to describe a secular civil assembly of citizens (Watson, 1978). There were similarities between the civil gathering and the Christian gathering, but also important differences. The most important difference is that the ekklesia of the civil gathering terminated when the meeting ceased, where as the Christian ekklesia continued with members not ceasing to be community. This terminology reflected the "mysterious" fellowship, enabled in Christ, that permits Christians to be united even when physically separated; it reflects the fact that the dispersed people of God do not cease to be the people of God because they are in community with God, and through that, in community with each other.

In considering the question of "what is the Christian church?," Julien's (1998) distinction between church "expression" and "essence" is useful. The "essence" of church is constant, transcending social or cultural expression, while "expression" relates to a particular setting. Thus, the New Testament church was just one expression of church. It had its own liturgy and protocol for gathering, typically meeting for teaching on the Jewish Sabbath (Saturday), and fellowship the first day of the week (Sunday) where the "love feast" would be celebrated in remembrance of the last supper that Christ ate before he was crucified. That expression was just one possibility for what a church did when it met. Today all over the world, there are differences between cultures as church communities meet in different ways; there are also lots of similarities, especially as the Christendom influence has permeated much of the developing world and imported "cultural baggage" with church expression that is unnecessary for the essence of church to be realised. For example, the tradition that a certain code of dress or certain style of music is not intrinsic to the essence of the church, but is often confused with "doing/being church" properly.

To understand what is church at the level of its nature, many Christians believe that the essence of the church is best revealed by the documents known as "Scripture" in either the Old or New Testament. These texts are regarded as the authoritative statement on "what is church" and many other topics. In scripture, there are numerous descriptive images of church, and each image prevents a narrow conception of the church or one aspect being magnified. Elwell (1988) reports that Minear lists 96 Scriptural images of the church. They are classified into five categories being minor images, the people of God, the new creation, the fellowship in faith, and the body of Christ. Saucy (1972) finds two main categories: the church is the people of God in a divine assembly, forming the body of Christ and also the temple of God constructed by Christ, inhabited by God, with the priesthood of believers. Watson (1978) points out that the most familiar picture of the church in the New Testament is the body of Christ. The picture of a body provides a good illustration of the church being united in love, commitment and service, each being equipped with gifts to serve, with Christ the head.

Tuning from scriptural images, Elwell (1988) reports that throughout most of history, the nature of the church has often been important for Christians trying to establish the validity of their own existence. Many of the descriptions do not capture essence so much as particular expression, although some do strike upon those aspects of nature that are perhaps necessary to emphasise in a given context. One of the earliest descriptions was Cyprian of Carthage, who saw the nature of church as the instrument of salvation, saying "outside the church there was no hope of remission of sins nor any salvation" (McGrath, 2001). Donatism grew out of his teachings, and after Diocletian's persecution there was a schism, with the Donatists seeing themselves as the only true church measuring up to the biblical standard. To the Donatists, "purity" was the vital nature of church.

At the Council of Constantinople (381 AD), Ephesus (431 AD), and Chalcedon (451 AD), the church affirmed itself to be "one, holy, catholic, and apostolic." These traditional marks of the church suggest organic unity is important, holiness (theologically affirming the calling of the church), universality (in geographical extent and across peoples), and apostolic (originating from apostolic foundations). Elwell (1988) sees that these four marks capture the major themes of the scriptural images, finding they describe the essential nature of the church, and yet allow for differences in expression, although it is difficult to see how the richness of all the various metaphors is captured by the marks alone.

Sects in the Middle Ages emphasised elements of church nature that would distinguish them from Roman Catholics, who leant towards papal institution. The Arnoldists emphasized poverty and identification with the masses as characterising the church; the Waldenses stressed literal obedience to Jesus' teachings and evangelical preaching. The Reformers sought to distinguish themselves form the Catholics, although Luther's ecclesiology was actually designed to justify a temporary withdrawal from the church (McGrath, 2001). The second generation of Reformers developed a systematic and coherent ecclesiology, and defined church in the loosest possible terms, to prevent further faction. For Calvin, church was where the word of God was preached and the sacraments rightly administered as expressed in the Augsburg confession (1530 AD), Article 7, "the congregation of the saints, in which the Gospel is rightly taught and the sacraments rightly administered." Again, elements of nature from scriptural images are lost. Calvin also distinguished between the "visible" and "invisible" church, differentiating between the community of believers on earth, and the assembly of the elect known only to God (McGrath, 2001). The "otherworldly" emphasis echoes some of the eschatological characteristics connecting church to the "kingdom of God." History has also witnessed church become confused with state, but this distinction reminds of the otherworldly component.

The Radical Reformers sought to distinguish themselves from Catholics and Protestants, and expressed their concept of church in the Schleitheim Confession (1527 AD). Schism and confessions continued. The Westminster confession (1646 AD), Chapter XXV, finds the church is "all those throughout the world that profess the true religion, together with their children," summarising the state of church after the reformation in England. However, whatever definition is provided for "church," it is inadequate in terms of capturing the nature as expressed in Scripture. As with the marks, the confessions appear to capture expression rather than essence. An interesting statement appeared in the 20th century, with the Barmen Declaration (1934) calling for resistance against German Christianity and the Nazi racial discrimination against the

Jews. Barmen made statements of Christian doctrine to which the "true church" would hold. This represents an interesting shift in articulating the nature of faith underlying the Christian church, rather than trying to define the nature of church.

In general, Protestant churches, since the reformation, have emphasised the proclaimed word and administration of sacraments, while the Roman Catholic Church has tended to emphasise institution. At Vatican II (1962 - 1965) this changed, and "Lumen Gentium" expressed the revised understanding incorporating biblical imagery. "The Pilgrim People of God" was the dominant model, capturing a renewed sense of "sacred history," pilgrimage, and equipping by the Spirit, although Catholics still acknowledge that the church is hierarchical by nature. Vatican II's revisions were combined with liturgical reforms, with liturgy regarded as the best expression of the "true nature of the real church" (Sacrosanctum Concilium). Fox finds "At liturgy, we are most what we are: the Church" (Fox, 1993). The reforms saw laity incorporated into church life and many revisions to the "expression" of church, especially how it related to the modern world (Gaudium et Spes), recognising that the Church must be intimately associated with the human community. Liturgical reforms made a significant contribution to enabling community aspects of the nature of church to be expressed.

Roman Catholic theologian Dulles (1983), presents five models of church that have operated throughout history, making it clear it is necessary to distinguish between the church as a sociological and theological entity. When a model is raised to paradigm status, it may eclipse other valid models, and all models must operate within the context of church being an eschatological entity. Dulles' models are "Institutional," which entails a clear social structure, emphasising authority and power. "Mystical communion" stresses the Spirit working in all and mutual dependence. "Sacrament" emphasises the Church as a sign and light to the world and community. "Herald" makes the Word primary. "Servant" defines the church as an agent for betterment of human community. Dulles suggests the models are evaluated according to various criteria, including their basis in Scripture, tradition, and fruitfulness in enabling members be church. While revealing elements of church nature, they also show its multifaceted extent and difficulty in that one element may be emphasised at the expense of others.

The Lausanne Covenant on world evangelism (1974) articulated an important emphasis on the essential nature of the church, stating it to be one of "community," stating that: "church is the community of God's people rather than an institution, and must not be identified with any particular culture, social or political system, or human ideology" (Covenant of Lausanne, Article 6). Lausanne stands in contrast to the "institutional" view, and brings out one scriptural image of church, although looses the richness of other images. Also, some find that "community" cannot be isolated from institution: "it is always both at the same time, and exactly here we find our real problem" (Runia 1984). Community may also be too vague, missing the relationship with God implied by Scriptural metaphors.

Rather than studying the church and producing models, Synder (1978) cites how Savage actually draws models of church from society (including lecture hall, theatre, corporation, and social club), and in doing so, may describe the expression, but misses the nature, moves towards letting the world define church. Synder also sees the essential nature of church is community through whom God is accomplishing his eternal plans. The biblical concept of community values "fellowship," where "the bond of love" distinguishes the church. Fellowship is a gift given by God (Ferguson 1946). The Methodists General Conference (2004) discussed the nature of the church in a preconference session, and found that "caring" was primary "The nature of the church is just that: the strength of gentle care for each other," perhaps echoing the concerns of society today where "belonging" and "acceptance" are one of the most widespread needs: from homosexuals to young children who just do not fit into Christendom worship. Although clearly, emphasising any one aspect of the nature of church falls short of capturing its entirety.

There are three theological definitions that relate church (1) to Christ and the believer's union with Christ, (2) to the eschatological "gathering" around Christ, of those in heaven and on earth and (3) to the Trinitarian communal being as an ontological model for church community. Clearly, each of these theological understandings bears upon church as a "community." The third particularly seeks to find within church the "community" that is supposed to exist within the Christian God: in the Father, Son, and Holy Spirit. The "mutual" cooperation, fellowship, and "prochoresis" (the idea of dancing round the same point) suggest that there is a deep unity within the persons of the one God. This unity is a model for the unity among believers upon earth. There is also community found in the concept of church being "believer's union with Christ." That union joins people sharing the same "status in Christ." Finally, the eschatological gathering around Christ refers to the entire community of the redeemed, present , past, and future, who will one day gather as the whole community of God's people in heaven.

In the context of community, Synder raises the question of whether church community is a lifeboat for the drowning, leaven to produce social change, dye penetrating society, or some combination, as it functions as an agent of the Kingdom of God. Packer (1993) partly answers this with a "community" view of church that also recognises an eschatological element. Packer describes the church as "a single "worshiping community, permanently gathered in the true sanctuary which is heavenly Jerusalem." Recognising the "otherworldly" element of church again reminds of the "supernatural" component of the "nature," and reiterates Calvin's distinction between "visible" and "invisible" church. Synder (1978) sees unity and growth as a component of church's nature. While these might be desirable properties, and scripturally supported, they cannot be definitive since it is clearly possible to have a church in decline that is still a church.

There is certainly evidence for decline in organised Christianity. Statistics on the changing patterns of religion are not actually that easy to come by. Since the 1930s, many countries have not included questions on religion in the national census. Countries that do ask citizens about religion have campaigned for fictional religions such as "Jedi Knight" to be recorded. Also, on a census, it is difficult to distinguish between an adherent and someone more nominal, leading to many "inaccuracies" in census results. Gallup poll surveys are also biased by this question of what is considered nominal vs. committed practice. We focus on the Australian, British, and American statistics, and see evidence that there is certainly decline.

The Australian bureau of statistics finds that "The proportion of all Australians stating an affiliation to some type of religion remained relatively stable from 1933 until 1971, at slightly less than 90%. This proportion dropped to 80% in 1976, then slowly declined to 73% in 2001." (http://www.abs.gov.au/Ausstats/abs@.nsf/0/fa58e975c 470b73cca256 e9e00296645?OpenDocument). This decline was accompanied by a rising tendency among all Australians to state that they did not affiliate with any religion, particularly evident since the 1970s (7% in 1971 and 16% in 2001). The National Bureau of Statistics in the UK found that "In the 2001 Census, 77 percent of people in England and Wales, 67 percent in Scotland and 86 percent in Northern Ireland stated that they had a religion." This was the first census to include a question on religion, and it remains to be seen what trend may emerge (http://www.statistics.gov.uk/STATBASE/ssdataset.asp?vlnk=7212). The American census does not include religion as a census question. Religious adherent statistics in the U.S. are obtained from surveys and organizational reporting. Gallup polls (http://www.adherents.com/rel_USA.html) also indicate a small decline, from 84 percent Christian in 1996 to 82 percent Christian in 2002.The American Religious Identification Survey 2001 (ARIS) indicated that in 2001, more than 29.4 million Americans said they had no religion: more than double the number in 1990.

In fact, many see the 21st century decline in Christianity presents a crisis in Christendom (Murray, 2002) for the Western "church." Jinkins (2002) perceives the death of the church to be a crisis that is a "gift" that will give the church identity and responsibility. The end of Christendom may provide a "crisis" in the sense of both judgment and opportunity: this double sense attached to the Greek noun from which our English word is formed. "Crisis" can, in fact, teach salutary lessons, suggest fresh possibilities, and be turned to constructive ends. In a general sense, this is the understanding of "crisis" that the end of Christendom presents to the church today.

There is no shortage of theologians and authors — Protestants and Catholics — who have been calling for "renewal" in the church. See, for example, Friend (1998) aiming to help readers discover new ways of understanding themselves and the mission of the church in the process of renewing the contemporary church. Many of those seeking renewal want to reestablish the "community" aspect, for example, Van Gelder and Mouw (2000), who promote church as a community of people governed by the Word and led and taught by the Spirit. Ludwig (1995) tries to bring people out of a legalistic view of the Roman Catholic Church to a view of its "sacramentality" mediating in the world. He notes from the moment it was institutionalized, Catholicism has been entangled in a struggle between the institution and the embrace of God's presence in the world. For Ludwig, the challenge is to reconstruct Catholicism within a postmodern paradigm. Most

Christians would also testify to the "permanence" of the church in that it is divinely guaranteed by Christ, its rock, and will not fail. The decline that Christendom churches may be experiencing is a "death" the can lead to "transformation" to a more glorious form. It is a "change" rather than an end. The question is, just what will come next?

One of the biggest difficulties of the 21st century is the way that contemporary church communities tend to segregate congregations according to age. The individualistic mind-set of contemporary society has permeated the church to the extent that families are hardly ever together, and the extended family nature of the church is undermined. There are programs for children, crèches and nurseries for infants, gatherings for youth, social events for the retired, a program for just about every segment of the congregation, but nothing that links them all together. Even the centre of church life in its corporate worship tends to fragment in a way that compromises what church is meant to be about. Some movements are addressing this, for example, Family Integrated Church, which is a biblically based model that strengthens the family unit and restores the Church's life as a family of families. Also, forums like "churchbaby" highlighting the division being caused by contemporary approaches of individual "ministry" to different ages.

6.5 References

Anti-Climacus (S. Kierkegaard). (1850). Indøvelse. In *Christendom (Practice in Christianity)*.

Barth, & Bonhoeffer. (n.d.).

Bonhoeffer. (n.d.).

Coplan, P. (2004). *Jesus, religions, and just war. Is there such thing as a just war? Discussion on religion, religious wars, and just war doctrine.* Retrieved from http://www.everystudent.com/wires/justwar.html

Dulles, A. (1983). *Models of the church: A critical assessment of the church in all its aspects.* Gill and Macmillian.

Elwell. (1988). The church. In *Elwell's evangelical dictionary.* Bible Library, Version 4.0. Ellis Enterprises Ltd.

Erickson, M. (1998). *Christian theology* (2nd ed.). Baker Books.

Ferguson, E. (1946). *The Church of Christ — A biblical ecclesiology for today.* William B. Eerdmans Publishing Company.

Fox, Z. (1993). The rise of lay ministry in the years since Vatican II. In P. M. Hegy (Ed.), *The Church in the nineties* (pp. 230-241). MN: The Liturgical Press.

Friend, Jr., H. E. (1998). *Recovering the sacred center: Church renewal from the inside out.* Valley Forge, PA: Judson Press.

Jinkins, M. (2002). The church faces death: Ecclesiology in a postmodern context (Review for the book). *Theology Today, 59*(1), 133-136.

Julien, T. (1998). The rssence of the Church. *Evangelical Missions Quarterly, 34*(2), 148-153.

Ludwig, R. A. (1995). *Reconstructing Catholicism for a new generation.* Crossroad Pub Co.

Marx, K. (1844). Selections from the *Contribution to the critique of Hegel's Philosophy of Right.* Retrieved from http://www3.baylor.edu/~Scott_Moore/texts/Marx_Opium .html

McDonald, W. (2001). Søren Kierkegaard. In *Stanford encyclopedia of philosophy.* Retrieved from http://plato.stanford.edu/entries/kierkegaard/

McGrath, A. (2001). *Christian theology: An introduction.* Blackwell.

Methodist General Conference. (2004).

Muggeridge, M. (1980). *The end of Christendom.* Eerdmans Pub Co.

Murray, S. (2002). *Christendom.* Retrieved October 27, 2004, from http://tce.dse.nl/members/lightandheat/pstermschristendom.html

NPR. (2004). *The Catholic Church and sex abuse: Commentary on the church in crisis.* Retrieved from http://www.npr.org/news/specials/priests/

Packer, J. I. (1993). *Concise theology.* Wheaton: Tyndale House Publishers.

Runia, K. (1984). Evangelicals and the doctrine of church in European history. *Evangelical Review of Theology, 8*(1), 40-57.

Saucy, R. L. (1972). *The church in God's program.* Chicago: Moody Press.

Schwartz, R. (1997). *The curse of Canaan: The violent legacy of monotheism.* Chicago: University of Chicago Press.

Sullivan, A. (2001). *This is a religious war, September 11 was only the beginning.* Retrieved from http://www.andrewsullivan.com/thewar.php?artnum=20011007

Synder, H. A. (1978). *The community of the King.* IL: Inter-Varsity Press.

Taylor, A., & Foner, E. (2003). American colonies. In *The penguin history of the United States.*

Van Gelder, C., & Mouw, R. J. (2000). *The essence of the Church: A community created by the spirit.* Baker Book House.

Vos, H. F. (1996). *Exploring church history.* Lightning Source Inc.

Walker, W. (1997). *A history of the Christian church* (4th ed.). Edinburgh: T&T Clark.

Watson, D. (1978). *I believe in the church.* Hodder and Stouchton.

Weber. (2003). *Anabaptists.* Retrieved from http://www.newadvent.org/cathen/01445b.htm

Chapter 7

Church and the Internet

"Human beings must be known to be loved; but Divine beings must be loved to be known."

Blaise Pascal

"This is my simple religion. There is no need for temples; no need for complicated philosophy."

Dalai Lama

7.1 Introduction

This chapter considers the topic church and the Internet. We start with outlining some directories for "virtual religion," defined earlier as that religion which finds electronic expression in the virtual world. We note that there are directories both for real-world churches with a Web presence, and those that are truly a stand-alone online initiative. The two types of "church" are often confused. We continue by looking at specific examples of entities that are solely based on the Internet. They call themselves :Internet church," or might be called "Internet church." The examples mentioned range from Internet ventures sponsored by official mainline churches (e.g., I-Church), providing paid staff for pastoral oversight, to those set up by self-help organisations for the blind (e.g., EChurch-UK), to satirical efforts at making religion humorous (e.g., Church of Fools), and sites that appear "scam-like," designed for collecting funds, offering schemes to "get rich," and giving ordination qualifications, and so forth.

Secondly, we discuss the question of whether these Internet entities can call themselves "church." We look at features/aims and unique "missions" of those solely online entities that have set themselves up with a web presence. We find that the main usage of the Internet is in fostering "community" through discussion, exchange of opinion, and theological debate at many different levels. Also increasingly, the Internet is being used for evangelism. The extent to which community and evangelism are aspects of the actual church, is the extent to which Internet entities and real-world churches overlap.

Thirdly, we investigate a typology for "Internet church." Bednell's typology for Internet church predicts six different types of church based on whether they are founded around "information" or "communication," and then whether they support current institutions, bridge to current institutions, or create new forms of institutions. Our approach to a typology seeks a classification according to the technological features and ecclesiological functions that a Web site supports. Cutting across these is the question of "accessibility," that is, the question of whether such an expression of Internet "church" is more or less "available" to those with special needs, to the geographically isolated, to children/young people, to a certain socioeconomic group. In some instances "Internet church" may facilitate a better "expression" of the essence of "church" than the real-world church is able, in that context. As the contemporary church seeks to "contextualise" itself, the Internet is a highly relevant place to do so.

The objective of this chapter is to summarise the range of Web sites that have sprung up as "churches," and what they are doing. We seek to understand the different ways that the Internet is being used in entities that might call themselves "church." We emphasise the important difference between churches that have a real-world presence and a Web page, and those entities that are entirely "virtual." We want to examine a typology for Internet church, and identify how the Internet is being used to both foster Christian communities and implement various Christian "missions." We aim to point out the range of different aims in having a Web presence — from dating to teaching, evangelism to prayer, children's ministries to discussion groups. We want to raise the question of whether the Internet church is a "valid expression," and if so, what features are required; if not, why.

7.2 Examples of "Internet and Church"

There have been various attempts to create a "community" directory for virtual Christianity. Hughes (2000) defines a community directory as an accurate organised list of resources, people, services, and places that are relevant to the purpose for which it is compiled. The term "virtual Christianity" encompasses a range of Internet entities, from churches, to historical documents, communities to commercial outlets, among other things. We specifically seek to consider those elements of "virtual Christianity" that may be considered to be "Internet and Church." For the present, we work with a loose definition of what "Internet and Church" entails, reserving judgement on whether there can be such a thing as "Internet church" or not. Directories for "online churches" or "Internet churches" or "virtual Christianity" often list Web sites from real-world churches. For example

- **Great Church Web sites (http://www.greatchurchweb sites.org/)**: complied by David Gillaspey, for American "Internet Churches." As of November 26,t 2004, he had reviewed 6,875 Protestant, Catholic, and Orthodox church Web sites, from which he chose 379 (5.5%) so far to include in the database, offering a "virtual gallery" of church home pages. The site not only collates information about "virtual churches," but also offers some useful tips for creating Web sites, including tips for disabled users.
- **Online Churches (http://online-churches.net/):** hosts a directory of online churches. They report "A growing number of churches are tuning into God through 'video cafes.'" According to *The Washington Post*, congregations across the country are offering services with TV sermons, in which a pastor preaches live in a more traditional service in one room, while people in the video cafe see only his talking head on a screen. "This melding of technology and religion in

> video venues is taking off," the newspaper observed. "Leaders of those churches say a video sermon used to be only for the homebound or for those who arrived late and had to sit in an overflow room. Now it has become an attractive option in its own right, especially among the young." This site reports the takeoff of technology and church life with the American "video café," linking many with "church" who would not normally go to the traditional church building

There is not a directory known to us that specifically lists those Internet entities that are entirely virtual and concerned with "being church" on the Internet. Whether an "Internet church" is, in fact, possible is open to debate, although elements of church can certainly be repeated. For example, there can certainly be virtual Christian "communities" and discussion groups and teaching resources and chat rooms; Internet can support a teleconference, or "shared white board" for a collaborative meeting and brain storming; it can contain video and audio recordings of worship services and present sacred images. But whether this is a "church" is still open to debate. Either way, a directory of such Internet entities is not available.

Thus, we start with surveying some examples of what may be called "Internet church." We want to make a chronological listing of the entities and when they appeared. Table 1 presents a summary of the different Web sites that might be called "Internet church" and when they went online. Unfortunately, not only is there no "community directory," but there is no "scam-list" of those entirely virtual entities that are "suspicious."

We find the examples range from Internet ventures sponsored by official mainline churches (e.g. I-Church), providing paid staff for pastoral oversight, to those set up by self-help organisations for the blind (e.g. EChurch-UK); to satirical efforts at making religion humorous (e.g. Church of Fools) and sites that appear "scam-like," offering instant ordination, requesting moneys for buildings, advertising schemes guaranteed to make money, and sites offering miracles. There are numerous sites whose aim is not entirely clear. We also make a brief summary of some of these Web sites, what they contain, and/or their aims:

- **1994, The First Church of CyberSpace (http://www.godweb.org/index1.html):** founded by Charles

Table 1. Chronological list of Internet churches

Date	Name	URL
1994	The First Church of CyberSpace	http://www.godweb.org/index1.html
1995, May 10	Virtual Church	http://www.virtualchurch.org/
1996, July 4	The Virtual Church of the Blind Chihuahua	http://www.dogchurch.org/index.shtml
1997, February 7	First International Church of the Web	http://ficotw.org/
1998, April 1	The Ship of Fools	http://shipoffools.com/church/
2001, May	EChurch-UK	http://www.echurch-uk.org/
2004, May	Church of Fools	http://shipoffools.com/church/
2004, July 30	I-Church	http://www.i-church.org/aboutichurch.php
2004	E-Church (version 2.1)	http://www.e-church.com/
2005	Church.co.uk	http://www.church.co.uk/
n.d.	Jesus Connect	http://www.jesus-connect.net/
n.d.	WebChurch	http://www.webchurch.org
n.d.	Vurch	http://www.vurch.com
n.d.	Church for All	http://www.churchforall.org/
n.d.	Churches of Christ	http://church-of-christ.org/
n.d.	Cyber Church	http://cyber-church.com/
n.d.	Grace Walk	http://www.gracewalk.org/
n.d.	The Internet Church	http://www.the-internet-church.com
n.d.	Big Church	http://bigchurch.com
n.d.	Internet Church for Christ	http://churchforchrist.com/mycustompage0001.htm

Henderson is one of the first, certainly earliest attempts at Internet congregations. Today, the homepage advertises: "Though there are many congregations, denominations and other religious groups that advertise their presence on the Web, we are the first to organize within cyberspace itself: making connections, constructing links, dropping clues that point to the presence of the Creator within the creative chaos of the Internet. We seek colleagues interested in collaborating with us as we envision those new forms of faith community that are emerging at the dawn of a new millennium. We are available to work with churches, campus ministry groups, and others interested in using computers to communicate the faith."

- **1995, Virtual Church (http://www.virtualchurch.org/):** is a church with separate "rooms." Each has something different to offer: the sanctuary features sermons by guest ministers, communion, and prayer; the library has Bible quizzes, links to Bible search engines, reference materials, and bookstores; the gallery contains images of fine art, stained glass, and photographs. There is a children's room with illustrated Bible stories and pictures to color, a music room with hymn lyrics and sound files, and a fellowship hall with links to other Internet resources.
- **1996, The Virtual Church of the Blind Chihuahua (http://www.dogchurch.org/index.shtml):** is another early example of Internet Church. It claims to be "a sacred place in cyberspace named after a little old dog with cataracts who barked sideways at strangers because he couldn't see where they were. We humans relate to God in the same way, making a more or less joyful noise in God's general direction, and expecting a reward for doing so. Hence our creed: We cannot be right about everything we believe. Thank God, we don't have to be!" It is a humorous attempt at a Christian community that touches on some deeper questions.
- **1997, First International Church of the Web (http://ficotw.org/):** Offers free ordination. They have also recently acquired a church building and request monetary donations be sent for it. It solicits no tithes from any of its members. Members are requested, but not required, to post a link to the church on their own personal Web pages and e-mail correspondence.
- **1998, The Ship of Fools (http://shipoffools.com/church/):** is hosted by a UK-based organisation. Their patron saint is "St

Simeon the Holy Fool," an eccentric desert saint who went into the desert for 29 years, living on lentils in an isolated cave next to the Dead Sea: at first struggling against temptation, and then advancing to an alarming degree of holiness. His life shows how God chooses "the foolish things of the world to shame the wise; the weak things of the world to shame the strong" (1 Corinthians 1:27). They originally produced a paper-based magazine that died, and rose again in Web form on April Fools day, 1998. The "Ship of Fools" organisation asks whether there is a better way to do Christianity than what the church is doing at the start of the 21st century. They appeal to people who feel alienated from conventional church and say "If you're ever wondering 'Where Would Jesus Surf' just look here." Their Web site includes thriving online community bulletin boards, including some attention grabbers such as (a) the Mystery Worshipper — volunteers who drop in on conventional church services across the world and make notes to report back, (b) the "Gadget for God" — a real world article that has a "cannot believe it" factor (e.g., the WWJD (What Would Jesus Do) boxer shorts with a false fly to relieve temptation), (c) the Ark — the world's first Internet reality game show, where Big Brother meets 12 biblical heroes, controlled on computer by contestants who battle it out to stay on board for 40 days and avoid the dreaded plank.

- **2001, EChurch-UK (http://www.echurch-uk.org/):** is a Web site designed to provide Christian fellowship for blind and partially sighted people, but is designed for all. The founding couple searched a long time for a church in London that wanted "two blind people and two guide dogs." The journeys to unknown places very stressful. Real fellowship was often impossible. In common with a lot of visually impaired people, the initiators felt a need for more regular fellowship than just on Sunday, and wanted to meet during the week. They also wanted to be able to share their faith with others in similar circumstances. They believed that God was leading them to use the Internet. Screen readers for Web documents make possible a speech synthesis of the textual content.

The most interesting potential of Internet church appears to be the "community" that it fosters, rather than the static repositories of information. Internet church has great potential to foster thriving virtual communities. Thomas (2004) reminds us "Membership of the body of Christ is not limited by four walls and a spire or tower. The Church is the fellowship of those who belong to Christ, and to one another in Christ, and I would argue that you can have fellowship with other members of I-church at least as fully, if not more so, as with those you sit next to on a Sunday, but whom you never really know deeply."

- **2004, The "Church of Fools" (http://shipoffools.com/church/):** is an initiative piloted in May 2004 by the "Ship of Fools." They produced a 3-month Web-based pilot of a 3-D virtual church. It is one of the most imaginative visual interactive environments for Internet church and a virtual community yet, complete with "avatars." The church was launched with a real-world service that was packed out; thousands of people engaged in the virtual world. The church is intended for people on the edges (and beyond) of faith and for Christians from all church traditions. The church is an attempt to create "holy ground" on the net, where visitors embodied as virtual characters can worship, pray, and talk about faith.

The church is divided into two areas: the sanctuary and the crypt. The sanctuary is a place for worship services, complete with

Figure 4. Impression of the sanctuary of the Church of Fools

message and music and personal prayer, outside worship times. As you wander around, you will find images on some of the walls. Clicking them will load a pop-up window with material for prayer and meditation. Figure 1 illustrates the virtual sanctuary space. It was taken from service (final service of 21st September, 2004 after a 3 month trial) recorded at http://www.shipoffools.com/church/. The crypt is a chat room with lounge and coffee machine. It is a relaxed place under the sanctuary where you can take a seat, trade views on the singing and the preaching, generally talk to others, and spark off lively debate. Outside regular service times, adherents could roam around the sanctuary or meet for an informal chat in the crypt, where the drinks machine and lounge area provided an environment for graphical online chat.

The Church of Fools has just started to explore the technical possibilities for virtual worlds. There is huge scope to improve the "technical" through virtual reality that technology fosters. With Internet-mediated voice communication, the potential for wearable computers, virtual reality headsets, haptic interfaces, and other technologies that influence "presence," there is scope to achieve a deeper reality in the "embodied" sense. Never mind the "social" presence that can be fostered through participation. One aspect of this virtual church is that there is no commitment with the members, and creating a sense of "belonging" is difficult. In its 3-month trial, Church of Fools also experienced many people simply entering church for fun outside the set service time (and services often reached full capacity), sometimes abusing the system, engaging in, at times, "unsavoury conversations," and other disruptive behaviour. There was a natural tendency for people to "push the system," and the pulpit eventually had to be made "out of bounds" to the virtual wanderers!

- **2004, I-church (http://www.i-church.org/aboutichurch.php):** is an example of a "private" community being fostered online: private in the sense that membership is restricted (at least during the "trial"). It was launched on 30 July, 2004 at St Mary the Virgin, Oxford, with a Eucharist led by the Bishop of Dorchester. It is sponsored by the Church of England, and under the pastoral care of the Bishop of Oxford. I-church is a serious attempt to connect people from all over the world

> into a Christian community. There are four main sections to I-church: the devotional life of the church, pastoral care, outreach, and technical/ administrative support. There are ways of controlling access to different parts of I-church to prevent "abuse," and people entering simply to be disruptive. The interactive parts will be restricted to members. The parts that are open to all will not be interactive, that is, allow one person to have online contact with another.

To attain membership of I-church, subscribers have to demonstrate a commitment to prayer, study, and social action. A person also has to disclose enough about themselves to be traceable and excludable. Paveley (2004) explains, "I-church is a real parish of real people who don't stop being members when they log out." One of the key discoveries about Internet communities is that their members soon express a desire to meet in the real world. The I-church suggests that real life is connecting and then meeting, and spotlights the frequent experience of attending and worshipping, but not really knowing others, thus not experiencing community! The belief and aim is that I-church members will experience a different and better community, because there is no building to focus upon. They aim to achieve "a sense of belonging" and the "devotional life of a distinctively Anglican church" together with new models of "pastoral care" in that setting. They consider that on the Internet, "people can form very deep contacts very quickly on the Internet, because there is an immediacy about this form of contact. You don't waste words: you tend to get to the heart of matters very quickly." In I-church, it is possible to know and to be known; it is an opportunity to really belong meaningfully to a supportive community without being limited to one place and one time.

Thomas (2004) explains the attraction of I-church being that "One of the defining features of our culture is the desire to self-resource. And the Internet is probably the ultimate expression of that self-resourcing." Thomas makes an important observation about the changing nature of a society that is consumer-oriented, and how that influences the sense of belonging, finding that "No longer do we belong to an organisation or an institution in order to serve that organisation or institution. We look to it to serve us. Instead of being contributors to our communities, we are consumers of them." It may be that the increasing failure to participate in organised religion is a direct result of a loss of faith in such institutions as places that are effective in their key tasks. Thus, he finds that it "should be no surprise to discover that there are some people, maybe more than a few, who want to be part of a Christian community, to commit themselves to one another in prayer, in learning, and in social action, without the hassle and clutter of participation in the local parish church."

In terms of organisation, the I-church community is organised in small "pastorates" of about 15 to 20 people who support one another. An authorised pastor leads each pastorate. To some extent, this arrangement perpetuates the "authority" of Christendom. Internet mediates the medium of the "control" in which the authority is exercised, and the "levelling" influence is enabled. Further, the emphasis on the control that the Church of England exercises over the arrangement is a continued assertion that both (1) the venture is "legitimate Christianity" and not the product of a sect or cult, despite being "alternative" in its nature, and that (2) the venture is going to perpetuate the polity of conventional church life. While suitably qualified and gifted people are naturally the most suitable to select as such leaders, the system is still open to abuse: just as "bad shepherds" can abuse their authority within conventional church life in ways that have plagued the church throughout history. Until those "control" and power structures are completely changed, even Internet church is open to the same problems of corruption that have destroyed the church within Christendom. The abuse of power is particularly horrific in religious contexts, since people are most "trusting" and "vulnerable" in those contexts. And it is also one of the contexts that is most likely to attract individuals who have the "sociopathic" inclinations for self-glory, power, and deceit, as their true colours are disguised, often all too cleverly from the unsuspecting "sheep" of their fold.

One comment notes that Internet church in I-church is not really new, but "What's new here is someone paying someone to do it." This arrangement of financing the leadership to operate the electronic forum continues the tension within the wider church between those people who do "serve" in a voluntary capacity, and those who are funded by the "faithful." Financing people to undertake specific tasks within the church has often been criticised as unfair and bad practice in terms of creating a community and ensuring that all people are involved and participative. When certain individuals are funded for certain tasks, the situation evolves where only those who are paid do the tasks, and where the wider community does not explore and venture into training to undertake those tasks themselves, and are not encouraged to. Such a practice of funding some, and not others, also opens itself to corruption with the selection and placement of those "funded" individuals, even when controlled by "committees" and others. Part of the Reformation was a protest at the way that the key leadership positions in the church involved strategically placed candidates. Often these were family members of already assigned leaders, so perpetuating the corruption of leadership. It remains to be seen how I-church will succeed where conventional church has failed in its polity.

- **2004, (version 2.1). E-Church (http://www.e-church.com/):** is a Web-based service that helps people publish their thoughts about God and engage in peer spiritual renewal. E-Church believes that it is the only spiritual blog service in the world. A blog is a frequently updated Web page where entries are listed in reverse chronological order (most recent first). Blog entries typically consist of links accompanied by commentary. Blogs encourage conversation through informality, enthusiasm for errata, comments (usually posted alongside the original entry), and reciprocal hyperlinks. They aim to help people: publish thoughts about God, listen to feedback, participate in peer spiritual renewal, meet like-minded people. They stimulate a "community" by having people post an image and description about themselves, and have had some 80 members.
- **2005, Church.co.uk (http://www.church.co.uk):** goal is to become: 24/7-providing a welcome to everyone whatever their situation, whatever the time, night or day; holistic-offering a breadth and depth of support, spiritually and socially, to the whole community and beyond; global-serving as the hub for the whole church.co.uk network as it grows around the UK and the world.
- **n.d. Jesus Connect (http://www.jesus-connect.net/):** aims to bring Christians together through high technology, while reflecting his light into cyberspace.
- **n.d. WebChurch (http://www.webchurch.org):** is the first virtual church outside the USA. It is interdenominational in the

sense that it has chapels for "Catholic, Orthodox, Episcopalian, Anglican, Non-Conformist, Presbyterian, Don't knows & Definitely nots."

- **n.d. Vurch (http://www.vurch.com):** is primarily a place of worship. There are three structured steps: (1) 30-second prayer/thought/notice, (2) an online discussion (room with a view, blue room, dream room), and (3) make a donation or buy some merchandise.
- **n.d. Church for All (http://www.churchforall.org/):** is a Web site aiming to be church without a building. They also encourage their members, as they grow spiritually, to consider having a regular meeting in their own home with other believers to pray, have fellowship, and discuss the Bible together, even if this is just your own family, or your friends and neighbours. They do all they can to furnish the member with wedding and funeral guidelines that they think will be helpful. They have a worship script online that takes the visitor through prayers and songs and a recorded message, and have opportunity for "giving" to their church.
- **n.d. Churches of Christ (Internet Ministries):** (http://church-of-christ.org/) has a unique flavour to their site in that there are many different language versions available — Italian, German, Swiss, French, and so forth. They include bulletin boards and discussion groups.
- **n.d. Cyber-Church (http://cyber-church.com/):** is designed to bring Jesus to the Internet, and to unashamedly present the Gospel of Christ all around the world to all who visit here. While Cyber-Church can never replace the fellowship of your own local church, it is our sincere prayer that we can become your "home away from home" church, and that you will find true Christian fellowship here, and that we can meet many of your ministry needs
- **n.d. Grace Walk (http://www.gracewalk.org/):** is a teaching and training ministry that exists for the purpose of sharing the life of Jesus Christ with others, and to help Christians discover the freedom of their new life in Christ.
- **n.d. The Internet Church (http://www.the-internet-church.com/theinternetchurch.htm):** has been established as a teaching and learning center.

Naturally, the Internet is changing daily, and the various "church" Web sites similarly change. The trend is that more and more entities called "Internet church" are springing up. While Gorn (2004) suggests that religious communities add depth and stability to the virtual environment because of the sense of history and reality that such communities provide, these communities themselves change. Their "content" may remain more static than a debate forum about current affairs, but other aspects of their identity are subject to the same "transience" of the virtual world. Gorn maintains that the "religious" material provides a link into real human experience and a more stable world. It reconnects people with reality through the content of its matter, and enables people to connect with their "humanness."

7.3 Function of the Internet and Church

Wilson (2000) coined the term "Internet church" in his book of the same title. He gives an insight into the power and potential of the Internet in Christianity, covering the basic history and principles of the Internet, as well as examples and resources for churches who want to utilise the Internet, plus the important motivational vision for taking up this new media. Typical resources of Internet church are a Web site with a bulletin board forum, or perhaps an online chat room. There may be an information page related to doctrine, and/or some other static resource for the members of the community. While it may seem straightforward that Internet church is, in some way, using technology to "be church," it is controversial whether they are indeed "churches," and not always clear what they are aiming to achieve. Half a decade after *Internet church* was written, there are plenty of Web sites and examples of online institutions that call themselves "Internet church." But simply having a Web site does not encompass all that Internet church is.

As we have seen, the question of "what is church?" is an involved question: the question of "what is Internet church?" is even more so!. Is it a room full of isolated people sitting in rows typing at computers? Is it something that must mimic "real-world" church? If so, which "style" or "expression" of worship should it implement? Does it have to repeat the structures of Christendom to be valid? Should it have a concept of "membership," or be an open forum? Can it ever capture the characteristics of a "real-world" Christendom church through technology? How? What about the sacramental life? Is Internet church even a church? Or is the phenomena of using technology as "church" really something entirely different from church? Is it questionable whether the phenomena can even be called "church?" If not, what constitutes Internet church? Is a text-based information resource with a blog sufficient to qualify for being a church? Or must there be a fixed worship time? Are children allowed on the discussion boards, or is that impossible in an unmoderated forum using open-source bulletin board technology, which requires users to be over 13 years of age, for its own legal reasons? If children are not included, how can the "Internet church" be the same entity as the "real-world" church? Or is having a separate forum for minors no different to the age-segregated ministry that is rife in real-world churches?

In 1999, the Society of Archbishop Justus offered the Anglican Church a tract on Church and the Internet and how the Internet could be used (http://justus.anglican.org/resources/tracts/nc/). The main advantages were cited as "it can help the church with its mission as no technology since the printing press has been able to help. Online communication is economically advantageous to the church. It can be used to bring more information to more people more cheaply. It allows people to form communities without needing buildings. And it will reach the young." Clearly, the Internet was seen as a tool to be seized and used by the church in its mission. It has certain economic advantages, and may appeal to the "young." However, the use of the Internet in Christian and church contexts has gone way beyond the simple "helping spread the Christian message": the "mission" of Internet entities is far wider than communicating the gospel. There certainly are other aims and "missions" of entities that have a Web presence; teaching and instruction is surprisingly under represented.

In many ways, the Internet has been used more for fostering the "life" of churches (in community) than its mission (in spreading the gospel message). At the start of the first appearance of Christian entities on the Internet, Ken Bedell (1999) identified that many entities were not actually calling themselves churches. Instead, Bednell called the entities "Internet congregations," and in doing so, focused in on one of the main uses of the Internet in creating virtual Christian communities. Today, this aim of creating community still seems a primary aim of the "Internet church." We find that the main usage of the Internet in entities that either call themselves church, or which are candidates for being such, are in:

1. Seeking a new expression of conventional church using discussion, exchange of opinion, and theological debate at many different levels through chat rooms, bulletin boards, blogs, and e-mail lists (e.g., I-church, Echurch-UK)
2. Fostering "community," perhaps especially appealing to those "disillusioned" with mainstream Christianity (e.g., The Virtual Church of the Blind Chihuahua; The Ship of Fools; Church of Fools).
3. Overt "evangelism" and spreading the Christian message (e.g., http://www.e-vangelism.com/)
4. Scam-like schemes offering instant ordination and qualification for religious leadership, requesting moneys for buildings (when other Internet Churches point out no buildings are needed), guaranteed personal money-making schemes, "healing," miracles, and supernatural bill paying.
5. Other function, not necessarily related to the life or mission of the church, including "Christian" dating (Bigchurch.com), counselling.

Clearly in the first aim, seeking a new expression of conventional church, we have the boldest assertion that the Web community is able to function as a conventional church. That is, there is such a thing as "Internet church"; that the virtual world can support all that is needed in the function of church. The entity is not just supporting the community life of the church, or assisting the main mission of the church, but is all that a church needs to be. One of the best ways of answering the question whether there could be such a thing as Internet church is perhaps to look at the function of the church, and what scripture says this is.

There are various understandings of what church should do and be. Four different functions can be identified (http://church-ministry.tripod.com/): (1) "Outreach" — The church reaching out to those outside the church. (evangelism, missions), (2) "Inreach" — The church reaching in to those inside the church. (encouragement, fellowship, accountability), (3) "Upreach" — The church reaching up to God. (praising, prayer) and (iv) "Downreach" — God reaching down to the church. (Bible study, listening to the Holy Spirit). This definition captures the "horizontal" and "vertical" aspects of community, as well as the two main biblical injunctions to "reach out" and "build up within." Matthew 28:19 suggests the function of the church is to "go," "make disciples," "baptise," and "teach." Ephesians 4.12 suggests it is "to equip the saints for the work of service, to the building up of the body of Christ." Those Internet entities that are candidates for being church are certainly attempting to fulfil these functions, and arguably succeeding.

The biggest "questions" about the possibility of Internet church revolve around the questions of "presence," that is, physical presence of other people; of tangible symbols (such as water and bread) that are used in "sacramental" ways to point to realities beyond themselves; even of God, who is believed to be "manifest" in a special way when even "two or three" are gathered. In a later chapter, we consider this question of "presence" and just what it means, how it is achieved, and whether "Internet presence" is any more or less "genuine" than physical presence. Especially, what "presence" means in a religious context, where there is recognition of the possibility of transcendence of the physical world, and that this forms a component of that which is "church."

However, it may be a mistake to set up "Internet church" as a separate entity from real-world church. We may feel more comfortable calling a separate room full of noisy children trying to sit in rows a "children's church," and less comfortable with calling a separate room full of adults sitting in rows at computers "Internet church," and if we take them out of their rows or put them in different buildings, we are even less comfortable with calling it church, but what has changed? If the computers were facilitating blind and deaf people engaging in worship, would we be more prepared to call it church? If they were facilitating noisy children focusing upon a "teaching," would we be more prepared to call it church? If a disabled person who could not leave the house was able to "be part of" the virtual network, would we be more prepared to call it church?

Andrew Carega (2002) notes " ... contrary to popular opinion, the Internet wasn't luring Christians away from their regularly scheduled church services. The Internet, according to the researchers, 'is a useful supplemental tool that enhances their already-deep commitment to their beliefs and their churches ... '" However, Carega found that pastors used the Internet differently: "clergy use the Internet quite differently. Most ministers don't see the Net as a space into which they can enter for community and relationship, but as a tool for research." At a conference on post-modern ministries, the Internet was still being defended as a "tool" and "One participant claimed it was impossible to create authentic community over the Internet." Carega reminds us "Howard Rheingold wrote the book on online community nearly a decade ago, and millions are online proving that virtual communities can and do exist. While we in the church are still asking, 'How can I make my Web site cool?' and debating whether or not people can develop relationships and community on the Net ... We in the church must change our way of thinking about the Internet. If we don't, we'll end up with our own subculture online, just as we have in 'real life.'"

In a final closing word on Internet church, we report two contrasting opinions. George Miller (2002) speaks favourably of church and the Internet, even pointing out the "theological" possibilities of fellowship beyond this physical world. Blake Atwood (2001) points out that the Internet cannot replace that physical gathering which is the church.

George Miller (2002) points out that the fellowship of believers is more than "this world"; more than sitting in the same church building or sharing the same pew. "The Internet church is like no other. Loving others through words is a new concept, a new blessing. Not face-to-face, the words we speak through the keyboards tells of the love in our hearts. I may never meet you in this human form, but God knows us both. We will have a place in heaven sitting by His side. Where our Spirit now concealed, will be the real insider-outside then you will know the real me. Neither you nor I will be disappointed, having new names. We will never lose the ability to love. Charity like eternity, is forever. In this new church of words with the online pews. No pastor, no elders, just God and us. Sharing these end-times together."

Blake Atwood (2001) writes " ... for the Internet to become one's sole place of soul-help isn't the answer. The church is the one brick-and-mortar place that the Internet can't replace. It seems absurd to even mention the idea that one could 'go to church' just by logging on ... Not attending a brick-and-mortar church means missing out on a lot of good things ... I encourage you to leave your computer and get to a church. Use the computer and find a church that looks like a place you'd like to visit." Thinking Anglicans comment "Congregations without the practice of discipline are not new to the Church of England. Congregations without biblical preaching are not new either. What is new is the idea of a parish without meeting together for the sacraments or to know who our brethren really are" (http://www.thinking anglicans.org.uk/ss/archives/000540.html). While the Internet has a part to play in the church, it is a tragedy that it should be seen as a substitute.

7.4 Typologies for Internet Entities and Church

Ken Bedell (1999) examines "Internet congregations" in order to ask just what are they. He does not call them churches, but has identified one of the main functions of the Internet in fostering virtual communities that may be called congregations. He defines Internet congregation as "a group of people must intentionally see themselves as part of a community where they interact with each other, support each other in what they understood to be their spiritual lives." He was looking for conscious and intentional religious community, not just those who used discussion lists to talk about religious themes or find spiritual support. An Internet congregation is designed to completely replace all of the functions of a traditional congregation. However, he explains, "this definition proved to be so restrictive that I was unable to find people who understood themselves to be participants in this kind of an experience."

Bednell identifies six possible uses of Internet and their relation to "bricks and mortar" congregations. He finds two often overlapping, but distinct approaches to forming community in "information" or "communication." Of these approaches, he says "The first assumes that information is the essential ingredient for community building. The second assumes that communication is essential for community development. Cutting across both of these assumptions are three strategies: support for current institutions, bridge to current institution, create new forms of institution." Bednell's typology includes the following categories:

- **Support current institutions (information):** for example, Grace Cathedral. Grace Cathedral is an example of a congregation that is physically based, but makes bold claims about being an Internet church. They invite people from around the world to join their effort and make a financial commitment.
- **Support current institutions (communication):** for example, Ecunet. Ecunet (http://ww1.ecunet.org) calls itself "The world's oldest global, ecumenical online conferencing community." From its inception in pre-Internet days, Ecunet has understood itself to be a communication tool that supports religious organizations.
- **Bridge to current institutions (information):** for example, Charles Henderson is the founder of The First Church of Cyberspace. Henderson works in a very secular setting, pointing people to religious institutions. He believes that the Internet is a place where religious people should be present to point people to religious organizations.
- **Bridge to current institutions (communication):** for example, people with a religious agenda are spending time in chat rooms or participating in discussion groups where the topic is not specifically religious.
- **Create new forms of institutions (information):** for example, WorldVillage.com. WorldVillage is a family of Web sites focused on providing a family-friendly Internet experience. The site makes no claims about being based on Christianity, nor does it claim to be creating a new kind of community, but has a Christian chat room with other general "information and services" including product reviews.
- **Create new forms of institutions (communication):** for example, Partenia, CyberFaith.International. The Partenia homepage (http://www.partenia.org/eng/index1.htm) is sponsored by Jacques Gaillot, who in 1995, refused the Vatican's request that he resign as a bishop. He was removed from his responsibilities to a diocese that no longer exists, but instead, is an ancient, ruined city covered by the Sahara desert since the Middle Ages. As the bishop of "no-

> where," he oversees a Web site that hosts electronic forums that are completely open to anyone on the Internet. The site fosters open discussion by Roman Catholics. It is the primer Web site of free Catholics who hold to the teachings of Jesus (Yeshua, Jeshua) rather than hierarchical churchianity.

Bedell finds "it is interesting to note that some of the people who seem to come the closest to forming Internet congregations deny that is what they are doing, while others make very bold claims. Stephen Rose, for example, encourages people to participate in an ongoing dialog with him, offers spiritual resource, and, for a period, even celebrated weekly Eucharist online. However, in a section of his Web site where he discusses CAP (Church for All People) he says, "Are we creating a church? Nope. Not desired. Not intended. We mean only to profess membership in a church created by Jesus and to maintain that all are members" (http://www.renewal2.com/cap5.htm).

Our approach to a typology seeks a classification that is driven by the actual "entities" in existence. It is also an approach that seeks to be adaptive to those "entities." We isolate two broad classes: (1) the technology utilised, and (2) the function in church life and mission supported by the technology, and seek to categorise examples of "Internet church" by the features they possess. In terms of the church life and mission, it is likely that Internet entities will reproduce all or some of the features of a real-world church. For example, preaching, social community, study, pastoral care, prayer, worship, sacramental life, corporate repentance, celebration, and so forth, may all be part of the Internet entity. To be an Internet church, the entity should not compromise that which is considered to be essential to the "essence" of a church. As we have seen, there may not be agreement over the essence of "real-world" churches, but the Internet church should only clarify or enhance the real-world expression of what is considered to be the essence.

In terms of the technology utilised, common examples at the start of the 21st century include discussion boards and e-mail distribution lists. More recently, a graphical 3-D virtual environment was piloted with audio. There is an increasing use of text-based communal "blogs," — with individual's entries linked in more and more sophisticated ways making networks of human relationships in the process. Andrew Carega writes about what if the

Bible was written today, and the writers were bloggers (http://www.e-vangelism.com/). He says "Jesus wrote in the sand with his finger. No doubt a wiki-man who would have preferred his own wiki Sandbox. Solomon would have sent out his proverbs with a daily RSS feed, perhaps using a blog as a home base for his feeds. Matthew. A hyperlink geek who would blog with a constant stream of links back to the original prophecies in the Hebrew Scriptures. Most blogging programs make that easy."

The future may see an increase in non-text-based environments, avatars, video, and so forth, as "new" ways of mediating both "presence" and "identity" in all manner of virtual interactions explored. By categorising Internet churches according to the technology they use, we can also make room for future technologies. Technology may not currently support teleporting personal identities into communal ether, but if and when that is possible, that will be a "feature" of those who use that aspect of the Internet for their "entity" that they call "church." The technology may intersect with the function of the church differently for different people: discussion on a text-based bulletin board may be sufficient for some, while others may find anything less than a video link to be insufficient.

Associated with these two broad classes of feature (the technology utilised and the function in church life) there is the broader question of "accessibility." The question is not just the socioeconomic accessibility of whether people have Internet access or not. It is not even whether the forum is private or public, supporting only those who meet in real-world churches or bringing together those who are isolated. It is not whether the technology can be used by minors (e.g. some open source bulletin boards used in virtual communities only permit those over 13 years to use the technology because of the unmoderated context. Thus, the "church" would be a church without children!). The questions of whether the Internet "entity" is accessible touches on all of these issues, but also includes the question of whether it makes church more or less accessible to those with special needs: the disabled, the blind, the deaf, the mentally retarded, the geographically isolated, and so forth. The possibilities of technology assisting the disabled, or the geographically isolated, make it very possible that Internet church may be more "accessible" to those with certain needs than the real-world church could ever be. Even if "Internet church" is not a perfect manifestation of the real

Table 2. Technological features and ecclesiological functions of Web sites

Church Function\ Technology	Discussion Board	Text Blog	Chat Room	E-mail List	E-mail private/ SMS	3-D Graphical Environment	Web site text	Web site image	Web site audio
Community	B	B	B		C	D			
Study									
Pastoral Care/ counselling									
Prayer		E			C		E	E	E
Evangelism									
Polity/ Organisation					C				
Preaching						D			
Worship Praise						D			
Social Action									
Family Devotion						F			
Information repository							A	A	A

church, it may be an expression doing a better job (in some instances) than current manifestations.

In Table 2, we shall give some specific examples of Internet church. Here we analyse them according to the technological features and ecclesiological functions. Of course the functions and features have a certain amount of overlap, since "preaching" may be a "prayer," "community" may be stimulated by creating an "information repository," "study" may be a form of "pastoral care" in meeting an intellectual need, and so forth. Web site images may be used for devotional purposes, or to build a sense of social community among the people. Such overlap in features and functions may be the main "difficulty" of such an analysis, but provides a much needed starting place in understanding "Internet church" Web sites.

Table 2 is explained as follows:

(a) This class of Web site is basically a repository of information about a real-world congregation or denomination. These Web sites primarily aim at promoting the real-world church, and do so through the medium of Internet. They have no real virtual community associated with the Web site. Technically, they include text, images, and audio about the real-world congregation

(b) This class of Web site is stimulating "interaction" in a virtual community using publicly accessible text-based contributions from members on discussion boards, blogs in chatrooms, and so forth, to do so. The only distinguishing element from any other virtual community is the content, which is assumed to be "Christian related" and/or facilitating a real-world Christian community.

(c) This class of Web site is a private, text-based community. It includes private e-mail/SMS messages that essentially build community, as the telephone used to do. It may facilitate the distribution of "confidential" prayer requests that cannot be made public, and be the means of implementing "nontransparent" polity.

(d) This class of Web site is about non-text-based communities. The Web site is steering away from solely text-based interaction, venturing into 3-D virtual worlds, and exploring ways of stimulating interaction and relationship, even worship through preaching and music.

(e) This class of Web site is about "vertical community" and "interaction" with God, whether this is a private prayer, music, study, a meditation, or other devotion. It may involve use of a private resource, or be a communal collaboration, for example, in blog. Such Web sites are distinguished by the emphasis on "interaction" with God.

(f) This class of Web site is about "family devotion," using a graphically based 3-D virtual environment to contextualise religious themes for children in a "game-based" scenario that facilitates interaction with parents, learning, and worship.

While we may attempt to isolate such "classes" of Web site, each will have its own "combination": some may be more interested in stimulating friendship and community, others in "praying" or "counselling," some may be interested in discussing theological issues, and others simply in transferring as many aspects of real world church as possible into the virtual world. There may be combinations of archived addresses, liturgies, prayers and meditations, even video and audio recordings of actual gatherings. A bulletin board may be used for prayer, or as a discussion forum to enable members to engage with each other. Some members may keep in touch privately through SMS, while others use a more public forum, blurring the distinction between "virtual" and "real" community, as well as the functions and features of the Web site.

Undoubtedly, the Internet enables a public sharing of resources far more effectively than religious resources in other media (e.g. one person may borrow a book, several thousand may download an electronic article and share responses to it in real-time). Web sites may contain "personal devotion" material intended for "personal exploration" and "personal faith" that many people may use at once, or over a period of time. Even the "sharing" of common information can itself contribute to building a community, and a "private" resource become a shared "public" expression of religiosity. As the contemporary church seeks to "contextualise" itself, the Internet is increasingly a highly relevant place to do so.

7.5 References

Atwood, B. (2001). *The postmodern christian — the Internet church*? Retrieved from http://www.suite101.com/article.cfm/postmodern_christian/87252/2

Bednell, K. (1999). *Internet congregations in 1999*. Paper presented at the 1999 meeting of the Religious Research Association, Boston. Retrieved from http://www.religion-research.org/RRAPaper1999.htm

Carega, A. (2002) The Church-Internet (dis)connection. *Next Wave Magazine*. Retrieved from http://www.next-wave.org/jun02/disconnection.htm

Gorn, E. (2004). *The ultimate diaspora: Religion in the perpetual present of cyberspace*. Retrieved from http://www.gracecathedral.org/enrichment/excerpts/exc_20010404.shtml

Hughes, I. (2000). *Virtual communities*. Retrieved from http://www2.fhs.usyd.edu.au/bach/pub/community/virtcom.htm

Miller, G. (2002). *Thoughts about Internet church*. Retrieved from http://www.soon.org.uk/thought/internet_church.htm

Paveley, R. (2004). Cyberspirituality: Running an Internet church. *The Door*. Retrieved from http://www.oxford.anglican.org/door/content.php?id=1096

Society of Archbishop Justus. (1999). Retrieved from http://justus.anglican.org/resources/tracts/nc/

Thomas, R. (2004). Why Internet church? *Thinking Anglicans*. Retrieved from http://www.thinkinganglicans.org.uk/archives/000499.html

Wilson, W. P. (2000). *The Internet church*. Word Publishing.

Chapter 8

Christian Community: Real and Virtual

"I link, therefore I am."

William Mitchell

"You can pray for someone even if you don't think God exists."

Anonymous

8.1 Introduction

This chapter focuses on Christian community. We start with a consideration of real Christian community, finding that it is unique because of the relationship that is expected to exist between members: this relationship is one of "love," in a "fellowship" dictated by the common status of "believer in Christ." Secular communities are broader in type, and do not necessarily have this bond underpinning. There is evidence that both secular and religious communities have largely broken down in Western cultures. Many have found that the computer and virtual communities that are emerging are actually assisting people to find community once again. Some of the helpful factors in kindling virtual communities are the "levelling" and organisational structure that virtual communities make possible. Increasingly, it appears that virtual communities are providing an alternative to conventional religious communities. Debbie Gaunt provides a useful comparison between six models of Christian community and virtual community. And while the possibilities of virtual Christian communities are exciting, they are limited in (1) the lack of physical presence within which to express the most primitive aspects of community and (2) lack of guarantee that the type of relationship is that "love" that flows from the mutual status in Christ.

One of the strengths of virtual communities is the "communication" and "interactive life" that underpins them. Pros and cons of virtual interaction have been identified in virtual communities of various domains, from business to social, to teaching and learning. General principles of successful interaction have been sought, as well as characteristics of virtual communities and the interactions supported. Parallels with face-to-face interactions extend even to malicious individuals who engage in "identity deception" to undermine a relationship and/or community. In this wealth of literature about virtual interaction, we find the interactions of Christian communities to have a special place. Isolating "congregational communities" from online theological debates, we find that one unique characteristic of the virtual Christian community is the aim of the interactions in that community. The interactions in "congregational communities" are for the sake of personal connectedness, and building community itself. To this extent, the most useful aspect of the virtual world is the extent to which it facilitates this "depth" of exchange, fosters trust, and provides an environment where personal "openness" is possible.

Presence is an issue to consider in virtual communities. The distinction between physical and virtual presence are useful to consider in the light of religious mandates to "meet together." It is possible to physically meet and yet fail to "meet" in other ways, raising questions of whether a virtual community is even better than a physical gathering. Nevertheless, technology has a long way to go before adequately mediating physical presence. As more sophisticated virtual interaction becomes possible, it will be possible to tailor virtual interactions, so achieving the best of real world and virtual communities.

The objective of this chapter is to consider the nexus of real and virtual Christian communities. We want to point out some unique characteristics of Christian communities in both the real and virtual worlds. In the real world we find that, ideally, Christian communities are underpinned by a type of relationship which is unique. We want to consider the important place of "interaction" in virtual communities, especially the aims of interaction in religious communities that are again, quite unique in "virtual congregations." We also want to point out the issue of presence in virtual communities. Physical presence is often emphasised in real-world Christian communities. As technology progresses, it may be possible to tailor a virtual community to achieve the optimal level of social and physical presence.

8.2 Real and Virtual Christian Communities

Stephen B. Clark (1976) identifies Christian community as a type of relationship rather than a type of organisational structure. Sometimes Christians use the term Christian community vaguely to refer to any group in which everyone is a Christian. In reality, Christian community is Christians who have a brotherly commitment to one another, who share their lives, and who live interdependently as members of a body. People working for church renewal, who want to know what Christian community is and how to build it, should begin by studying the depth of the relationship among Christians that the scriptures envision. He examines three terms in the New Testament that communicate the scriptural vision of this relationship: brother, fellowship, and "body of Christ."

- **Brother:** The scriptures consistently use "brother" to describe situations where there is a definite relationship between people who are joined to one another in Christ. In the early church, oneness with brothers and sisters in the Lord was more important than relationships with fellow citizens, even with members of the same family. Clark notes the unauthenticity of community today, finding that "Most Christians today make limited commitments to other Christians. They can be counted on for a number of carefully specified activities. The remaining parts of their lives are private. Our commitments as Christians are usually no different from our other commitments such as our jobs."

- **Fellowship:** The word "koinonia" describes the fellowship of early Christian community who "shared" together. The first thing they shared was the Holy Spirit. They also shared possessions and assets. Everything was at the disposal of the community for the common good. Clark also notes the unauthenticity of community today finding that "sometimes Christians are more likely to make great financial sacrifice to help each other than they are to talk about their prayer life, their experience of God, or their love for the Lord. Our spiritual lives are the most important things we have in common." He also notes "Many Christian groups have found themselves in serious difficulties because they have started by developing community in material terms."
- **Body of Christ:** The phrase the "body of Christ" is found in the letters of Paul. The term is used to refer to the universal church and a local Christian assembly. Clark says: "Being the body of Christ means much more than running orderly worship services or establishing proper procedures to make decisions and resolve disputes. It is a daily, living relationship that embraces our whole lives. We are members of the same body all the time. The relationship goes beyond the things we do in common." The key to this aspect of community is to be interdependent. Western people can have trouble with interdependence because in our culture, growing to maturity means cutting ties that bind us to others and becoming independent: yet God's plan for our maturity is not individualistic.

Undoubtedly, in early Christianity, the Christian life was, in essence, community oriented. Among other things, covenant theology informs us that God's purpose in redemption was understood to be the formation of a people, a corporate entity. Christian community was believers living together in the same locality with common goals, principles, and identity: a group of people who, corporately, are committed to becoming like Christ (Eph. 4:11-16). For the Christian, the church is the structure for experiencing community, and calls the believer to a committed participation in its worship, instruction, mission, and into submission to its government. As we have already seen, this "community" in the church was "confused" in the political arrangement of Christendom. The Latin term "Corpus Christianum" is often translated as the "Christian body," and describes the community of all Christians united under the Catholic Church in Christendom. While such a community was to be guided by Christian values in its politics, economics, and social life, it had no "guarantee" of the kind of "intimacy" that the scriptures speak of for community. The loss of community in the church has affected our definition of the church, seeing people turn to other institutions for community.

The basis for Christian community is often taken to be the Trinity. The Trinity consists of three persons-Father, Son, and Holy Spirit-in loving and caring relationship. Each of them dwells within each other. Even before man was created, and before the heavens and earth were created, there was community in the Trinity. Community is also based upon a correct view of ourselves. We are God's image-bearers, who should reflect His character in all areas of life. Community is also based upon a correct view of ourselves. We are God's image-bearers who should reflect His character in all areas of life. The term "perichoresis" is sometimes used to refer to this "unity" within the Trinity. It comes from the words "peri" meaning "around" and "chorea" meaning "dance." Perichorea is "to dance around" and "perichoresis" is the divine dance of the persons of the Trinity. Perichoresis is us, crossing our boundaries and living our lives in their lives, and they living their lives in ours. This is just as Christ crossed the divine-human boundary to live his life in us.

In terms of building community, commitment is essential to community. It will include: (1) individual commitment to Christ (Rom. 10:9-10), (2) individual commitment to a body of believers (Acts 2:42-47), (3) corporate commitment to Christ's lordship (Rom. 15:5-6; I Cor. 1:10; Phil. 2:2; Col. 2:19) and (4) corporate commitment to the individual (I Cor. 12:24-26; I Thess. 2:7-12). This kind of commitment cannot be based on convenience. Natural and spiritual gifts should be dedicated for use in building the community. Community is often not adequately expressed in large groups. Out of this context, ongoing relationships can be developed. Community is not synonymous with communes, although hospitality and associations with the weak and poor will be required. Community will call for one's time, money, and energy. All possessions belong to Christ and are used for His glory. The idea of Christian community may differ to the understanding of community in wider society, although there is much overlap.

In the secular world, community can take on many definitions including (1) a group of people living in a particular local area (2) a group of people having ethnic or cultural or religious characteristics in common, (3) common ownership, (4) a group of nations having common interests, (5) the body of people in a profession, (6) agreement as to goals, (7) residential district, (8) in ecology a group of interdependent organisms inhabiting the same region and interacting with each other. In most definitions, a community can be thought as a place of belonging, although there is not necessarily the commitment, "fellowship," shared belief, and mutual "status in Christ" that communities of Christians ideally share. While Christian communities ideally have a stronger bond between its members, there is evidence of breakdown in religious communities, just as there has been in wider society.

Many have found that since the 18th century, there has been increasing community breakdown in the secular world due to the increase in division of labour, individualism, competition, and so on. Born (2003) cites poverty as one of the commonly presumed causes of community breakdown, one which has certainly led to a "gulf" between the first and third world, although also recognizing a deeper aspect that "community breakdown is related to public attitudes and society's weakening belief in the power of community and communal responses." Beaudoin (1999) also identifies the current generation as being highly suspicious of authority and hierarchy and institution. It is as if society has come to distrust community. Many people mourn the loss of a secular community: the form that they had known in earlier times. Fernback and Thompson (1995) identify that the primary factor inhibiting the formation of communities, no matter what their scale or nature, is that they are difficult to organize. Usually, some institutional framework is necessary within which to establish the community. The development and maintenance of such institutions often sap the energy of the members of the would-be community, and confuse the ideals inherent in the notion of community with the project of the institution itself. Among other things, there is commonly a tension between "doing" and "being," and between individualism and communalism.

Metcalf (1995) finds in a post-industrial world "increasing numbers of people choose to drop out, into small, personalised communities more in harmony with ecological values." Metcalf calls these communities "intentional communities." Size ranges from four or five adults to about 160 permanent residents. Many communities are rural, and others are in the cities or suburbs. A few have explicit political ideologies, some are avowedly nonpolitical, and many are indifferent to national politics. Some have shared wealth, and most are based on private ownership, but Metcalf found some important similarities. All the Australian communities described in Metalf (1995) describe spirituality as important to the lives of the communities and their members. All place importance on the ecology, and most combine these two principles into a central concern that may be called "ecospirituality." They all report that the dynamics of interpersonal relationships are still one of their biggest challenges, along with the recruitment of new members and continuation of the community beyond the original founders. The "intentional" community is a reaction against the "institutionalised" community. In this rejection of institutionalised authority and corresponding difficulty in community organisation, the virtual community sits.

A virtual community is a community of people sharing common interests, ideas, and feelings, over the Internet or other collaborative networks. A possible inventor of this term, and one of its first proponents, was Howard Rheingold, who created one of the first major Internet communities, called "The Well." In his book, *The Virtual Community*, Rheingold (1998) defines virtual communities as social aggregations that emerge from the Internet when enough people carry on public discussions long enough, and with sufficient human feeling, to form webs of personal relationships in cyberspace. Before the Web, virtual communities existed on bulletin boards, and many still do. In general, there are two kinds of communication among virtual community members: message postings and real-time chat.

Some contend that the virtual community has blossomed in part due to a general public lament over the disappearance of informal public spaces in our real existence, combined with a rising distrust of powerful institutions that accompany those communities. Virtual communities are different. People are building virtual communities in reaction to the disintegration of traditional local communities. Hughes (2000) suggests "the world's industrial and technological societies are organised as states with hierarchical bureaucracies. Yet the Internet is not organised or controlled by state bureaucracies or industrial corporations. Perhaps it is a new form of social organisation, with opportunities for structures that are not bound by the hierarchical relationships of the state." Far from destroy community, the e-world is actually enhancing it.

While there is certainly the potential to use the virtual community to perpetuate the "institution" of the real world, the "levelling" influences remains true; the electronic presence of an institution with a million members is as visible as the homepage of a teenager in their backroom. People are put on an equal footing in a way unprecedented in the real world. Additionally, there may be a levelling among "personality" types, since there is evidence, as discussed in an earlier chapter, that the "introverted" may even be more inclined to participate in the virtual world than the "extroverted," so reversing the patterns of the real world, and bringing into balance the contribution that both personality types may make in a combination of forums. There is also the observation that, for period of time, those who are less technically minded (perhaps stereotypically the older generations most likely to perpetuate Christendom) may be disadvantaged in the virtual community simply because they are more unfamiliar with the technology, until it becomes so common place and "user-friendly" that people the world over are on an equal footing. The "flatness" of the virtual world, and its "levelling" influence on humanity, is at once liberating and alarming, as the new possibilities and rules emerge.

Yet despite all the "social levelling" influences a virtual community may have, there is still the reality that it leaves basic economic levelling unchanged. Cruikshank (2000) reminds us that international research firm Ipsos-Reid found "billions of people have neither heard of the Internet nor have any intention of going online anytime soon." He points out the obvious "in lesser developed countries, where access to the Internet is a significant problem because of poverty and lack of a modern communications infrastructure, cost and access are cited as barriers more often than they are in major industrialized countries." Those with access to the virtual community are, themselves, in a particular, and still privileged, position, in that computer equipment and Internet access and education to use it are assumed prerequisites. While more and more Web pages are designed for multilingual viewers, and automatic translation is available, there is also the linguistic reality that the Web originated with "English" material, and it still dominates it. The means of interacting with a virtual community itself requires certain underpinning values, and many (not necessarily gender or age related) are still averse to participating in such a world.

Increasingly, it appears that virtual communities are providing an alternative to conventional religious communities, and there is evidence that the virtual community is more successful than the institutional church in achieving Christian community. Charles Henderson (1997) describes the emerging faith communities of cyberspace. He refutes the idea that computers isolate. Rather, computer networks can strengthen and enhance community. This is all the more important as real-world communities are breaking down, Christian communities included. Virtual communities provide an interesting option of "organisation" where the community elements do not have to be lost. For a long time, both within the church and in its relation to the state, the Christendom mindset has perpetuated hierarchical arrangements that often make the "community" elements of the church in opposition to its governmental and "institutional" elements. Many consider the church to be both a community and an institution (Runia, 1984), and therein lies the "tension." In many ways, it is not surprising the virtual religious communities are forming as a response to the breakdown in established religion, the abuses of power that have been demonstrated there and other deficiencies of "hierarchical" structures imposed upon what should be the most "intimate" web of relationships.

The virtual communities of the WWW provide an interesting example of "community" that is separate from "institution." Marc A. Smith and Peter Kollock (1998), in *Communities in Cyberspace*, examine four main issues in virtual communities, being (1) the question of online identity in an environment where individuals cannot be seen; (2) the question of social order and control in what is, at least on the surface, a largely anarchic environment; (3) the structure and dynamics of online communities; and (4) the virtual community as a foundation for collective action. The Christian community sees a unique relationship between the real and virtual in terms of social order and control and dynamics where, potentially, the models of Christendom are broken.

Certainly, the virtual world may be used to simply repeat the "power" roles of conventional communities. Some have noted that in virtual religious communities, the authoritarian leadership of a single member controlling the group tends to be maintained in the electronic environment, just as there is a dominant, controlling leader in many face-to-face religious gatherings (Schroeder,

Heather, & Lee, 1998). This is not surprising since for centuries, Christendom has encouraged and perpetuated "passive" religion for the worshippers who are lead by the "dominant" leader. and it will take time to remove this false component of religion from worship. The power setup creates a situation where so often, the authority the leader has been given is abused and misused to the detriment of those they are meant to be "serving." This mindset is unlikely to change overnight, until the structures of Christendom are eroded from the generations: yet the possibility now exists.

Debbie Gaunt (1998) has looked at some Christian paradigms of community, and used them to evaluate the way people group themselves online. Fascinating parallels are drawn between Christian communities and virtual communities. The real challenge is to find a way of doing religion that makes sense in the computer-mediated environment. She observes "People, for one reason or another, associate closely with one another to the point where their collective identity is recognised by themselves and by others." The elements, which are "recognised" as parameters of community, depend on other models of community from the culture and experience of those involved. Gaunt has found six models of Christian community, and has drawn parallels with virtual communities.

- **Model 1:** "I will take you as my people (Exodus 6:7)." This model relates to God's covenant with his people. Gaunt finds two levels on which CMC involves notions of contract that may serve as a parallel for the Christian concept of covenant. Firstly, access to the Internet and bulletin board systems usually involves a contract. Secondly, there is a strong sense within Internet communities of an unwritten, informal contract between each individual and the community.
- **Model 2:** "You are the body of Christ (1 Cor 12:27)." The New Testament describes a community that is socially, racially, and geographically diverse, yet is bound together so closely that Paul uses the body as a metaphor. Gaunt says "The early church had to overcome geographical, social and racial divisions to forge a unity of belief and purpose." This is equally true of computer-mediated communication where social aggregations emerge "when enough people carry on ...

public discussions long enough, with sufficient human feeling, to form webs of personal relationships in cyberspace."

- **Model 3:** "All who believed were together (Acts 2:44)." The book of Acts is the earliest document we have that gives a retrospective portrait of the emerging Christian community. One of the sociological peculiarities of the population of cyberspace is the fact that all users are relative newcomers, so how we relate to one another is changing as we go along. There is a sense of all being in the same boat.
- **Model 4:** "Abide in me as I abide in you (John 15:4).". The Johanine epistles depict a community or communities bound together by faith expressed in a love ethic that affects a communion between believers and Christ in the Spirit. Gaunt says, "Most members of most virtual communities never meet one another face to face. This means that they meet and develop a relationship entirely mediated by electronic text. The effect of this is that each party to such a relationship is a cognitive construct in the imagination of the other person." CMC users live out Christ's injunction to "live in me as I live in you" by necessity. This is not a mystical experience, it is simply the only way a relationship can be sustained in an environment wholly mediated by text-based computing
- **Model 5:** "That Trinity which is God (Augustine, De Trinitate IX.1.i)." The most potent image of community in Christian thought is the concept of Trinity: "a trinity of persons mutually interrelated, and a unity of equal essence" (Augustine). This mutual indwelling (perichoresis) is a potent model for Christian community. Perfect unity in diversity of autonomous individuals, in which the whole is found in each fraction, is both the reality of trinity and the hope of the church. There is nothing consciously Trinitarian about computer-mediated community. What does exist is a clear sense of mutuality and equality.
- **Model 6:** "Being as communion." The fullest Christian understanding of community is communion. Communion is also the unity between people, as vested in the church. The sacrament of Eucharistic communion is a symbol of this unity. Gaunt explains the term is frequently used in CMC "Rheingold uses the term, citing Marc Smith, to describe one of the 'collective goods' which bind isolated individuals into a community."

In a closing consideration of real and virtual Christian communities, these models may provide some inspiration that the Christian entities are indeed genuine models of Christian community. However, the models do not guarantee the "type" of relationship that exists within the communities, that is, the models do not guarantee that the relationships are underpinned by "love." And even if the relationships are "committed" and "caring," the expression is "limited" to the nonphysical. The smallest Christian community, the marriage, would be hard to sustain in a virtual world! And, while the Internet may present interesting possibilities for the "organisation" of communities — possibilities that move away from that which is "unhelpful" in existing power structures–they do not guarantee even a believer's "status in Christ" for those in the community. These limitations — in physical presence and the type of relationship — are perhaps the biggest limitations of virtual life.

8.3 Interactive Life

There are many different reasons why people engage in virtual communities, and some may be more appropriate than others for virtual interaction. Some studies have compared "virtual teamwork" vs. "face-to-face" teamwork, and found that the face-to-face relationships were better for the team task (e.g.Warkentin & Sayeed, 1997). Others have found that perceptions of virtual communication are enhanced when the existing environment did not include adequate communication opportunities (e.g. Ziegler & Mindrum, 2002) finding "virtual experience that was, according to participants, better than many 'real' conference experiences, where people often sit passively in a dark room and listen to a single speaker with little, if any, opportunity for interaction." It appears that "engagement, feedback, humor and sharing of insights were amplified through the use of a virtual chat room and instant messaging service, which ran parallel to the video feed. Participants could communicate with one another and with meeting organizers, who monitored the chat and interrupted the meeting from time to time to give the speakers and participants a richer sense of how the meeting topics were being received." Others have examined pedagogy in virtual and face-to-face environments, and found similar pros and cons for learning in virtual vs. real worlds.

In general terms, some find it a paradox that virtual interaction could be better than face-to-face interaction. Face-to-face interaction has many additional "communication" cues, including nonverbal communication and the physical presence of another, that have traditionally aided human communication. There is certain "accountability" in face-to-face exchanges since identities are more "exposed" than in virtual exchanges. Face-to-face encounters for what ever purpose, social, business, learning or other, have been the norm for many years in society. However, virtual communication is a rising phenomena. Whether conducting business, learning, solving a problem, or other, virtual communities offer "interactive life," and pros and cons have been identified in the respective domains. Religion is one domain where interaction remains to be examined.

First, we consider some general comments about virtual interaction. In terms of successful interaction in online communities, Peter Kollock (1998) notes that the principles underlying successful online communities reduce to the principles underlying interactions, the most basic of these being two people faced with the decision of whether to cooperate or behave selfishly. If this is the only time someone will be interacting with another person, or if this is the last time, there will be a great temptation to behave selfishly. Thus, successful communities promote ongoing interaction. Godwin (1994) makes a similar point in his essay on principles for making virtual communities work, when he stresses the importance of promoting continuity in online groups. Kollock continues to report the second condition for successful online communities is "that individuals must be able to identify each other. The third condition is that individuals must have information about how the other person has behaved in the past. If identity is unknown or unstable and if there is no recollection or record of past interactions, individuals will be motivated to behave selfishly because they will not be accountable for their actions." To some extent, these are "implicit" rules of interaction in virtual worlds.

More explicit rules of interaction are sometimes given. There is an interesting instance of "interactivity rules" within online religious communities in the UK Pagan site. The site particularly aims to promote discussions, and goes to lengths to assure potential members that they will be "accepted" in the community. They claim the Web site is "a place where we can speak freely and express ideas without censure or without being laughed at." They explain that they are not interested in "converting" people, or saying other religions are bad or evil, or have launched a crusade on the church, but are interested in "honesty," saying "we at least listen to the other side of the argument and try to articulate why we disagree. And if, when all is said and done, we still disagree, well ... we let it lie." Paradoxically, they want to promote a form of paganism that is "about what you want to do — there are no rules," although without recognizing the contradiction in their implicit "rule" that there is no right way, either about practicing paganism or "interacting" to discuss it. And they do suggest a set of communication "rules" with guidelines (http://home.freeuk.net/magickcauldron/urp/guidelines.html), intended to be "inclusive" of all, and promote discussion that takes place within these boundaries where "no one is wrong." That itself is a rule! Social interaction within virtual communities is more than a set of "interaction" principles, but contains the whole spectrum of rituals and history and identity.

The general features that lead to successful communities have been examined by Kollock (1998), investigating graphical virtual worlds that have added a 2-D or 3-D visual representation of a space to go along with interactivity mediated through more traditional text communication. Kollock rightly notes "There is no algorithm for community ... what makes for a successful online community is often poorly understood." He notes: "the tendency of those involved in building graphical virtual worlds is to create visually compelling worlds that look good, but do a poor job of fostering social interaction." He notes "Worldsaway" as a successful online community. "The community succeeds not because of flashy graphics, but because it contains many of the requisite elements for a successful community: identity persistence, a sophisticated set of rituals, an internal economy with a monetary system, property rights, a rich set of documents recording the history of the community, a coherent sense of space, casual interaction caused by the fact that one must 'walk' most places, and a moderate level of risk."

Second, we consider the problem of "identity deception," or perhaps more accurately "malicious identities." The web has introduced various types of computer crime, those who intentionally spread viruses, and also those who "troll" and otherwise seek to breakdown community. As we have already noted, these malicious types will be found in virtual worlds just as they are in the real world. And these malicious types will simply repeat their destructive behaviour in the virtual world. There have been many instances of virtual deception having real world implications. For example, the "encounters" made through virtual chat rooms having real-world implications, sometimes for the worse of people who meet face to face. Whether for personal gain, a hidden agenda, or simply pure mischief, those malicious individuals can destroy lives and communities just as they can in the real world. In virtual worlds, "malicious identities" are likely to engage in some form of "deception," as they do in the real world, whether overtly pretending interest in a community in order to become a part of it and undermine it, or covertly leading astray those easily influenced (e.g. children) through more subtle tactics.

Turning now to virtual interaction in religious communities, we consider some specific elements that are relevant to virtual Christian communities. We start by considering the types and purposes of interaction in virtual Christian communities, especially those that would approximate "congregational community." At this point, we make a distinction between such communities and say, an online theological forum, where academic discussions were conducted as they would be in any other domain from philosophy to current affairs. The "congregational community" is engaged in more than academic debate. Some find that the idea of human beings connecting powerfully to one another out in the ether is inherently spiritual; "interactions" in a virtual world may have, and convey, this metaphysical quality!

In such "congregational communities," one of the primary reasons for interaction is for the building of "community itself." It is not for playing a game, or solving a business task, or learning, or teaching, or even socialising. The building of community may take place through these tasks, although it is the "personal relatedness" that underlies the interaction in a Christian community. It is a forum where deep human concerns are to be revealed: "sins" and "failings," weaknesses and struggles. As we have already identified, the type of relationship ideally underpinning Christian communities is one where, among other things, there is a high degree of "trust." We have also noted how this is sometimes paradoxically difficult to achieve in face-to-face encounters. Thus, face-to-face encounters are often inhibited by the fear of rejection. However, the virtual environment offers certain "safeness" in exchanges. A person who is in any way "threatened" by the level of identity disclosure in a virtual communication can walk away, in a way that is not possible in face-to-face encounters. There is the real possibility that they will not walk away, but go on to levels of intimacy that would just never be achieved face to face. Even in ongoing virtual relationships, there is the "removedness" from the real world identity that creates a similar "security" underpinning the exchanges. This is, perhaps, the essence of what the virtual world offers interactive Christian life: the extent to which it facilitates this "depth" of exchange, fosters trust, and provides an environment where personal "openness" is possible and encouraged.

While the virtual community may facilitate an individual coming to "trust," there is the result that some still consider face-to-face encounters as irreplaceable for both building trust and repairing shattered trust (e.g., O'Hara-Devereaux & Johansen, 1994). Cummings and Bromiley (1996) maintain that a person trusts a group when that person believes that the group (a) "makes a good-faith effort to behave in accordance with any commitments both explicit or implicit, (b) is honest in whatever negotiations preceded such commitments, and (c) does not take excessive advantage of another even when the opportunity is available." Several factors, such as shared social norms, repeated interactions, and shared experiences, have been suggested to facilitate the development of trust (e.g., Mayer, Davis, & Schoorman, 1995). Another factor asserted to promote trust and cooperation is the anticipation of future association (Powell, 1990). Such anticipation of future association is higher among group members who are colocated than among physically dispersed members. The possibility of physical meeting reinforces social similarity, shared values, and expectations, and increases the immediacy of threats from failing to meet commitments (Latane, Liu, Nowak, Bonevento, & Zheng, 1995). Thus, we return to the question of real-world communities and the interrelation of the virtual and real world.

Schroeder et al. (1998) report on the social interaction among participants in a church service in an online, multiuser, virtual-reality environment, interacting in a text-based context. It examines some of the main features of prayer meetings in a religiously oriented virtual world, and also what sets this world apart from other virtual worlds. Next, it examines some of the issues of research ethics and methods that are raised in the study of online behaviour in virtual worlds, and then analyses the text exchanges between participants in a virtual church service, and some of the ways in which these compare with the content of a conventional church service. They find that virtual church does not look especially remarkable in comparison with the other virtual worlds. Particular differences are that social interaction is more tightly or formally structured. Encounters are less haphazard, conversations are more focused and sustained, and the roles and structures within the group are more defined.

Some of the characteristics they note include the service takes place at a fixed weekly time and in a fixed locale, other e-worlds seem to be less rigid. This "structuredness" also pertains to the organization of the prayer meeting itself, referring to movement and behaviors of the avatars. The leader is clearly "primus inter pares" during the service. He/she clearly has the right to lead the conversation and to speak in a generally uninterrupted manner. But apart from this group identity, there is also a clearer sense of hierarchy in the virtual church than in other multiuser virtual worlds. There is also a clearer sense of "insider" and "outsider." While the relationships between participants in virtual church are stronger than in other virtual worlds, they are, of course, in another sense, quite weak and unidimensional: what believers know about each other is typically limited to, for example, the difficulties they are seeking relief from (which form a large part of the service), their religious ideas, and the like. To these shared religious feelings, we can add other forms of sociality that are common throughout multiuser virtual worlds: the "smalltalk," for example, surrounding the way people typically introduce each other to establish a rapport ("Where are you from?," "What's the weather like over there?," etc.). But these forms of social interaction do not add up to the multifaceted face-to-face relations of a real church community.

Schroeder et al. (1998) further find that the language and general ethos of religious meetings in the virtual church bear all the hallmarks of informal, interactive, charismatic-style worship. This type of worship had its roots 35-40 years ago. Since then, the movement has spread worldwide, and has heavily colonised many of the mainstream churches. The movement has created strong bonds between otherwise disparate groups in both the Catholic and Protestant communities, though its influence has been most pervasive among the latter. In virtual church meetings, members are typically from different traditions, though not from ones which are very disparate doctrinally. The general charismatic style is quite evident: informal, open, and interactive. Some practices, however, are transformed by the technology, and may detract from the sense of a religious gathering: verbal exchanges become shorter, emotional solidarity with coparticipants is weaker, and there is less orderliness to the prayer meetings. But the technology also brings certain gains: the virtual church allows for more candid exchanges between participants, it enables a kind of access from all over the world that is not available in conventional services, and it permits experimentation in the use (and prior to that, the design) of the virtual space that is less constrained than a church in the real world.

8.4 The Question of Presence

A diverse group of people, not just religious communities, are interested in presence: how to create it, how to use it effectively, and how it mediates a variety of responses face to face and remotely. As we shall see, there are many understandings of "presence" and definitions and opinions. For example, the physical presence of being in the same room may be experienced at the same time as a total isolation of social presence among others in that room. Presence is particularly important in some religious communities where "physical gathering" is emphasised, or required, or desired, in order to be that community. For example, faithful Christians are invited to gather and not cease to meet together. The synagogue, as a Jewish place of worship, literally means a "meeting place" where people would come together. However, this requirement of a physical presence within the religious community may, in fact, prohibit those communities from any virtual existence, even though social presence and other forms of presence may more effectively be mediated.

The Roman Catholic Church has faced particular questions of "presence" relating to its worship and liturgy in light of "virtual" and "remote" communication possibilities. In particular, the question has arisen as to whether "sacraments" can be administered over the Internet. Normally, sacraments are physically shared experiences that involve some tangible aspect of the material world that is a pointer to a reality in the spiritual world, such as "water" in a ceremony called baptism pointing to "cleansing of sin" or "bread" in a communion celebration representing "the body of Christ sacrificed," Especially with communion, the celebration depends "on the physical presence of the gathered faithful," and the Catholic church has a very particular theology of the "presence" of the divine among the gathered faithful, raising some interesting questions when the faithful are gathered virtually!

The ruling of the U.S. bishops' Secretariat for the Liturgy was that no sacrament could be received by electronic communication. The same ruling was found for the ritual involving "adoration of the cross," which also was not permitted to be done via a Webcam without physically being in the church building (http:// www.monksofadoration.org / webadore.html). This has implications for all "remote" links — "live" telecast, Internet transmissions, Web cams and video links — since technology cannot replace the physical presence among gathered people. Perhaps the rationale for banning sacramental "remote worship" is that if God takes the trouble to manifest among the people, then the people can at least take the trouble to manifest among each other.

Conceptualisations of presence can be divided into two basic categories: (1) physical presence — referring to the perception of being physically located in a medium and (2) social presence — referring to the feeling of being together and communicating with someone in a medium. Most research on presence has focused on technologies that use a variety of sensory inputs to simulate a real environment and foster both "social" and "physical" presence, with less attention paid to presence in the context of text-based virtual worlds, where the issue and questions of "social" presence are just as real. One can experience a high degree of physical presence without the transmission of any kind of reciprocal communicative signals. At the same time, one can also experience a high degree of social presence in virtual environments that only supply minimal physical representation, like Internet chat rooms. Copresence refers to a mix of both physical and social components, thereby supporting both social and physical presence. Since a "virtual (text-based) community" mediates "social' presence" rather than a "physical" or "embodied" presence, if ever a physical presence was required, there are certainly implications. For example, in Christian contexts, physical presence does play an important role for many people in the "gathering together" of believers.

Apart from the distinction between physical and social presence in virtual communities, there is a more general concept of "presence" applicable to all manner of electronic media, including television and radio. This type of presence is sometimes called "telepresence," "virtual presence," "being there," and even "a perceptual illusion of nonmediation." Marvin Minsky (1980) coined the term telepresence, initially in reference to teleoperation technology for remote manipulation of physical objects. Telepresence refers to the "phenomenon that a human operator develops a sense of being physically present at a remote location through interaction with the system's human interface, i.e. through the user's actions and the subsequent perceptual feedback he/she receives via the appropriate teleoperation technology." (Ijsselsteijn et al., 2000). Telepresence is the extent to which one feels present in the mediated environment rather than in the immediate physical environment, whereas presence is defined "as the sense of being in an environment." (Steuer, 1992). So, in other words, telepresence is the experience of presence in an environment by means of a communication medium.

Lombard and Ditton (1997) recognize six interrelated, but distinct, conceptualizations of presence: (1) Presence as social richness — presence is the extent to which a medium is perceived as sociable, warm, sensitive, personal, or intimate when it is used to interact with other people. (2) Presence as realism — the degree to which a medium can produce seemingly accurate representations of objects, events, and people: representations that look, sound, and/or feel like the "real" thing, (3) Presence as transportation — Three distinct types of transportation can be identified: "You are there," in which the user is transported to another place; "It is here," in which another place, and the objects within it, are transported to the user; and "We are together," in which two (or more) communicators are transported together to a place that they share. (4) Presence as immersion — the idea of perceptual and psychological immersion in a virtual reality experience. (5) Presence as social actor within medium — people respond to interpersonal distance cues in, and even talk to the pictures of people on the television screen. The mediated nature of the "interaction" is ignored, and the media personality is incorrectly perceived as a social actor. (6) Presence as medium as social actor — social responses of media users not to entities (people or computer characters) within a medium, but to cues provided by the medium itself.

In addition to the specific definitions, presence has also been described as a "mental manifestation" (Sheridan, 1992), as a general "existential phenomenon" and a "cognitive state" that results from attending to, and evaluating, incoming sensory information (Barfield, Zeltzer, Sheridan, & Slater, 1995). Another similar concept that is a quantifiable aspect of display technology of a virtual medium is "immersion." Immersion is not user-centric, and is determined by the extent to which displays are (a) inclusive, or the degree to which stimuli from the real world are excluded from the user, (b) extensive, or the number of sensory modalities accommodated by the system, (c) surrounding, or how panoramic the displays are, and finally (d) vivid, or the resolution of the displays (Slater & Wilbur, 1995). Slater's model predicts that the higher the level of immersion, the higher the level of presence. Two other types of presence are subjective presence and objective presence. Subjective presence is the likelihood that a person judges himself to be physically present in a remote or mediated environment, and objective presence refers to the likelihood of successfully completing a given task (Schoerb, 1995).

Most research on presence has focused on technologies that use a variety of sensory inputs (e.g., visual, auditory, haptic) to create a simulacrum of a real environment, a virtual reality that mimics perceptions in the physical world. Less attention has been paid to presence in the context of text-based virtual worlds. Jacobson (2002) presents a brief overview of theories that identify factors that promote or undermine a sense of presence in text-based virtual worlds. He finds that preconceived ideas influenced the sense of presence "in the case of virtual partners who formed impressions of one another before seeing photographs, idealized images did not match reality, and the difference was disappointing." Lombard and Ditton (1997) outline existing research about the factors that encourage or discourage a sense of presence in media users, as well as the physiological and psychological effects of presence.

There is a real possibility that one day, it will be possible to tailor interactions in the virtual world, and combine the best of the virtual world and real world interactions. This would mean that interactions in the virtual world would have to grow in sophistication of communicating "presence." Then, at one end of the spectrum, virtual world interaction would have the possibility of virtually replicating face-to-face interaction-perhaps through some "holographic" transmission of a person into a common space with another person — where all elements of face-to-face communication could be reproduced. At the other end of the spectrum, the virtual world would have a text-message posted to a bulletin board read asynchronously by the parties. In between, various levels of "intimacy" could be selected to optimise "exchange," according to the context and preferences of the parties involved. However, before such a "sliding scale of presence" could be offered, technology has many problems to solve.

In summary, "presence" is a concept relevant in electronic environments. It concerns how both physical and social relationships are mediated. Physical presence refers to the perception of being physically located in a medium, and social presence refers to the feeling of being together and communicating with someone in a medium, even if text-based and primitive. The depth of physical presence that can be mediated in a text-based community is restricted, compared to that which can be mediated in a more sophisticated virtual world. It may be that a virtual community may be more successful at mediating social presence. The "meeting together" that is important in Christian communities includes this depth of encounter that the enhanced social presence of virtual worlds brings. However, the absence of physical presences creates a barrier for many religiously minded. Whether sophisticated virtual environments would ever alleviate the "lack of signal" in physical presence remains to be seen. However, there are many possibilities for mediating a virtual encounter.

In the virtual Christian community, we find one instance of the intersection of religion and technology. It is an instance where technology is being used in a certain way, and impinges upon theological questions: what is church, what is a community, what is an acceptable type of "presence" in order for there to be authentic corporate life, and other such questions surrounding a religious use of technology. Another instance of the intersection of theology and technology is when theology, and a theological perspective, is used to impact technology. It is this aspect of the nexus of religion and technology that we next examine.

8.5 References

Barfield, W., Zeltzer, D., Sheridan, T., & Slater, M. (1995). Presence and performance within virtual environments. In W. Barfield & T. A. Furness, III (Eds.), *Virtual environments and advanced interface design* (pp. 473-541). New York: Oxford University Press.

Beaudoin, T. (1998). *Virtual faith: The irreverent spiritual quest of Generation X.* Jossey Bass Wiley.

Born, P. (2003). *Poverty and community breakdown.* Retrieved from http://www.tamarackcommunity.ca/downloads/clife/pborn/community_breakdown.pdf

Clark, S. B. (1976). *Mere Christian community.* Retrieved from http://www.rc.net/sos/clark1.htm

Cruikshank, B. (2000). *Technology: Why aren't more people online?* Retrieved from http://www.galtglobalreview.com/infotech/people_offline.html

Cummings, L. L., & Bromiley, P. (1996). The Organizational Trust Inventory (OTI): Development and validation. In R. M. Kramer & T. R. Tyler (Eds), *Trust in organizations: Frontiers of theory and research* (pp. 302-330). Thousand Oaks, CA: Sage Publications.

Fernback, J., & Thompson, B. (1995). *Virtual communities: Abort, retry, failure*? Retrieved from http://www.well.com/user/hlr/texts/VCcivil.html

Gaunt, D. (1998). *Wherever two or three are gathered together. Christian community in cyberspace.* Retrieved from http://www.gnacademy.org/~napoli/activity/workshop/02/religion.html

Godwin, M. (1994). Nine principles for making virtual communities work. *Wired, 2*(6),72-73.

Henderson, C. (1997). The emerging faith communities of cyberspace. *CMC Magazine: Special Focus Spirituality.* Retrieved from http://www.december.com/cmc/mag/1997/mar/hend.html

Hughes, I. (2000). *Virtual communities.* Retrieved from http://www2.fhs.usyd.edu.au/bach/pub/community/virtcom.htm

Ijsselsteijn, & Ridder, (1998). *Measuring temporal variations in presence.* BT Presence Workshop BT Labs. Retreived from http://www.tue.nl/ipo/people/ijsselsteijn/btpaper.html

Ijsselsteijn et al. (2000).

Jacobson, D. (2002). On theorizing presence. *Journal of Virtual Environments 6*(1), 2002.

Kollock, P. (1998). Design principles for online communities. *PC Update, 15*(5), 58-60.

Latane, B., Liu, J. H., Nowak, A., Bonevento, M., & Zheng, L. (1995). Distance matters: Physical space and social impact. *Personality and Social Psychology Bulletin, 21*(8), 795-805.

Lombard, M., & Ditton, T. (1997) At the heart of it all: The concept of presence. *Journal of Computer-Mediated Communication, 3*(2).

Mayer, R. C., Davis, J. H., & Schoorman, F. D. (1995). An integrative model of organizational trust. *Academy of Management Review, 20*(3), 709-734.

Metcalf, B. (1995). *From utopian dreaming to communal reality.* Sydney, Australia: University of NSW Press.

Minsky, M. (1980). *Telepresence.* Omni. NY: Omni Publications International Ltd.

O'Hara-Devereaux, M., & Johansen, R. (1994). *Global work: Bridging distance, culture, and time.* San Francisco: Jossey-Bass Publishers.

Powell, W. W. (1990). Neither market nor hierarchy: Network forms of organization. *Research in Organizational Behavior, 12,* 295-336.

Rheingold. (1998). *The virtual community.* Retrieved from http://www.rheingold.com/vc/book/intro.html

Runia, K. (1984). Evangelicals and the doctrine of church in European history. *Evangelical Review of Theology,* 8(1), 40-57.

Schloerb, D. W. (1995). A quantitative measure of telepresence. *Presence: Teleoperators and Virtual Environments, 4*(1), 64-80.

Schroeder, R., Heather, N., & Lee, R. (1998), Religion in multiuser virtual reality. *JCMC, 4*(2).

Sheridan, T. B. (1992). Musings on telepresence and virtual presence. *Presence: Teleoperators and Virtual Environments, 1*(1), 120-126.

Slater, M., & Wilbur, S. (1997). A framework for immersive virtual environments (FIVE): Speculations on the role of presence in virtual environments. *Presence: Teleoperators and Virtual Environments, 6*(6), 603-616.

Steuer, J. (1995). Defining virtual reality: Dimensions determining telepresence. In F. Biocca & M. R. Levy (Eds.), *Communication in the age of virtual reality* (pp. 33-56). Hillsdale, NJ: Lawrence Erlbaum Associates.

Warkentin, M. E., & Sayeed, L. (1997). Virtual teams vs. face-to-face teams: An exploratory study of a Web-based conference system. *Decision Sciences.* Retrieved from http://www.findarticles.com/p/articles/mi_qa3713/is_199710/ai_n8758806

Ziegler, R., & Mindrum, C. (2002). *The subtle power of virtual collaboration.* Retrieved from http://www.accenture.com/xd/xd.asp?it=enweb&xd=ideas%5Coutlook%5C7.2002%5Chuman_perf_1.xml

Chapter 9

The Theology of Technology

"Theology ... is searching in a dark cellar at midnight for a black cat that isn't there."

Robert A. Heinlein

"Our scientific power has outrun our spiritual power. We have guided missiles and misguided men."

Martin Luther King, Jr.

9.1 Introduction

In this chapter, we consider another aspect of the nexus of religion and technology. This is the idea that theology can actually inform technology. We start off distinguishing the term "theology of technology" from "cybertheology." Cybertheology still waits an adequate definition, but it is some vague notion that there is "theology" happening with technology simply because we call it such, and have a religious theme. Thus, we may find "theological" significance in the way the Internet "connects" people, as they may be "connected" in a spiritual bond, and call it "cybertheology." However, the "theology of technology" is concerned with "conventional theology" being applied to technology. We examine six different patterns for the way that science and theology have been related, and consider how in AI, technology and theology are related in some special ways.

One of the most obvious ways that conventional theology can be applied to technology is to provide ethical input into the moral use of technology. The moral use of technology, or the morality of scientific method, is still essentially concerned with the moral judgement of people. However, within AI, we are faced with some unique questions of the "morality" of a scientific product itself. AI engages in the task of creating machines that mimic human action; as such, it cannot escape the question of what is moral machine action. "Friendly AI" is concerned with creating intelligent machines that benefit humanity in their action. Thus, "friendly AI" is a concept that cannot really operate without ethical input. Theology is a traditional source of answers for such questions. Morality is one component of human identity. In their morality, theology tells us that human beings were created "perfect," and after sin, this nature was corrupted. Restoration of the image can be achieved through faith in the atoning work of Christ. Thus, the "morality" of human action (and even the possibility of moral behaviour) is a profoundly theological question. The morality of machine artefacts imitating human action is no less so.

The question of human morality is intimately related to the question of human identity. Morality is a unique part of being human. A machine, which is expected to behave in a human like way, must imitate at least this aspect of human identity. For many years, human identity was understood in terms of rational, logical thought. At the start of AI, Turing was interested in the question of "whether a machine could think?" His method involved a game of "identity" in the Turing test. However, thinking is only one aspect of what it is to be human and behave in a human-like way. AI will benefit from broadening its conception of human identity; in particular, the insight that theological input can give about that identity. The biblical concept of the "image of God" (Imago Dei) has been foundational for understanding human identity. People have been understood to bear the image of God, among other things, in their moral, spiritual, intellectual, emotional, social, creative, and relational natures, and in the capacity for faith itself.

The objective of this chapter is to consider the "theology of technology." We particularly aim to examine the nexus of religion and technology from how technology may be impacted by theology, having seen the converse in the way that technology is influencing religious expression through virtual religion. Our objective is to demonstrate that conventional theology has input to give to AI. We want to contrast this nexus with "cybertheology"; we want to demonstrate that AI requires moral input in quite a unique way. It is not just another technology that raises other ethical questions about the use of scientific knowledge. AI is attempting to create machines with human like behaviour; morality cannot be ignored, since that is a component of human behaviour. In fact, morality is just one of the evidences of that identity, which is human. For a long time science, and especially AI, has focused on "thinking" as the distinguishing aspect of humanity. From Descartes conclusion of "I think therefore I am," to Turing's infamous question "Can a machine think?," the Western world has sought to answer this in machine intelligence. It is time to broader the conception of that which AI is modelling.

9.2 Theology and Cybertheology

What is theology? Theology is, literally, rational discourse concerning God (Greek θεος, theos, "God," + λογος, logos, "rational discourse"). Theology is defined in various ways. Here are some definitions:

- "(a) The study of the nature of God and religious truth: rational inquiry into religious questions; (b) A system or school of opinions concerning God and religious questions" (Houghton Mifflin Company).
- "(a) the rational and systematic study of religion and its influences and of the nature of religious truth; (b) a particular system or school of religious beliefs and teachings; (c) the learned profession acquired by specialized courses in religion (usually taught at a college or seminary)" (Wordnet).
- "The science of the knowledge of God. Theology seeks to think God's thoughts after Him, insofar as He allows man through the Scripture to enter into His thinking" (www.dtl.org/trinity/misc/glossary.htm).

Theology generally assumes the truth of at least some religious beliefs and is, therefore, to be distinguished from the philosophy of religion, which does not presume the truth of any religious beliefs. It is to be distinguished from religion since theology is more "objective," while religion is subjective. Often theology is taken to mean Christian theology, especially when it is considered to be "faith seeking understanding," and faith is appropriated in the Christian sense of relationship, encounter with the divine.

Sometimes theology is considered to "start with God" and be "about God" rather than humanity, although humanity in relation to God is a topic of concern. Karl Barth was keen to point out we can only start with God's revelation; to go from some human construction to God is an idolatrous worship of that which our hands and mouths have made. To the extent that humanity invents "theology," it is a human construction that may hinder God's self-revelation. When "theology" becomes a focus on the human and not the divine, we may find it a "hindrance" to God's revelation. There is the danger that "theology" becomes "about man" rather than "about God," and becomes dominated by that, which is not useful.

Recently, the term "cybertheology" has come into usage, although there are no real attempts to define what this is. The term is used widely. Here are some examples of usage:

- "Theology of the Internet and advanced technologies (cybertheology) is a new plot in theology of the means of social communication" (http://www.amen-dir.net/Cybertheology/index.htm).
- "What is necessary instead is to find a way of communicating the gospel which harnesses the strengths of the Internet itself — a cybertheology, if you will." (http://www.ecic.info/archive/icic1/gaunt.html).
- "What is cybertheology doing on a geography web site? First, because it happens to interest this geographer. More importantly..." (http://webhost.bridgew.edu/jhayesboh/teilhard.htm).
- "Cybertheology: Surfing the Noosphere — did a nineteenth century Jesuit Priest, who was also a paleontologist, invent the Internet?" (http://www.actionweb.co.nz/futuresphp/article.php?article_id=151).

The Cybertheology Web site (http://www.cybertheology.net/) provides some of the most useful distinctions in the field. It presents a list of resources "in," "of," and "for" cyberspace. The section "theology in cyberspace" contains journal and periodicals, documents, text, and other resources; church Web sites; and other forums where theology is the content. The "theology of cyberspace" gives a list of sites that contribute to the study of cyberspace, mostly from the perspective of theology. It includes experimental churches and communities, some of which seem rather frivolous. The "theology for cyberspace" contains ways in which people are doing theology or religious praxis in cyberspace: ways that are only or mainly relevant to the medium of computer-mediated communication.

Cybertheology is certainly connected with the Internet and computer-based communication. It usually has a Christian perspective. Eva Borowik-Dabrowska (2004) states that: "The task of the theologians of the mass media is to serve others to understand anthropological and moral consequences of existence of the World Wide Web." In *Cybergrace,* Jennifer Cobb Kreisberg (1998) expands some of her particular ideas about emergent technologies and spiritual evolution that point to the same metaphysical process in which humanity participates. This process dissolves the subject-object nature of human reality, and promotes a Buberian I/Thou relationship with one's self and, by extension, with one's God. However, it is not immediately clear that in the interest in computer-facilitated life, there is necessarily any "theology" at all, in the sense that there is any "study of the nature of God."

However, that which might be called "cybertheology" is trying to make some references to God. For example, Charles Henderson explains how the Internet is coming to be seen as a metaphor for God. He explains how "Paul Tillich, pointed out several decades ago, the effectiveness and power of a religious symbol can be measured in two very different ways. In the first place religious symbols become powerful because there is perceived to be a connection between some finite object in the world and the infinite realm to which that object points. So today the Internet is perceived to be offering humanity a new window looking out upon the Infinite. Yet, said Tillich, there is also a very different and in some ways contradictory standard by which the power of a religious symbol can be measured. An object from the real world can become a potent religious symbol only when its 'meaning is negated by that to which it points.' If then, the Internet is a good metaphor for God, it will not betray us by becoming a new, more powerful, opiate, but will continue to draw us out, beyond ourselves, and beyond whatever it is that Internet is now or ever could become, to that which actually is the Web of God's own creation. In the end, God may in fact be that Web greater than which none other can even be conceived." That is, the Internet may help point people to God.

Another reference in cybertheology to the "nature of God" that elevates the field from a study of humanity, and its very literal constructions, is the association that is made with the ideas of a Jesuit priest named Pierre Teilhard de Chardin. He is often quoted as a "predictor" of the Net half a century before it arrived. He "imagined a stage of evolution characterized by a complex membrane of information enveloping the globe and fueled by human consciousness." God was seen at work in this "evolutionary process." Teilhard believed this vast thinking membrane would ultimately coalesce into "the living unity of a single tissue" con-

Figure 5. The theology of technology

taining our collective thoughts and experiences. Both scientists and the church scorned his writings, with the Catholic Church on the verge of excommunicating Teilhard. Yet his work is now being interpreted as a "theology of the Web," see, for example James Hayes-Bohanan (2005). And the "integration" of science and theology regarded as "god," as a goal and end of evolution. Suggestions such as these force a return to the question of how, and perhaps whether, has God revealed transcendence within the human (and/or machine) realm.

In this chapter, we discuss the "theology of technology," and seek to distinguish it from the various notions of "cybertheology," or that which is specifically about the Internet, or human communication in computer-facilitated environments, or ways of expressing religion and "faith" within those environments, or metaphors that that environment might provide about God. Figure 5 illustrates the "impression" that theology makes upon technology, aiming to help visually distinguish the "theology of technology" from cybertheology, where the "theology and technology" aligns with conventional theology, as represented by the Christ and the cross, and continues to be paramount.

Indeed, "cybertheology" may be an example of "pseudotheology." The American Scientific Affiliation (ASA) defines pseudotheology as "a discipline that looks like authentic Christian theology but fails the basic tests for authentic theology. It applies bad hermeneutics, done irresponsibly, and makes claims to produce results that authentic theology cannot (such as identify physical mechanisms for phenomena), or sets out to theologically demonstrate the validity of some previously chosen philosophical or scientific position" (http:// users.stargate.net/ ~dfeucht/Seven%20Patterns.htm).

The "theology of technology" that we speak about is the idea that "conventional theology" might be applied to further the goals and aims of technology, and assist understanding, development, and pursuit of technical goals without ceasing to be that which is "conventional theology." Conventional theology can so assist technology, and science, in that realm known as artificial intelligence (AI), where it can suggest a new philosophical paradigm for the pursuit, and also the way that progress might be made.

In Richard Bube's (1995) book *Putting it All Together: Seven Patterns for Relating Science and the Christian Faith,* he describes a definition for "authentic Christian theology" as "a particular way of knowing, based on descriptions of the world obtained through the human interpretation of the Bible and human experience." Bube then goes on to examine seven different fundamental patterns he finds in relating science and Christian theology. These conceptions are relevant to the way that we may relate conventional theology and technology. These patterns are as follows

- **Pattern 1, Science has destroyed Christian theology:** there is conflict, both science and theology cannot be right and science always wins.
- **Pattern 2, Christian theology in spite of science:** there is conflict, both science and theology cannot be right and theology always wins
- **Pattern 3, Science and Christian theology are unrelated:** science and theology tell us different kinds of things about different things, so there is no common ground and no possibility of conflict. Neither has anything to say about the other. This pattern is perhaps the most commonly chosen pragmatic pattern of all.
- **Pattern 4, Science demands traditional Christian theology:** there is conflict, science and theology cover the same ground in the same way, but science provides all the evidence concerning the truth of traditional Christian theology.
- **Pattern 5, Science redefines Christian theology:** because science and theology cover the same ground in the same way, traditional theology must be redefined and rewritten to agree with modern science.
- **Pattern 6, A new synthesis is needed for a redefined science and a redefined theology:** science and theology should tell us the same things about the same things, but they both need to be reformulated to make this possible.
- **Pattern 7, Science and theology offer complementary insights:** science and theology each provide valid insights into what reality is, according to its own perspective. Integration of insights from each allows us to have an adequate and coherent view of reality.

In a "theology of technology," we are concerned with a slightly different exercise. First, we are examining "theology" and "technology," not "science." Secondly, in "technology," the exercise is, by nature, "applied"; we are not merely trying to describe the world and reconcile scientific vs. religious understandings. In the "theology of technology,"we are engaged in a more practical endeavour in "creating" behaviours and artefacts artificially. Some may find that creating certain behaviours in machines is also an impossible exercise, although with a theologically informed technology, we find a similar synthesis to Pattern 7 in that two or more different, but valid kinds of insight are needed to more fully comprehend something. There are also similarities with Pattern 4. However, instead of "science providing all the evidence concerning the truth of conventional theology" the roles are reversed; it is "theology" which provides the stimulus for what occurs in the technical realm. That is, at least some parts of theology offer some insights to "truth" in the technical realm, and are their underpinning.

9.3 Moral Machines or People?

One of the most obvious ways that conventional theology can be applied to technology is to provide ethical input into the moral use of technology. Technology, unlike science, cannot escape the question of what is done with the "product." Science has traditionally been conducted in a "moral vacuum." There is, of course, the question of the morality of scientific method itself, which may prohibit certain "means" to the "end." However, in a climate where the end product knowledge is "objective," there is little room for "morality" in the knowledge itself. Natural objects and physical laws are considered neither "good" nor "bad," and science is pursued to "discover' these laws. The "neutrality" of science is largely due to the influence of positivist philosophy, which dominated science in the 19th century, and excluded reference to teleology (that is, purpose) in scientific discourse. The knowledge created is isolated from any "purpose" to which the science may be put. Hence, we have the situation where machines and products are developed with no moral guidelines on their use. Technology cannot escape moral questions.

Various organisations are set up to monitor the appropriate use of technology at various levels. Groups that do monitor the application of science often have a religious or political affiliation. Sometimes these groups, especially religious groups, are seen in negative terms, representing people who are resistant to change, reinforcing the false dichotomy of "science" vs. "religion," rather than presenting a body reflecting upon the application of science. But they undertake an important task, since clearly the ramifications of a certain piece of technology, in terms of benefit or harm, may not always be apparent at the outset: even those that appear beneficial. These monitoring bodies include the Institute for Religion, Technology, and Culture (http://www.religion-research.org/irtc/irtc.htm), which aims to promote discussion and reflection on technology from a theological and philosophical perspective. They see technology as impinging upon how people understand themselves, the world, and God. The "science, religion and technology group" of the Church of Scotland (http://www.srtp.org.uk/srtpage3.shtml) was set up to monitor unexpected risks and side effects, unintended social consequences, and changes in moral outlook arising from technology. Thus, monitoring bodies are particularly valuable to ensure that the desired outcomes of "benefit" are attained.

Religious voices have also warned about the unwitting influences of technology, suggesting a reflective view is necessary. A Roman Catholic religious address of half a century ago gives a general warning of the dangers of technology in terms of "exalting technology" and "blinding intelligence" (Pius, 1953). The address points out that technology can beautifully reveal God, and also cause humanity to once again sink itself into the first sin of self-sufficiency and independence. Once again, the angle is what using technology will do to us — whether it is used for good or evil-and what it will do without us realising. The key is to being aware and willing to stop when things have gone too far, whether technology threatens to either reduce us to objects or exalt us to gods. Whenever technology makes us deny our humanity, it robs us of our authenticity and is a problem. The view of the Catholic Church was not simply a condemnation of technology outright. Following the 1953 address, the Second Vatican Council (1965) produced a document on "Relating to Modern World" ("Gaudium et Spes") that acknowledges an awareness of the Church's relation to the secular modern world.

The Vatican II document, "Gaudium et Spes," (1965) surveys several themes on the relation of the Roman Catholic Christian church to the modern world, including its relation to technology. "Gaudium et Spes" identified that there is a certain emptiness underlying technology affirming the dignity of the human person, in that people were created in "the image of God," capable of knowing and loving their Creator, and appointed by that Creator as master of all earthly creatures. Technology potentially erodes this aspect of human dignity. The document also finds that humankind exists in a community, and has social laws written into people's moral and spiritual nature. The greater a human's power becomes, the farther his individual and community responsibility extends. They perceive the role of the church in such a world as being a "leavening" agent in human society.

The moral use of technology, or the morality of scientific method, is still essentially concerned with the morality of people. However, within AI, we are faced with some unique questions. AI engages in the task of creating machines that mimic human action; as such, it cannot escape the question of what is moral action. While secular sources can provide ethical input to moral questions, theology is a traditional source of answers for such questions. In *Computer Power and Human Reason*, Joseph Weizenbaum (1976) demands that the scientific community consider ethical and moral issues associated with the development of machines that can imitate human behaviour.

Weizenbaum created ELIZA in order to demonstrate natural language processing in computer systems. Though ELIZA was capable of carrying on a human-like conversation, Weizenbaum never intended for ELIZA to be a substitute for human interaction. He was appalled when psychiatrists suggested that the program might be an acceptable substitute for human therapy. Even Weizenbaum's own secretary, who was intimately aware that ELIZA was a machine, conversed with the computer on a number of personal matters. Horrified, Weizenbaum began work on the philosophical problem presented by the mechanization of human characteristics and talents. He finds that the real question for AI is not what computers will be able to do, but what we, as human beings, should allow them to do.

Science fiction writer Isaac Asimov, inventor of the term "robotics," was concerned with the principles by which machines should operate so that they did not threaten humanity. He proposed the infamous "three laws of robotics" (Asimov, 1942). Many of his stories revolve around the conflicts that arise from the "three laws," and the sobering conclusions there are drawn. The laws state (1) a robot may not injure a human being, or, through inaction, allow a human being to come to harm, (2) a robot must obey the orders given it by human beings, except where such orders would conflict with the First Law and (3) a robot must protect its own existence as long as such protection does not conflict with the First or Second Law. In 1985, a "zeroth" law was created that placed humanity's interests above that of any particular individual, giving us: (0) a robot may not injure humanity, or, through inaction, allow humanity to come to harm. The moral dilemmas raised by Asimov in a fictional context make an important observation for AI, in that morality is a component of "simulated behaviour." The fictional origins of such "machine morality" concerns are now being translated into technical design decisions. However, interactions between moral beings in the real world are far more complex than a set of basic safety rules.

There is a term coined by the Singularity Institute for AI called "friendly AI." "friendly AI" refers to the production of human-benefiting, non-human-harming actions in AI systems. It is especially important that those systems that have advanced to the point of making real-world plans, in pursuit of goals, are indeed friendly. Friendly AI describes design features for benevolence and analyses, the ways in which AI and human psychology are likely to differ, and the ways in which those differences are subject to our design decisions (http://www.singinst.org/friendly/guidelines.html). They believe creating "ethical machines" does not even remotely resemble the task of ensuring ethical behaviour in a possibly hostile human, or the task of instilling ethical behaviour in a growing human child. It is not clear just how "design guidelines" for friendly AI could ever be achieved without some "reference" for what is moral. In religious terms, the question is, at essence, the question of what is "sin," since any "sin" is non-human benefiting action. Thus, "friendly AI" moves into theological ground.

The very consideration of "morality" in a technology such as AI sets it apart as a unique endeavour. Morality and ethical action is not relevant to technology at some meta-level where or how it is used. rather, morality and ethical action is bound up in the aims of the technology itself. At this point, theology intersects with technology in a unique way. AI cannot escape the necessity to "model" human morality. In that endeavour, there is a whole new set of questions that are raised. When we admit that AI is aiming to reproduce human behaviour, and that human behaviour is subject to "ethical" principles, we most certainly venture into the realm of theology. We are driven to the question of "what it is to be human?" Morality is just one component of that human identity. The protestant reformer, Martin Luther, understood the theological concept "image of God" to be man's "moral substance, or nature." In this morality, people were created to be like God. However, human sin, and the Fall, resulted in the corruption of this moral nature. Restoration of the image can be achieved through faith in Christ. Thus in theology, we may study and understand the nature of human identity, especially the "morality" of what it is to be human.

It could be said that ethics apply only to conscious entities, and that a machine cannot have ethics (and neither, perhaps, can a lower animal). But it is possible to model some part of ethics logically and build this into a computational system.

9.4 Artificial Identity: The Image of God

The question of human morality is intimately related to the question of human identity. Morality is a unique part of being human. Animals do not have morality. A machine that is expected to behave in a human-like way must imitate at least this aspect of human identity. For many years, human identity was understood in terms of rational, logical thought. Descartes' famous conclusion was that his existence could be known because he was conscious and thinking; this is, "I think therefore I am" (cogito ergo sum). At the start of AI, Turing was interested in the question of "whether a machine could think?" His method involved a game of "identity" in the Turing test. However, thinking is only one aspect of what it is to be human and behave in a human-like way. AI will benefit from broadening its conception of human identity; in particular, the insight that theological input can give about that identity. The biblical concept of the "image of God" (Imago Dei) has been foundational for understanding human identity. In this image is found the moral, intellectual, rational, emotional, relational, and social essence of humanity.

In both the Jewish and Christian traditions, the biblical concept of the "image of God" (Imago Dei) has been foundational for understandings of the nature of personhood. The term image of God is applied uniquely to humans, and has its roots in Genesis 1:27, where God created people in His own image. People have been understood to bear the image of God, among other things, in their moral, spiritual, intellectual, and creative natures. Human beings have free volition, making possible the "choice" of sin. There are also aspects of humanity, distinct from animal and plant life, that are uniquely human: intellect, language, morals, the capacity for "faith," and other, which are in this "divine image." While "image of God" has been foundational for understandings of the nature of personhood, the concept encompasses more than "rational thought": it is far more. This theological conception of personhood contrasts with other fields that are also interested in "identity" and the question of "what is it to be human?"

Philosophers have also asked: "what is the basis of a person's identity?" The traditional conceptions of identity certainly do point to "rationality" being a popular distinguisher. Descartes (1641) famous conclusion was that his existence could be known because he was conscious and thinking: this is, "I think therefore I am" (cogito ergo sum). Since then, the human has been defined by, or closely associated with, cognitive ability; rational and logical thought. Descartes promulgated the principle of "science without presuppositions." His famous conclusion was a product of his method of universal doubt being applied to "all things," and the four Cartesian laws: (1) accept nothing as true which is not clear and distinct, (2) analyze a problem into its parts and discuss it part by part, (3) arrange thoughts from simple to complex as the order of study and (4) enumerations must be full and complete and nothing must be omitted. The statement "I think therefore I am" was found to be a self-evident proposition, intuitively grasped and not an inference.

More recently, philosophers have turned away from rationalism as the basis of identity and looked to "functionalism." Macmurray (1995) is one who believes that action, rather than thought, is primary. The human being is conceived of as an agent. Activity is intentional and includes reflection as a secondary component. Also, the possibility of action requires that there be something to act upon, and so the existence of the other is also presupposed. Thus, agency entails embodiment and relatedness. To exist is to be part of the world, in relation with other parts of the world. To treat another person as a person, then, implies the recognition of their agency. Moreover, the expression of agency implies the freedom to act. Consequently, the individual engaged in heterocentric action will avoid curtailing the freedom of the other. For MacMurray, it is more accurate to say: "I do think and therefore I am." Human identity is agency and action.

In the context of identity based upon functionalism, we are immediately faced with the question of whether humans are qualitatively different from machines. Others we have already reviewed, such as Weizenbaum (1976) and Heidigger (1977), have addressed this argument, warning and aiming to demonstrate the importance of retaining distinctive human identity. Bruce Mazlish (1993) sees this question as one of four identity discontinuities with which the human race has had to grapple. Beginning with Copernicus, human beings had to bridge the gulf between the earth and the universe to accept the fact that the sun, not the earth, is the center of our solar system. Darwin compelled humanity to examine its evolutionary past, and rethink the alleged great divide between itself and animals. Freud showed that reason is not even master of its own domain: its operations being determined by the will, instincts, affects, unconscious, and life history. The notion of the "fourth discontinuity" involved the perception that humans are not qualitatively different from machines, and are imploding into machines.

Mazlish (1993) has also identified a "fifth identity discontinuity" arising as technology advances to the point of creating human-like computers and robots, and people become ever more like cyborgs; humanity is forced to question its self-proclaimed ontological divide from machines. As we have examined, some transhumanists believe that the human race, as it currently is known, will degenerate or disappear as an offspring of evolution. In each of the identity discontinuities that Mazlish describes, Best and Kellner (2004) assert that in each case, "rational man" had to rethink its identity to overcome false dichotomies and illusions of separation from the cosmos, the animal world, the unconscious, and the machines it invented. So where may humanity find its identity? Conventional theology provides an answer in the Imago Dei.

Early Christian writers such as Irenaeus, Clement of Alexandria, and Augustine, identified that humans were made in the "image of God." This image was primarily located in human intellect and the power of reason, distinguishing humans from the lower creation. Theologian Thomas Aquinas, finds the human is said to be the image of God by reason of the intellectual nature. The mind distinguishes people from the lower creation, and the intellectual nature imitates God (Aquinas, 1947). While rational thought and cognitive function is clearly a vital component of personhood, it is not the only definitive aspect of humanity. Martin Luther understood the image of God to be man's "moral substance." As a result of humanity's sin, aspects of the image have been corrupted, though not destroyed, and can be restored through faith in Christ (Luther, 1966).

For theologian John Calvin, the image of God was essentially spiritual in nature, extending "... to the whole excellence by which man's nature towers over all the kinds of living creatures." Because of human sin, this image is now confused and mutilated. It is partially restored through conversion and faith, but will regain its full splendour only in heaven. The Christian concept of election, where the individual is enabled to have a special personal relationship with God, is relevant since a person is given value not by any innate quality or achievement, but by divine initiative in establishing the relationship. The identity, purpose, and value of the "elect" person is defined by the electing and choosing purposes of God. The concept of adoption offers a similar redemptive action of God, where salvation involves being made a part of the family of God. In adoption, the emphasis is upon the benevolent and gratuitous initiative of God, and not any innate qualifications of the person. In both cases, personhood is found in the divinely grounded relationship.

In the post-Reformation and modern periods, scholars have suggested a variety of meanings for the "image," usually seeing in this concept a reference to some quality intrinsic to humans, such as a "feeling," or sense of the transcendent, or even humanity's upright walking. Clearly this would have implications for the "insect like" robots and "flying agents" that seek to avoid some of the navigational difficulties of the biped! Natural language has been cited as one faculty with which humans are endowed but which other creatures are not, and therefore, it is language that is the distinguishing component between humanity and the rest of creation. Karl Barth identified the image with the relationship of man as male and female. Yet this does not adequately distinguish people from animals. Even though Turing included a male/female gender aspect in the test of whether a computer could deceive a human converser about its true identity, gender was not the primary factor.

Berkouwer gives a relational understanding of humanity as "image of God" (Berkouwer, 1962). That is to say, humans bear the image of God by their unique capacity for a personal relationship to God. In this view, humans are unique not so much in terms of innate capacities, but rather through being uniquely gifted and capacitated for such a relationship with God (in the traditions of Jewish, Christian, and Islamic theology). There is no abstract or innate defining "essence" of the human such as intelligence or rationality: the nature of the human is understood in terms of relationship to God, and this relationship is human nature. To some extent, MacMurray (1995) supports this "relational" understanding of personhood.

Kenneth Gergen, Professor of Psychology at Swarthmore College, asserts that human beings are formed socially, and that all human knowledge is relational. Rather than "cogito ergo sum" as the definitive aspect of humanity, it may be "Relatio, ergo sum" (I relate, therefore I am) that is closer to the truth. Seeing the world through relational lenses requires a gestalt shift, a personal transformation not unlike a religious conversion. Noreen Herzfeld (2000) is one who argues for a correlation between the pursuit of AI and a relational interpretation of the Imago Dei. Herzfeld argues that the history of failure in symbolic AI provides strong support for a relational model, where the image of God is not viewed in terms of properties or functionality, but with a relational interpretation.

Macmurray distinguishes between social and personal relations. Essentially, social relations are found in the work place, where people are related on the basis of their instrumental worth, whereas personal relations are grounded in the appreciation of one another's intrinsic worth. In the former case, the relationship is founded on the basis of a common purpose, whereas in the latter case, the relationship exists for its own sake. Macmurray refers to functional relations as "societies," and to personal relations as "communities": the former is comprised of the association of members, while the latter describes the fellowship of friends. Fundamentally, therefore, personal relations involve the treatment of persons as persons, and not merely as objects. MacMurray says that we cannot fully understand individuals in isolation, but only in relation to others. Relationship is constitutive of human living for Macmurray: "We need one another to be ourselves. This complete and unlimited dependence of each of us upon the others is the central and crucial fact of personal existence." The idea of an isolated agent is self-contradictory; any agent is necessarily in relationship with others. Macmurray corresponded with Martin Buber, and his thought essentially extends Buber's vision.

Colin Gunton, professor at King's College, London, describes an ontology of relation that involves a "vertical" relationship with God, and a "horizontal" relationship with each other. Gunton believes that we need a view of our relations to God that doesn't simply see us as souls, but as personal beings. The concept of redemption is to be concerned with an embodied life in social relation to other beings as well as to God. Shifting from functional to relational moves from what a machine might be able to do and achieve, to its capacity for relating. Gunton believes that it is the relational capability that is the key to understanding the Imago Dei, not the ability to think or reason. Personhood is an eschatological concept, something we only truly achieve in full in the bodily resurrection of the whole person promised in Jesus Christ.

In the context of "relational" comprehension of personhood, we have already discussed how Anne Foerst at MIT has worked on the Kismet project — a "social robot" — demonstrating the elements of relatedness. Kismet is able to respond to human interaction with basic human emotions. Foerst believes that human beings are entirely relational and do not develop as rational, individual beings. She believes that "It is absolutely crucial that babies are in relation, because without relation, they don't learn anything." Self-image can be defined by the way others treat us. Racism, sexism, or some other form of prejudice can all deny personhood, but the Imago Dei given by God supersedes human-constructed personhood. Foerst is just one researcher who sees embodiment as vital. In the Kismet and Cog projects, which seek to demonstrate the vitality of relatedness, the social, and emotional, she sees that most crucial assumption of all is that "without body there is no being, without body there is no mind, no thought, nothing." The trend towards embodied, situated intelligence is consonant with this embodiment of the human. In fact, much of the artificial life paradigm is built upon the physical realisation of robots that interact directly with the world about them.

Again, arguing for a relational understanding of personhood we find William Hurlburt, from Stanford University, who believes that mind is embodied in such a way that our conceptual systems draw largely upon the commonalities of our bodies and the social environment we live in. The result is universal, common, shared understandings across languages and culture, enhanced by fundamental emotions. Facial expressions are nearly a universal language that not only generate physiological changes in the person expressing the emotion, but similar responses in the human observer-the beginnings of empathy. The human mind is formed and defined, grounded by empathy experienced in community. This community is also evidenced in the Christian doctrine of the Trinity. The Cappadocians elaborated the idea of the Trinity as "Father, Son, and Spirit bound up in each other's being" so that we may say there is one God, but three persons. The persons of God in the trinity give to and receive from one another what they uniquely are, that is communion, and eternal love. Through their relation comes their genuine otherness to one another. Being made in the image of God would also entail having this capacity for relating in social community: not only capacity for relating, but it would be the very means of definition of who we are.

Returning to more ancient theologians, Thomas Aquinas (1947) sees in the image of God, the basis for a person's loving relationship to God. Our humanity is more defined by our capacity to love — God and others and our selves-than to think. This kind of love is expressed by the Greek word "agape." No one has dared to ask "can a machine love?" in the sense of an ethical, moral, embodied, agency with purpose to influence another for the good. Thinking becomes secondary to the ethical and moral constraints within which the freedom of will is exercised. Ultimately, it may be "I love therefore I am" that defines humanity. Maybe AI should be pursuing the question of "can a machine love?," as popularised by the Warner Bros film "AI."

Thus, we see that human identity is not solely defined by the capacity for rational thought: theology brings out the social, related, interactive, moral, situated, embodied aspects of human nature. Focusing upon the functionality of a system, especially functionality that produces rational behaviours misses, as theology would inform us, what it is to be human. Cognitive power alone is insufficient for "describing" that which produces intelligent behaviour. While AI may gain some important inspirations from the theology of personhood, we should remember that our human capacity to relate to the divine was capacitated by God, and in a very important way, people are fundamentally different to any intelligent machine that could ever be produced.

Furse (1996) does speculate about the possibility of a robot coming to Christian faith due to its intellectual capacities, ability for mental ascent to "know God," and even pray. Yet it seems that fundamentally, God has chosen humanity, and therein lies the ultimate aspect of human personhood and identity: that God chose us. This is an aspect to our identity that could never be replicated: we have personhood by divine initiative, not by any attribute or work, function, or relation of our own. While we seek to engender intelligent machines to be as similar to humans as we can, there is this fundamental difference that whatever we "create," we can never endow it with that which can be only given by God. Machines have just never been elected by God for salvation, and will never be able to have a faith relationship with God.

In this brief survey, we see a range of theological conceptions on human identity in the "Imago Dei," ranging from conceptions that focus upon the intellectual and rational, emotional and social, to the moral, relational, and interactive. Some of the theological contributions certainly have cast doubt upon the worldview that says "I think therefore I am" as the basis of our existence, worth, and identity. Theology shows us that thinking is just one component of the relating, agency, and moral acting that is embodied in the human being. An AI informed by theology would do well to recognise that rational thought is not the sole definition of personhood; that the question of "can a machine think?" is just one aspect of what we may enquire about in intelligence. Within AI, we may do a better job of mimicking some aspects of our (socially defined) intelligent behaviour by taking this broader concept of personhood into account.

9.5 References

Asimov, I. (1942). Runaround. Reprinted in *I, robot.* (1968) London: Grafton Books.

Aquinas, T. (1947). *Summa Theologica* (Pt. 1, Q. 93, Art. 4. Tr.). New York: Benziger Bros.

Berkouwer, G. C. (1962). *Man: The image of God* (D. W. Jellema, Trans.). Grand Rapids, MI: Eerdmans.

Best, S., & Kellner, D. (2004). *H.G. Wells, biotechnology, and genetic engineering: A dystopic vision.* Retrieved from http://utminers.utep.edu/best/papers/phiecosoc/hgwells.htm

Borowik-Dabrowska, E. (2004). *Cybertheology.* Retrieved from http://www.amen-dir.net/Cybertheology/index.htm

Bube, R. H. (1995). *Putting it all together: Seven patterns for relating science and the Christian faith.* University Press of America.

Descartes. (1641).

Foerst, A.

Furse, E. A. (1996). *Theology of robots.* Retrieved December 11, 2001, from http://www.comp.glam.ac.uk/pages/staff/efurse/Theology-of-Robots/A-Theology-of-Robots.html

Gergen, K. (n.d.).

Gunton, C. (n.d.).

Hayes-Bohanan, J. (2005). *Toward a theology of the Web: Pierre Teilhard de Chardin and cyberconsciousness.* Retrieved from http://webhost.bridgew.edu/jhayesboh/teilhard.htm

Heidegger, M. (1977). *The question concerning technology and other essays* (W. Lovitt, Trans.). New York: Harper and Row.

Henderson, C.

Herzfeld, N. L. (2000). *Imago Dei/ Imago Hominis: Creation in one's own image in Genesis and artificial intelligence.* Doctoral dissertation, Graduate Theological Union, Berkeley.

Hurlburt, W. (n.d.).

Kreisberg, J. C. (1998). *Cybergrace: The search for God in the digital world.* Crown.

Luther, M. (1966). Commentary on Genesis. In H. T. Kerr (Ed.), *A compendium of Luther's theology* (pp. 82-83). Philadelphia: Westminster Press.

MacMurray, & MacIntyre. (1995). *The concept of the person and the future of virtue theory, the self as agent.* London: Faber.

Mazlish, B. (1993). *A new science: The breakdown of connections and the birth of sociology.*

Pius XII, Pope (2000, April). 1953 Christmas message of Pope Pius XII (December 4, 1953). *The Angelus, XXIII,* (4), (Original work published in 1953). Retrieved from http://sspx.ca/Angelus/2000_April/On_Modern_Technology_and_Peace.htm

Weizenbaum, J. (1976). *Computer power and human reason.* San Francisco: W. H. Freeman.

Chapter 10

The Philosophy of AI

"If the human brain were so simple that we could understand it, we would be so simple that we couldn't."

Emerson M. Pugh

"Reason is our soul's left hand, Faith her right."

John Donne

10.1 Introduction

As we shall see, the "theology of technology" can help inform the philosophical underpinnings of AI. We start with elucidating the idea of computation, and describe the idea of Turing machine computation. Its equivalence with Post systems and the lambda calculus are explained, and the way that these systems may be regarded as "rule based" and "generative" are brought out. All the equivalent formal models define enumerable languages. However, as Turing's original definition demonstrated, there are definable numbers that are not computable, that is, a computer could not be used to write some numbers down, yet they exist. The presence of "unsolvable" computational problems also reveals the limitations of Turing machines, and suggests the current limits of computation. While the "intuitive" understanding of computation is one of "step-by-step" algorithmic procedure, it will be hard to conceive of any other computational model.

Much of AI operates with the assumption of computationalism. This is the idea that computation can offer an explanation for cognition. We continue to examine some of the claims of computationalism and why there are problems with an "algorithmic" description of the mind. We consider some of the arguments for why cognitive functions are non-algorithmic, particularly noting the refutations based on the limitations of formal systems and the fact that Turing machine computation is just such a mathematical system. Other conceptions of computation, such as Putnam's "everything is computation" and Searle's "observer-related" computation, start to move away from the Turing machine conception. And depending on what does define computation, there may or may not be scope for computationalism.

Finally, we consider other "aspects" of human intelligence that are just as important as "thinking," and highly likely to be non-algorithmic. Recently, we have seen a shift in AI away from "thinking" as the definitive task, towards "emotional" and other intelligences. These are especially important for "relating" and human communication, with emotion being a vital aspect of semantics in language. Yet the "emotional" and "relational" is poorly understood in AI, evidenced by the fact that interactions with machines are often frustrating. Emotion, combined with the idea of consciousness makes it very questionable whether a mathematical model, ala Turing machine computation, could adequately capture intelligence. Even if thinking is basically algorithmic, it is not necessarily possible to devise a Turing machine to move the "human system" through a set of "emotional" and "consciousness" states from the start to finish, nor capture that in a set of "rewrite" rules that reduce the workings of a human being to a lambda calculus expression, or equivalent Post system/Turing machine.

The objective of this chapter is to outline the understanding of computation that dominates AI, as well as computer science and much of mathematics. This understanding of computation is essentially rule-based, expressed through formal systems such as the Post system, lambda calculus and the Turing machine. In this mathematical paradigm, the idea of algorithm is intuitively understood to be a "step-by-step" procedure. We also hint at the possibility of other understandings of computation, such as Putnam's "everything is computation." We introduce the idea of "computationalism," the suggestion that the (Turing machine) computations of a machine are, in fact, a mind. However, for many people, the mathematical model is the undoing of computationalism since formal systems have inherent limitations (in expressivity and deductions that can be made). The human mind is not limited in the same way that the formal systems are. We aim to highlight a couple of other properties of the mind and aspects of human behaviour that also appear to defy (Turing machine) algorithmic description: these are emotional awareness and its consequential social/relational outworking and consciousness itself. This chapter is necessary to provide the philosophical background to the implications that the "theology of technology" has for AI.

10.2 What is Computation?

Before modern computers were invented, Turing (1936) formulated a very important conception of "computation," He did so in fairly abstract terms, reasoning about what numbers could be "computed." A number is considered computable if a machine can write down its decimal: that is, they are real numbers whose expressions as a decimal are calculable by finite means. The class of computable numbers is very great, and in many ways similar to the class of real numbers, but it does not include all definable numbers. The class of computable numbers is, nevertheless, enumerable. In this definition of computability, Turing presented the universal Turing machine. This is a mathematical model that could generate any computable sequence. The Turing machine is considered to be the most general model of computation known, although Post systems and lambda calculus are two other "equivalent" systems.

Intuitively, a task is computable if one can specify a sequence of instructions that, when followed, will result in the completion of the task. This is an effective procedure, or algorithm, for the task. Mechanistically, a Turing machine is a simple computer whose operations are limited to reading and writing symbols on tape, or moving along the tape, to the left or to the right, one symbol at a time. Its behaviour at a given moment is determined by the symbol in the square currently being read, and by the current state of the machine. More precisely, a Turing machine consists of:

- **A tape that is divided into cells, one next to the other:** Each cell contains a symbol from some finite alphabet. The alphabet contains a special blank symbol (here written as "0") and one or more other symbols. The tape is assumed to be arbitrarily extendible to the left and to the right, that is, it is infinite, having as much tape as necessary for its computation. Cells, which have not been written to before, are assumed filled with the blank symbol.
- **A head that can read and write symbols on the tape and move left and right.**
- **A state register that stores the state of the Turing machine:** The number of different states is always finite, and there is one special start state with which the state register is initialized.
- **An action table (or transition function):** that tells the machine what symbol to write, how to move the head ("L" for one step left, and "R" for one step right), and what its new state will be, given the symbol it has just read on the tape and the state it is currently in. If there is no entry in the table for the current combination of symbol and state, then the machine will halt.

This Turing machine can be abstracted into a "finite-state automata": that is, a mathematical model that consists of a start and finish state, a set of rules determining the valid transitions between states. The finite-state automata makes the Turing machine essentially a "rule-based" paradigm. If the rules determining valid transitions between states have, at most, one entry for each combination of symbol and state, then the machine is a deterministic Turing machine (DTM). If the action table contains multiple entries for a combination of symbol and state, then the machine is a non-deterministic Turing machine (NDTM or NTM). It is always possible to turn the non-deterministic into the deterministic.

There is a formal equivalence between Turing machines and Post systems (Post, 1943; Monell & Margineantu, 1996). The Post-system is a rule-based grammar of rewrite rules that generates a finite enumerable language. The set of "sentences" generated by the Post system is identical to the sentences that a Turing machine can "compute." Formal equivalences can also be demonstrated between Turing machines and lambda calculus. Lambda calculus was developed by Alonzo Church (1936) to explore the problem of computability. The lambda calculus consists of a single transformation rule (variable substitution) and a single function definition scheme. It is thus, a simple, context-free grammar and a special-case Post system. The lambda calculus has been called the smallest universal programming language.

The importance of the equivalence between Turing machines, Post systems and lambda calculus is found in the question of "what can be computed?": that is, whether there is an algorithm for the computation. Not all problems can be solved. An undecidable problem is one that cannot be solved by any algorithm, even given unbounded time and memory. Many undecidable problems are known. The Entscheidungsproblem (German for "decision problem") is an example of an undecidable problem. As is the halting problem: determining whether a Turing machine will halt. The existence of undecidable problems means that there are some things that cannot be computed.

The widely held view that Turing machines completely express the intuitive notion of computation led researchers to assume that questions of expressiveness of finite computing agents had been settled once and for all, so that exploration of alternative models of computability seemed unnecessary. It was accepted that there were some problems that are simply undecidable and no (Turing machine) algorithm exists to compute them. However, recently researchers have considered alternatives to this formalised computation model. One is Copeland (1998), who suggests that accelerated Turing machines are able to compute the halting function augmenting within the current paradigm. Others have considered connectionist models as an alternative paradigm that "may possibly even challenge the strong construal of Church's Thesis as the claim that the class of well-defined computations is exhausted by those of Turing machines" (Smolensky, 1988).

The Turing machine is essentially a rule-based paradigm. As we have seen, the lambda calculus and Post system are also essentially "grammars" that dictate how "sentences" of a formal language may be produced by rules. A formal grammar consists of a finite set of terminal symbols (the letters of the words in the formal language), a finite set of non-terminal symbols, a set of production rules with a left- and a right-hand side consisting of a word of these symbols, and a start symbol. A rule may be applied to a word by replacing the left-hand side by the right-hand side. A derivation is a sequence of rule applications. Such a grammar defines the formal language of all words consisting solely of terminal symbols that can be reached by a derivation from the start symbol.

Chomsky has a hierarchy of languages and corresponding grammars in the Chomsky hierarchy. The Chomsky hierarchy consists of the following levels:

- **Type-0 grammars (unrestricted grammars) include all formal grammars:** They generate exactly all languages that can be recognized by a Turing machine. These languages are also known as the recursively enumerable languages.
- **Type-1 grammars (context-sensitive grammars) generate the context-sensitive languages:** These grammars have rules of the form $\alpha A \beta$ -> $\alpha \gamma \beta$, with A as non-terminal and α, β, and γ strings of terminals and non-terminals. The strings α and β may be empty, but γ must be non-empty. The languages described by these grammars are exactly all languages that can be recognized by a non-deterministic Turing machine whose tape is bounded by a constant times the length of the input.
- **Type-2 grammars (context-free grammars) generate the context-free languages:** These are defined by rules of the form A -> γ, with A a non-terminal and γ a string of terminals and non-terminals. These languages are exactly all languages that can be recognized by a non-deterministic pushdown automaton. Context free languages are the theoretical basis for the syntax of most programming languages.
- **Type-3 grammars (regular grammars) generate the regular languages:** Such a grammar restricts its rules to a single non-terminal on the left-hand side and a right-hand side consisting of a single terminal, possibly followed (or preceded, but not both in the same grammar) by a single non-terminal. The rule is also here allowed if S does not appear on the right side of any rule. These languages are exactly all languages that can be decided by a finite state automaton. Additionally, this

family of formal languages can be obtained by regular expressions. Regular languages are commonly used to define search patterns and the lexical structure of programming languages.

In linguistics, generative rule-based grammar assumes that in any natural language (a) the length of any sentence is finite (whether letters, phonemes, morphemes, or words.) and (b) there is no longest sentence (because of recursion). From these two assumptions, it follows that the cardinality of the set of sentences in any natural language is denumerably infinite. The set of such "sentence strings" from a Post system (or equivalently lambda calculus or Turing machine) is also considered to be an enumerable set, and one that is countably infinite. Given a particular finite "sentence string,"the rule base can be used to see whether the "string" was generated by the grammar or not: the task of determining this is the "parsing" problem. Parsing is applicable to formal and natural languages, and determining whether a string is generated from a language is a computational problem: a decision problem, just as deciding whether a Turing machine will halt or not is a decision task.

This formal, mathematical, essentially rule-based understanding of computation has dominated computer science for many years. The Church-Turing thesis (1936), Church's thesis, Church's conjecture, or Turing's thesis is a thesis that claims that any calculation that is possible can be performed by an algorithm running on a computer, provided that sufficient time and storage space are available. A common formulation of the Church-Turing thesis is that a Turing machine can carry out every effective computation. The limits of Turing machines describe the theoretical limits of all computers (McArthur 1991).

An intuitively acceptable algorithm for a task that is not Turing computable would refute the Church-Turing thesis. However, the idea of an "intuitively acceptable algorithm" often defaults to that which is essentially rulebased. The problem with refuting the thesis is within the task itself, with the "intuitive" nature of what is considered an algorithm. When algorithm is considered to be a step-by-step procedure, a string generated by rules of a Turing machine, or Post system, or entailed in a lambda calculus expression, then it will be hard to escape the paradigm, and find "computational" solutions for unsolvable problems.

10.3 Computationalism: Can a Machine Think?

Since the start of AI, people have been keen to demonstrate that machines think: that is, machines can perform operations that, if performed by a person, would require rational intelligence to achieve. AI has pursued tasks in many different problem areas ranging from expert systems that can diagnose disease, to programs that can discover mathematical formulae, planning systems that can navigate a robot, and natural language understanding systems that can summarise newspaper articles. At the start of AI, philosophical questions surrounding what is thinking, can a machine think, and is the human mind the same as a machine, abounded. Turing formulated the infamous Turing test as the means to answer the question "can a machine think?" (Turing, 1950), finding when the functionality of thinking has been achieved, we may say the machine thinks.

For many, these philosophical questions of AI have taken a backseat as practical problems were addressed and solved, although arguably, it is the philosophical side of AI that continues to provide the main "guides" that drive the field. Those concerned about the philosophy of AI may fit into the school we call "real AI." Earlier, we distinguished "virtual AI" from "real AI," finding "virtual AI" to be the intersection of AI and ICT technologies. Virtual AI would find natural partnership with ambient intelligence and ubiquitous computing to create intelligent environments. As such, the goals of "virtual AI" have shifted slightly from the goals of AI's pioneers. And the more philosophical questions, have become "irrelevant" to those simply concerned with producing "gadgets" with intelligence: decision support tools, or biometric verification systems, automatic diagnostic aids and other technologies that are not so much about reproducing human behaviour as augmenting and supplementing and supporting what people do.

However, within "real AI," there are still those who are, and must be concerned with, the philosophy of AI. The idea that thinking is a mechanistic computational process is certainly not new. It goes back to at least the 17th century, and some trace it as far back as the philosopher Aristotle. With the advent of the digital computer and its computational power, the possibility of "machine thought" became more than an abstract question. The "computational theory of mind" was proposed by Hilary Putnam (1961), and developed for philosophers by Jerry Fodor (1975). It is to be distinguished from various attempts to model features of the mind using computational modelling techniques, and from using the computer as a metaphor for understanding the mind. Computational theory of mind assumes that intentional states involve symbolic representations, and combines an account of reasoning with an account of the mental states.

With "the computational theory of mind," Jerry Fodor made a claim for "computationalism." This is the view that cognition essentially is a matter of computation. In particular, a mental state is a computational state embedded in a complex network of inputs, outputs, and other mental states. This type of computationalism is also referred to as psychofunctionalism. Fodor's claim went much further than anything a successful demonstration of the Turing test might imply, since Fodor's claim was that the "computations" were identical to "mind." Fetzer (1994) explains that computationalism is the proposal that people are Turing machines. Computationalism became a school in both cognitive science and AI. Computationalism raises simultaneous questions of "what is computation" and "what is mind."

Paul Davies (1991) explores the question of "what is mind" in the book *Theories of the Mind*, where he begins by examining the different philosophical categories of understanding the universe, and particularly the mind. We have already mentioned the materialist philosophy, which holds that if something exists (e.g., a mind), then it is physical. One version of materialism is physicalism, which sees the laws of physics as the algorithms that determine the informational states of particles (velocity, position, spin, etc.) from previous states, making the universe one large Turing machine. This includes the human mind. Such mechanistic materialism teaches that there is no spiritual dimension to human life, and the basic process of the universe is "evolution." Algorithms explain day-to-day life — there is no other underlying, unifying process — although evolution through time is regarded as such a universal process.

Davies elaborates on other philosophies that explain "mind." He informs us that idealists hold that only minds exist. Behaviourists hold that being in a mental state means being in a behavioural state, and functionalists hold that being in a mental state is being in a functional state and attempts to bypass the mind-body problem. The double aspect theory holds that the mental and physical are two aspects of the same underlying reality, denying mental and physical substance. Dualists agree that there are two different "types" of substance in the world: the immaterial and material, creating the "mind-body" dualism in the human being. Not all dualists share the same beliefs about how these two fundamental substances relate.

Some dualists think that causal relations hold between the mind and body (e.g., epiphenomenalists who believe that physical events cause minds), others deny this: some think that there is a simultaneous event (parallelism). Epiphenomenalists claim that consciousness and thought-processes exist as epiphenomena generated by the physical activities of the brain. Consciousness is solely a by-product of events in the nervous system (http://www.ai.mit.edu/people/marill/consciousness/node7.html). It is perhaps ultimately unknowable as to how the neural firings in the brain do relate to the human "being." If the mind is purely a product of neural firings in the brain, then questions about the possibility of free volition are raised. The human being is, at best, "constrained" by those firings and limited in the "choices" they may make, that is, there is no free will, although some consider free will to be an illusion.

In AI, computationalism is also known as philosophical AI or strong AI. It brings out the view that all human mental activities are reducible to algorithms, and could therefore be implemented on a computer. Strong AI often looks for biological plausibility in the implementation of algorithms, but does not require it. Always, strong AI would maintain that machines actually have cognitive states, or mind. Not many practitioners of AI would actually subscribe to this claim, although there are some who do find that computation is identical to mind. For a summary of the main philosophical arguments in favour of strong AI, and that human cognition may be, or has already been, duplicated by machinery, see Robinson (1988).

There are plenty of arguments to dispute computationalism. The claim that mental states are computational states has recently come under heavy attack from various directions. Some of the aspects, which make it unpopular, include the way computationalism suggests there is a complete deterministic account of the mind, with no room for free will, moral responsibility, or individual creativity. It also hinges upon materialism, and the view that if something exists, such as a mind, then it must have a physical cause. The behaviour of the universe is so reduced to laws of physics and mathematical descriptions, and the human brain is a physical process in neurone firings.

John Searle (1980) made significant contributions to the philosophy of AI with the Chinese room thought experiment. Searle used the Chinese room thought experiment to illustrate that computers just manipulate symbols, and demonstrate that there could be no "cognition." He asked us to imagine a person in a room with rules about how to manipulate Chinese symbols, but no knowledge of the language. As they manipulated symbols and output new combinations, they may appear intelligent to a Chinese speaker. But just as the person in the room cannot be said to understand those symbols, so a computer does not understand the symbols it manipulates. Symbol manipulation alone may achieve impressive results in terms of the cognitive operations it simulates, just as the demonstrated ability of a calculator to perform speedy and accurate arithmetic operations shows the power of symbol manipulation. However, we would probably not call a calculator "intelligent," just as we would not call a computer doing other symbol manipulation "intelligent." With this example, Searle distinguished between strong and weak AI.

The school of weak AI maintains that computers are doing no more than symbol manipulation. Most AI researchers subscribe to the weak AI school, believing that underlying any "machine," there is only symbol manipulation, whatever the machine is doing. The human being is the intelligence that interprets that manipulation. Sometimes an effort is made in AI to find mechanisms that do parallel the "reasoning" of humans, and mimic in some way what occurs in the human mind. But generally, weak AI does not seek any computational parallels with the human mind. Even if there are "biologically plausible" algorithms, the impossibility of cognitive states in a machine is still the distinguishing feature of the school. Clearly, weak AI would perceive many "limiting" reasons why a machine cannot implement a mind, and find many reasons why intelligence is non-algorithmic. If any activity or property of the mind can be demonstrated that cannot be simulated by algorithms and data structures, then the computationalist's worldview is shown to be incomplete.

One of the most important arguments of the non-algorithmic nature of intelligence comes from trying to formalise thought as a formal system. Many contradictions arise when the mind is construed as a formal system, as Gödel and others explain. Gödel's (1931) incompleteness theorem demonstrates that within any given branch of mathematics, there would always be some propositions that could not be proven either true or false using the rules and axioms of that mathematical branch itself. The implication is that all formalised systems of any complexity are, by definition, incomplete: each of them contains, at any given time, more true statements than it can possibly prove according to its own defining set of rules of design. Gödel's theorem has been used to argue that a computer can never be as smart as a human being because the extent of its knowledge is limited by a fixed set of axioms, whereas people can discover unexpected truths. What it seems to say is that rational thought can never penetrate to the final ultimate truth. Gödel showed that provability is a weaker notion than truth, no matter what axiom system is involved. The only versions of formal number theory that assert their own consistency are inconsistent. For more detail on these arguments, see Lucas (1988).

Penrose (1994) notes, the mathematical truths are true because of their meaning, not because of their syntax relation to an axiomatic system. The thesis of Penrose is that computers cannot, in principle, duplicate the workings of the human brain: all digital computers now operate according to algorithms, rules that the computer follows step by step. However, there are plenty of things in mathematics that cannot be calculated algorithmically. We can discover them and know them to be true, but clearly we are using some devices of calculation ("insight") that are not algorithmic, and that are, so far, not well understood, certainly not well enough understood to have computers do them instead. This simple argument is devastating to the algorithmic nature of intelligence and computationalism, where "cognition is computation." If the nature of computation is one component of computationalism, the nature of mind is another.

In summary, the question of "rational thought" has dominated AI for many years, and before that, philosophers have also pondered the nature of thought processes. Computationalism is the view that machine states really do implement a mind. This idea can be refuted with a number of arguments. Those that revolve around showing the limitations of formal systems that are implementing the "computation" will be most relevant to us. The question of "machine thought" ultimately reduces to the nature of mind and the nature of computation. We shall consider this further in the next chapter, but outline here two contrasting perspectives of computation that start to move away from the idea of computation being solely defined by a formal system. When we move away from computation being so defined, the possibilities of a machine implementing that which would be called a mind are interesting.

Both Putnam and Searle move away from the idea of computation being solely defined by a formal system. Putnam (1988) suggests that computation is all pervasive. According to Putnam's proof (in the appendix of his *Reality and Representation*), any open system, for example, a rock, can compute any function. If true, this would render void the computationalist's claim that cognition is simply a particular class of computation, since everything, even a rock, would be capable of cognition! Searle (1992) argues that computation is observer relative, that syntax is not intrinsic to physics. The relation between the physical implementation of computation and abstract computation is highly constrained, but it is still up to the observer to decide what constitutes a system state, and where to draw the boundaries of the system. It is also the observer who interprets the system being modelled in terms of the physical states and thus, corresponding abstract computational states. This makes computation, like beauty, largely in the eye of the beholder.

Within AI, the questions of "what is computation" and whether "computation in a machine is thinking" remain framed by a philosophical understanding of the universe, which believes that minds are ultimately products of physical processes. Whether it is the dualistic belief that minds, as mental entities, somehow emerge from the brain, or a purely materialistic understanding that there are no non-physical entities, the possibility of a "non-physical" explanation for "thinking" is frequently not entertained. The philosophical underpinnings of AI, whether the strong or weak AI camps, hardly entertain other philosophical possibilities. And while the role of "thinking" may be one of the primary aspects of the human being, as we have seen, it is not definitive of identity.

10.4 People, Machines, and the Non-Algorithmic

Finally, we consider other "aspects" of being human that are just as important as "thinking," but currently difficult to define in Turing machine algorithmic terms. In so doing, we move from those aspects of intelligence, such as creativity, that are just considered hard to define algorithmically, to those that may be fundamentally impossible. These aspects of "being human" include consciousness, emotion, creativity, and life itself. They entail the philosophical difficulties of assigning "meaning" and intentional states that may forever render AI impossible. Perhaps the ultimate difficulty is describing free will, algorithmically. The associated question is whether human identity entails a "spiritual" dimension that would render mechanical simulation impossible.

These considerations of the non-algorithmic elements of "intelligence" are at a different level to the question of whether other "algorithmic" mechanisms may be necessary to reproduce them. For example, Hecht-Nielsen argues that cognition in humans and many animals occurs in a very different, non-algorithmic, and less-complex way than has been widely assumed until now; but does not challenge the possibility of some mechanism reproducing them. The Hecht-Nielsen theory posits that "all aspects of cognition — seeing, hearing, understanding, planning and so on — are carried out using a single type of knowledge (antecedent support) and a single information processing operation called 'confabulation' which is carried out between the brain's cerebral cortex and thalamus. The scientist's theory hypothesizes that confabulation is the only information processing operation used in cognition" (http://www.physorg.com/news3358.html). "In short," Hecht-Nielsen concluded, "brains carry out cognition using a simple, universal, information-processing operation — confabulation — in concert with vast amounts of accumulated knowledge of a very simple kind." This kind of hypothesis is merely a statement that the current algorithmic methods are not really adequate and a different type of algorithm is necessary, rather than a challenge to the possibility of algorithmic description at all.

We start by considering "emotion" as a non-algorithmic element of human intelligence. Pickard (2001) recognised the role of emotion in AI systems. Emotion is, of course, a key ingredient of human communication, facilitating relationships and communication. It is a vital part of achieving "human-like behaviour." Some aspects of emotion may be algorithmically defined, with a mechanistic relationship between the physical and emotional. For example, "fear" is associated with certain physiochemical reactions. It is debatable whether the physical causes the emotional, or whether thinking itself can control the emotional. While there may be some simple relationship between emotion and behaviour at the lowest level, very quickly, emotion becomes more complex, and has important results in social interactions, perceptions of meaning, and human relationships. It is not clear that there is an algorithmic explanation for the role of emotion in human beings. Emotion is related to the "inner life" and qualitative states that are hard to quantify and measure and express. It may even be meaningless to have a simulation of emotion.

However, AI has attempted to simulate emotion in machines. Pickard (2001) describes prototype systems that can begin to detect and label aspects of human emotional expression, and respond to users experiencing frustration and other negative emotions, with components of human skills such as active listening, empathy, and sympathy (Pickard & Klien, 2001). A proper understanding of emotion creates the possibility for more sophisticated interfaces. Adaptive user interfaces may be able to do more than just optimise for data entry efficiency. There is the potential to respond to the user's perceived mood (Help aids like Microsoft "paperclip" may be endowed with a renewed user empathy that knows when not to appear without being told!). And of course the "emotion" behind speech is a vital component of its meaning. So while the lowest levels of emotional behaviour in people may be physiologically easy to comprehend, the higher levels — the social outworkings, the semantic implications, and relational consequences — are far more complex. Emotional intelligence may even mean that the ultimate question in AI may not be "can a machine think?," but "can a machine relate?" Appropriate behaviour within a social (relational) setting will then become evidence for intelligence, rather than rational cognitive thought. While recent work is pursuing "emotional machine intelligence," there are clearly limited results.

Another non-algorithmic aspect of human intelligence is creativity. Bunge (1983a, 1983b) points out that there is no algorithm for scientific discovery. The creative process of writing algorithms also does not, in itself, appear to be algorithmic. Artistic expression, like being able to compose a symphony or write a poem, is non-algorithmic. But what does it mean to be creative? New creation appears to involve something old in part: a new item could hardly be called a work of art if it had nothing in common with other such works. But what part is not "computerizable?" One cannot will, for example, a scientific discovery, but one can do things that are conducive to producing it. Creative thinking, according to Treffinger (1994) is a matter of "making and expressing meaningful connections." Thus perhaps in part, creativity is programmable, but the precise steps not definitive. Perhaps it is a huge search procedure, although that does not explain the "out of the blue" discoveries that do occur in human intelligence. Whether algorithmically programmable or not, creativity is not well enough understood to be programmed at present.

Perhaps the best-known attempt to reproduce creativity and discovery programs in AI is found in AM (Lenat, 1976). AM is a program that discovers concepts in elementary mathematics and set theory. It is a theory driven discovery system. AM has two inputs: (1) a description of some concepts of set theory (in LISP form). For example, set union, intersection, the empty set. (2) information on how to perform mathematics, for example functions. AM employed: a frame-based representation of mathematical concepts; slot and filler notations to create new concepts (slots) and fill in their values; heuristic search with 250 heuristics represent hints about activities that might lead to interesting discoveries and an agenda control of discovery process. BACON is another discovery program (Langley, Simon, Bradshaw, & Zytkow, 1987). It employs a data-driven approach based on the idea that many discoveries are made from observing data obtained from the world and making sense of it. BACON holds some constants, and attempts to notice trends in the data. While recent work builds on these earliest discovery systems, there are clearly limited results and much further work to undertake before "discovery" and "creativity" is understood and reproduced.

We continue the consideration of the "non-algorithmic" with a focus on consciousness. And consciousness is another "aspect" of the human being for which there may just not be an algorithmic possibility. Neuroscience has indicated that consciousness is the synergy generated with the interoperation of various parts of the human brain, what have come to be called the "neuronal correlates of consciousness." Currently, there is no general consensus as to how to define or measure conscious awareness. Despite this, many feel that consciousness is a fundamental determinant of what it means to be human. A definition of conscious can be cited as "having an awareness of one's environment and one's own existence, sensations, and thoughts." The possibility of artificial consciousness has been discussed in various forums.

One forum where consciousness is discussed is the philosophical forum, and the debate between physicalism and dualism. Dualists believe that there is something non-physical about consciousness, whilst physicalists hold that all things are physical. The term "digital sentience" is used to describe the concept that computers could someday be capable of independent thought through artificial consciousness in devices that appear conscious. These devices might either simulate consciousness or actually be conscious, but provided they appear conscious, the desired result has been achieved. Skeptics point out that a fundamental component of consciousness is subjective phenomenal experience, which may be beyond the scope of computational simulation.

In AI, one fundamental issue is whether or not conscious awareness is simply a by-product of complex intelligent system. Those who assume that consciousness is simply a by-product or an emergent property argue that in humans, a single neuron has nothing resembling intelligence. Yet in combination, billions of neurons combine to form a mind that does possess intelligence. It would appear then, that the brain is more than the sum of its parts. Intelligence emerges with sufficient configural complexity of neurons. So it is not inconceivable that other attributes, such as consciousness, creativity, and emotionality, may emerge as a by-product of complex artificially intelligent systems. In general then, the idea is that consciousness is just a by-product of any sufficiently complex brain, and AI engineers need not try to isolate and recreate it specifically: it will emerge automatically as needed.

Daniel Dennett (1994) said in his article, "Consciousness in human and robot minds," "It might be vastly easier to make an initially unconscious or non-conscious 'infant' robot and let it 'grow up' into consciousness, more or less the way we all do." He explained that the robot Cog, described there, "Will not be an adult at first, in spite of its adult size. It is being designed to pass through an extended period of artificial infancy, during which it will have to learn from experience, experience it will gain in the rough-and-tumble environment of the real world." Researchers are essentially asking: "can a machine know?" Ultimately, that question would have to be applied to the machine's consciousness of self, that is, is the machine self-conscious? Descartes battled with the question of knowing our being many years ago, and of course defined the nature of personhood in terms of thought: "cogito ergo sum." It was because the person could think that they knew they existed! This becomes circular when we are attempting to go beyond the basis of cognition alone to define personhood, and it is at this point that theology can make a more useful contribution.

Related to the idea of consciousness is the question of the nature of life itself. Life is a multifaceted concept. In biology, an entity has traditionally been considered to be alive if it exhibits all the following phenomena at least once during its existence: (1) growth, (2) metabolism, consuming, transforming and storing energy/mass; growing by absorbing and reorganizing mass; excreting waste, (3) motion, either moving itself, or having internal motion, (4) reproduction, the ability to create entities that are similar to itself and (5) response to stimuli — the ability to measure properties of its surrounding environment, and act upon certain conditions. Unfortunately, it is not difficult to find counterexamples and examples that require further elaboration. For example, male mules are not alive as they are sterile and cannot reproduce, while fire would be considered living. There is a certain conceptual distance between AI and biological or organic intelligence, in that it still remains only a simulation of real intelligence. Therefore, AI bears no resemblance to natural intelligence, whose many dimensions are beyond the grasp of science. The successes so far have only been in the simulation of intelligence, not the creation of true intelligence.

Finally, in a consideration of the non-algorithmic, philosophically, there are difficulties with assigning meaning to any object. As Searle has introduced, many processes involving semantics, as distinct from syntax, appear to be non-algorithmic. Also internal, subjective, qualitative states, such as the redness of red, aesthetic experiences of beauty and revulsion, are also inherently non-algorithmic. Searle takes the position that there is something fundamentally different between brains and computers, which allows brains to have these intentional states (i.e., understand) while computers cannot. The "semantics" of an object or event may be related to the concept of "free will." Much of the debate about free will centers on whether we human beings have it and what it is. Free will is often considered to be the capacity of rational agents to choose a course of action from among various alternatives. Some have defined "free will" as an impression. Most philosophers suppose that the concept of free will is very closely connected to the concept of moral responsibility. Philosophers who distinguish freedom of action and freedom of will do so because our success in carrying out our ends depends, in part, on factors wholly beyond our control. Philosophically, the possibility of "free will" presents an inherent difficulty with the algorithmic, which suggests as it does that all is determined in advance. The possession of "free will" is related to the question of whether human identity entails a "spiritual" dimension that would render mechanical simulation impossible. That is, not only whether a machine can think, but also whether it can have a soul (in a humanistic sense rather than a religious sense), have an inner life, have semantics (as distinguished from "mere syntax"), have content (as distinguished from "mere form"), and have personhood.

In summary, the earliest concern in AI was with rational human thought. Concern has recently shifted to "emotional intelligence" and the relational ability of machines. Whether this can be defined algorithmically or not remains to be seen. Human consciousness itself presents a new challenge, as this dynamic of the human realm is also considered. Whether a machine can think or not is just a small question in the bigger context of whether it can be conscious, and whether this can be achieved algorithmically. These other aspects of human "intelligence" — emotion and consciousness — make it questionable whether a mathematical model, ala Turing machine computation, could adequately capture intelligence. Whatever "computations" and "algorithms" we may posit are in operation in the human mind, they are not necessarily the "algorithms" and "computations" that would be understood by formalised mathematics. It is not necessarily possible to devise a Turing machine to move the "human system" through a set of states from the start to finish; nor capture that in a set of "rewrite" rules that reduce the workings of a human being to a lambda calculus expression, or equivalent Post system/Turing machine.

10.5 References

Bunge, M. (1983a). *Treatise on basic philosophy (Vol. 5): Exploring the world.* Dordrecht: Rediel.

Bunge, M. (1983b). *Treatise on basic philosophy (Vol. 6): Understanding the world.* Dordrecht: Rediel.

Church, A. (1936). An unsolvable problem of elementary number theory. *American Journal of Mathematics, 58,* 345-363.

Copeland. (1998).

Coplan, P. (2004). *Jesus, religions, and just war: Is there such a thing as a just war?* Discussion on religion, religious wars, and just war doctrine. Retrieved from http://www.everystudent.com/wires/justwar.html

Davies, P. (1991). *Theories of the mind.* London: Penguin Books.

Dennett, D. (1994, September 1-3). Consciousness in human and robot minds. *IIAS Symposium on Cognition, Computation and Consciousness, Kyoto.* Retrieved from http://ase.tufts.edu/cogstud/papers/concrobt.htm

Fetzer, J. (1994). Mental algorithms: Are minds computational systems? *Pragmatics & Cognition, 2*(1), 1-29.

Fodor, J. (1975). *The language of thought.* New York: Thomas Crowell.

Gödel. (1931). Über formal unentscheidbare Sätze der Principia Mathematica und verwandter Systeme. *Monatshefte für Mathematik und Physik, 38,* 173-198. Retrieved from http://home.ddc.net/ygg/etext/godel

Langley, P., Simon, H. A., Bradshaw, G. L., & Zytkow, J. M. (1987). *Scientific discovery: Computational explorations of the creative process.* Cambridge, MA: MIT Press.

Lenat, D. B. (1976). *AM: An artificial intelligence approach to discovery in mathematics as heuristic search.* PhD thesis, Stanford University.

Lucas, J. R. (1988). The Godelian argument. *Truth, an International, Inter-Disciplinary Journal of Christian Thought,* 2.

McArthur, R. P. (1991). *From logic to computing.* Belmont, CA: Wadsworth.

Monell, J. & Margineantu, D. (1996). *The equivalence of Post systems and Turing machines.* Retrieved from http://citeseer.ist.psu.edu/34521.html

Penrose, R. (1994). *Shadows of the mind: A search for the missing science of consciousness.* New York: Oxford University Press.

Pickard, R. W. (2001). What does it mean for a computer to "have" emotions?. Chapter to appear in R. Trappl, P. Petta, & S. Payr (Eds.), *Emotions in humans and artifacts.*

Pickard, R. W., & Klien, J. (2001). Computers that recognize and respond to user emotion: Theoretical and practical implications. To appear in *Interacting with computers.*

Post, (1943). Formal reductions of the general combinatorial decision problem. *American Journal of Mathematics, 65,* 197-215.

Putnam, H. (1961). Brains and behavior. *American Association for the Advancement of Science, Section L* (History and Philosophy of Science).

Putnam, H. (1988). *Representation and reality.* Cambridge, MA: MIT Press.

Robinson. (1988).

Searle, J. (1980). Minds, brains, and programs. *Behavioral and Brain Sciences, 3,* 417-424.

Searle. (1992).

Smolensky, P. (1988). On the proper treatment of connectionism. *Behavioral and Brain Sciences, 11,* 1-23.

Treffinger, D. J. (1994). Productive thinking: Toward authentic instruction and assessment. *Journal of Secondary Gifted Education, 6*(1), 30-37.

Turing, A. (1936). On computable numbers, with an application to the Entscheidungsproblem. In *Proceedings of the London Mathematical Society* (Series 2, Vol. 42). Retrieved from http://www.abelard.org/turpap2/tp2-ie.asp

Turing, A. (1950). Computing machinery and intelligence. *Mind, 59*(236), 433-460.

Chapter 11

Principle-Based Engineering

"As far as the laws of mathematics refer to reality, they are not certain; and as far as they are certain, they do not refer to reality."

Albert Einstein

"If scientific reasoning were limited to the logical processes of arithmetic, we should not get very far in our understanding of the physical world. One might as well attempt to grasp the game of poker entirely by the use of the mathematics of probability."

Vannevar Bush

11.1 Introduction

This chapter discusses a new conception of computation. The conception is one of constraints rather than rules. In contrast to the rule-based approach of Turing machines, Post systems and lambda calculus, the constraint-based approach "models" the constraints in operation in the system, and between the system and the environment. There are similarities with Putnam's idea that "everything is computation" because (1) computation must be "situated" in a profound way, embedded in its environment, but, there is also (2) a move away from the intuitive idea of "algorithm" as a step-by-step procedure, modellling the behaviour of the system in its environment, requiring a mapping of the abstract "algorithm" states to the physical states of "reality."

The importance of physically realising a constraint-based system gives rise to principle-based engineering (PBE) as a new conception of computation. It requires intelligent systems are situated in the world and embedded in context, just as human beings are. There is no attempt to model relevant aspects of the world, but the world is a part of the system. We find some theological themes emerge in the importance of (1) "incarnating" computation; Incarnation is an important component of humanity: people have physical bodies and isolating "intelligence," and an abstract model, separate from the physical world, is not helpful in capturing human identity. There is also a theological theme in moving towards (2) a constraint-based understanding of the universe. The popular and prevailing underlying "mechanism" in many domains, especially artificial life and emergent AI, is that of "evolution." Theology recognises that evolution is limited in the explanation that it gives about phenomena, and a constraint-based vision is even more helpful in many instances.

Finally, we contrast more fully PBE, with the prevailing artificial life approach to AI, showing the similarities and differences between constraint-based systems and evolutionary systems as paradigms for intelligent systems. We consider why a constraint-based approach to AI is more powerful than evolutionary methods, and when the constraint-based approach is situated within a physical context, evolutionary methods are a special outworking of a more general constraint-based paradigm. Thus PBE, as a constraint-based understanding of computation, firmly situated as a physical system in the world, interacting with the world in that situation, is a more promising paradigm of AI. It is not symbolic AI, or sub-symbolic AI, or artificial life, but a new school in PBE.

The objective of this chapter is to outline principle-based engineering, motivating it as a situated, constraint-based paradigm of AI that can be compared and contrasted with aymbolic AI, sub-symbolic AI and artificial life. We find that a constraint-based conception of computation makes an important distinction from the rule-based paradigm that characterises Turing machines, Post systems and lambda calculus. We emphasise the importance of situating computation when an intelligent system is being designed, and situating that intelligent system within the physical world, with the world a part of the system. We are keen to consider the theological underpinning of such "incarnated" computing; reminding that the physical body is a vital component of human identity; being situated in the human context is vital for semantics and appropriate human-like behaviour.

11.2 Constraint-Based Computation

In this section, we consider a new conception of computation that is different to the Turing machine. It is a conception of computation particularly applicable to "intelligent machines," recognising that "intelligence" needs to be embedded within the world, and that the world (in its entirety) cannot be modelled. It is not Putnam's idea, where every physical system could be considered to be a computational realisation, although does involve situating the computation, with the world as an integral part of the system. Neither is it Searle's suggestion that the "interpretation" of the physical system depends upon the observer. This would mean computation is a matter of individual interpretation, although it does recognise that there are an infinite number of "interpretations" of the physical world, making it impossible to abstract.

The new conception of computation bears some resemblance to the "implementation" question raised by Matthias Scheutz (1998). Scheutz sees that one weakness of computationalism is its conception of computation itself. Specifically, the "implementation" of the computation, that is, relating physical systems and abstract objects. There is an explanatory gap between abstract "computation" and concrete "physical systems." A "good" theory of implementation should deliver a constrained link between the concrete and the abstract, not depend upon it. Implementation normally finds a state-to-state correspondence between physical systems and abstract objects. A better theory of implementation would exploit descriptions of certain properties of concrete systems and abstract formalisms in such a way that a state-to-state correspondence results. Scheutz is seeking a concept of implementation that is able to relate the abstract model and concrete world.

To some extent, the problem with relating the abstract model of computation with the physical world is with the intuitive notion of algorithm as step-by-step procedure. The algorithm is a computational model. A model is something that stands in for, and that "corresponds" in relevant ways to the system being modelled. It is an abstraction of the components of the system that is "relevant." Models are useful when the system is too large to manipulate directly, or when it might be dangerous or expensive to actually do so. Models often bear a physical resemblance to the system they represent, being scaled down or having only key features included. A computational model, which is a step-by-step procedure, is not necessarily a true abstraction of what is occurring in reality. Forcing reality (e.g., the human mind) into that mold may be impossible.

With such a "model" of computation, it is the intuitive notion of "algorithm" and "procedure" that is inadequate, with "computable" being defined as a step-by-step specification. This idea of "computable" makes the mapping between the "model" and "reality" difficult. As we have seen, such computation in Turing machines, Post systems and lambda calculus are all essentially equivalent forms because they are rule-based forms. In linguistic terms, they are "generative grammars." They are systems of rewrite rules that generate a formal language. The formal language corresponds to an "algorithm" defining the computation. It is a step-by-step procedure that moves the abstract system, and supposedly its implementation in the physical realisation, through a series of states. The conception of computation is essentially rule based. However, rule-based "descriptions" are not the only descriptions that exist: they are not the only "models" of reality that can be found.

An alternative to the rule-based paradigm is found in the constraint-based paradigm. Within linguistics, their differences can be appreciated by considering their application to languages and grammars. Rules are generative, and describe how to produce sentences of a language from the underlying symbols. Constraints are non-generative, and describe how to verify sentences of a language when presented a string of symbols. Constraints provide a series of "tests" that make it possible to determine whether an item, for example, a sentence, is part of the language or not. In the simplest language consisting of pairs of characters, a set of rules might dictate the valid form of a sentence, S, for example, "S -> pairs; pairs -> a a; pairs -> b b; pairs

-> &," and so forth. A constraint-based description would simply have a cardinality constraint on the sentence, S. For example, "card(S) == 2," where "card" was a count of the length of S, dictating it must be 2. There may be other constraints in operation as well, such as the constraint that the symbols of S must be a member of numbers or letters, or some other symbol. The more that is known about the reality, the more constraints that can be specified. Some constraints may be unimportant. Constraints make it possible to "test" whether a sentence is an example of a language; rules make it possible to "generate" a sentence that is an example of a language.

Linguistic theory was, for many years, dominated by generative grammars. Attempting to describe the "form" of natural languages in terms of rules. For example, specifying that a sentence had the overall form of "subject," "verb" followed by "object." In the late 1980s, Noam Chomsky (1986) proposed a constraint-based approach to language description in "Government and binding theory." The approach was later called "Principles and parameters," reflecting the idea that a set of principles operated with parameter settings that determined the form of different natural languages (e.g., whether the "subject" did come before the "verb" or not). This grammar explains the general structure of language via a set of principles. There are particular parameter settings that vary according to the particular human language being described. Linguistic analysis of languages became an attempt to articulate these "constraints" in operation, rather than create a set of rules that described how to generate the language.

The important difference between the rule-based and constraint-based approach comes when the cardinality of the language is considered. Natural language had always been considered a "countably" infinite set of sentences. Langendoen and Postal (1984) challenge that perspective. They provided a mathematical argument disproving the "cardinality of the set of sentences in any natural language is finite." Using the possibility of conjunction to conjoin any number of possibly infinite clauses, they found natural language to be "uncountable." It was a non-denumerable set, in contrast to languages that were denumerable. This was the natural language vastness theorem. Thus, an optimal grammar would make no constraint on the length of sentences, not even a requirement that each sentence be finite. Of course, a principle-based grammar was exciting because it was not restricted to describing denumerable languages, as was the rule-based approach.

We may wonder what use such a constraint-based approach has (for language), when in reality, we are not going to encounter any sentences of infinite length, let alone encounter the distinction raised by different orders of infinity in uncountable sets. The strength of the constraint-based approach lies in its usefulness for explaining ungrammatical sentences: sentences that nevertheless, can often be understood and retain semantics. The explanation of the sentence is made in terms of constraint violation and constraint satisfaction. Generally, one or two constraints may be violated in an ungrammatical sentence. Constraint-based systems (either in syntax or semantics) can deal with these ungrammatical but meaningful sentences, while the rule-based descriptions are generally at a loss for explaining ungrammatical sentences since the string is outside what would be generated by the set of rules, and unless another set of rules is constructed for generating the possible ungrammatical sentences, any parsing system does not know how to deal with the sentence. This makes the constraint-based approach more "flexible."

Translating this "constraint-based" approach into the realm of computation opens up all sorts of possibilities. The paradigm is simply outside the current conception of computability. The Chomsky hierarchy defines the grammars and languages that are generated all in rule-based terms; every grammar in the hierarchy is essentially a finite-state machine, specifying how to generate strings of an appropriate type of language. A constraint-based approach makes no such generative description, but provides a series of tests by which membership of a sentence in a particular language can be verified. The constraint-based sense of "computation" is non-rule-based, and not comparable to the rule-based approaches to Turing machine, Post systems and lambda calculus.

Translating this "constraint-based" approach into the realm of computation is called principle-based engineering (Spenceley, 1992; Stender, Addis, & Spenceley, 1993). Computation is not moving a system through a set of states: rather it is constraint-satisfaction. This means the intuitive notion of "algorithm" is one of "constraint satisfaction." For example, if there is a system that can determine whether a Turing machine will halt (such as a human mind exerting a series of constraint-tests on the example to see if they are satisfied or not), then there is a solution and the problem is no longer undecidable, although there may not be a step-by-step algorithmic description of the solution. There is also the possibility of "fuzzy" computation as constraints are or are not satisfied within a system, and between the system and the environment. Thus, PBE is a constraint-based conception of computation.

PBE is distinct from the constraint-based approach of traditional AI. In classical AI, constraint satisfaction may be considered a particular technique of symbolic AI ,where it is a method of problem solving called constraint satisfaction. A constraint is simply a logical relation among several unknowns (or variables), each taking a value in a given domain. A constraint thus restricts the possible values that variables can take: it represents some partial information about the variables of interest. Constraints arise naturally in most areas of human endeavour, for example, the three angles of a triangle sum to 180 degrees. The main advantage of constraint satisfaction is the declarative nature of the task. It also makes it possible to integrate a variety of special-purpose algorithms, while presenting a coherent view to users.

Constraint satisfaction is a general problem in which the goal is to find values for a set of variables that will satisfy a given set of constraints. It is the core of many applications in artificial intelligence, and has found its application in many areas, such as planning and scheduling. In symbolic AI, a constraint satisfaction problem is characterized by:

- a set of variables $\{x1, x2, .., xn\}$,
- for each variable xi a domain Di with the possible values for that variable, and
- a set of constraints, that is relations, that are assumed to hold between the values of the variables. These relations can be given intentionally, that is as a formula, or extensionally, that is as a set, or procedurally, that is with an appropriate generating or recognising function.

The constraint satisfaction problem is to find, for each i from 1 to n, a value in Di for xi, so that all constraints are satisfied. A CS problem can easily be stated as a sentence in first order logic of the form: $(\exists x1)..(\exists xn)\ (D1(x1)\ \&\ ..\ Dn(xn) \Rightarrow C1..Cm)$. A CS problem is usually represented as an undirected graph called constraint graph, where the nodes are the variables and the edges are the binary constraints. Unary constraints can be disposed of by just redefining the domains to contain only the values that satisfy all the unary constraints. Higher order constraints are represented by hyperarcs. In the following, we restrict our attention to the case of unary and binary constraints. The operation of a constraint satisfaction system in symbolic AI consists in searching for combinations of variables that satisfy those conditions, this being the solution. There are various possibilities for algorithmic solutions:

- **Generate and test:** We generate, one by one, all possible complete variable assignments, and for each we test if it satisfies all constraints. The corresponding program structure is very simple, just nested loops, one per variable. In the innermost loop, we test each constraint. In most situations, this method is intolerably slow.
- **Backtracking:** We order the variables in some fashion, trying to place first the variables that are more highly constrained or with smaller ranges. This order has a great impact on the efficiency of solution algorithms and is examined elsewhere. We start assigning values to variables. We check constraint satisfaction at the earliest possible time, and extend an assignment if the constraints involving the currently bound variables are satisfied.
- **Consistency driven:** Consistency-based algorithms use information from the constraints to reduce the search space as early in the search as it is possible.

PBE is also distinct from constraint programming, that is, the programming paradigm in which a set of constraints that a solution must meet are specified, rather than a set of steps to obtain such a solution. Constraint programming is the study of computational systems based on constraints. The idea of constraint programming is to solve problems by stating constraints (conditions, properties) that must be satisfied by the solution. While programming with constraints makes it possible to model and specify problems with uncertain, incomplete information and to solve combinatorial problems, they by no means solve all difficulties. Perhaps the biggest difficulty is the computational complexity involved in exhaustive searches for variable combinations that satisfy the requirements. There is also the criticism that at one level, constraint programming is too high-level. There is a need for constraint programming to be more open and extensible; at another level constraint programming is too low-level. The gap between the description and the program is non-trivial. Constraint programs are not incremental. Upgrading an off-line solution in a reasonable fashion, and in a reasonable time, to absorb unexpected events is a fundamental challenge for the constraint community. Constraint propagation is too local. Cooperation between solvers is still primitive. There is a strong need for new theoretical and experimental results on cooperation between independent solvers.

PBE does not seek to instantiate variables; it does not necessarily entail a formal specification of constraints (that reduce the system to a logical problem, that is a formal system). As we shall see, PBE systems are based on physically realised components situated in the world. There are similarities with agent-based systems and some aspects of artificial life, although we explain how there are also differences, and PBE does not entail the "emergence" that artificial life often requires.

11.3 Situated Computation

The distinction between "physically realising" a system and mathematically describing that system through an effective procedure was one that Turing never found to be important. It did not matter whether the Turing machine was implemented through the electronic circuitry of digital computers or the "biological stuff" of DNA, whether cardboard paper and glue or silicon. The point of importance was the formalised mathematical description (the model). The notion of algorithm was a mathematical concept that could exist entirely separate and in isolation of any implementation. With PBE, the emphasis is upon the reality, not the model. Computation must be "situated" in a profound way, embedded in its environment. We may call it "incarnational computation." It shares similarities with Putnam's idea that "everything is computation," although we do not attempt to make the mapping from physical states of reality to "algorithmic" states. Rather, we locate the model with the implementation.

With rule-based computation, there are the on going questions of how to explain breakdowns of this correspondence between "model" and "reality." It is not just that algorithms "fail" under "unusual conditions" that were never anticipated, or that computer components suddenly malfunction, rendering even algorithms that have been "proved" useless, or that real world power failures that bring the electronic universe to a total standstill (in complete disregard of the abstract model). While these are genuine aspects of reality that defy modelling, there are deeper problems with modelling and abstracting "relevant" parts of the universe that AI hit on a long time ago in the frame-problem, in expanding microworlds to the real world, in providing "intelligence" that contained "common sense reasoning," in integrating robotic devices with the abstracted planning systems, and in many other facets of its endeavour to create intelligence that have assumed mathematical modelling of the world is both possible and necessary.

While PBE shares similarities with emergent agent-based AI and artificial life systems, the philosophical perspective of PBE does not permit "simulation" or "model" apart from the realisation. This makes PBE distinct to these more general models that can be reduced to Turing machine computation, because they are simulated. PBE requires a direct realisation in the world. PBE requires a system of any significant complexity is made of a number of interacting components that interact with each other and with the world. Additionally, PBE entertains the possibility for non-evolutionary processes to be the fundamental processes of the system, making it broader in scope from artificial life and evolutionary AI. This represents a shift from the Darwinian ideas that have permeated many different fields, with principles that are often greatly twisted from the context of natural evolution, where Darwin originally introduced them.

PBE is different from artificial life because it entertains other possibilities for "fundamental processes" over and above Darwinian evolutionary principles. In much of the artificial life paradigm, "evolutionary" principles are deemed to be the fundamental processes of the universe, creating the behaviour of the system. Artificial life takes Darwinian principles, such as "environment tailoring its forms" and "fittest forms surviving" to be the main mechanisms of all systems. Almost two centuries later, Darwinian principles are still popular, but no matter how worthy they were as ideas, they are not the only processes of the universe. The evolutionary paradigm of artificial life is narrowly, and often loosely, focused upon Darwin's postulated mechanisms. PBE examines other possibilities for "fundamental processes," and combines these with the crucial element of embodiment, or physical realisation. There is great potential for such "non-evolutionary" processes to account for phenomena in the natural world and the human situation. Indeed, Fodor (1975) proposed the process of "interacting modules" to explain elements of human cognition in the mind. While the behaviour of the system may develop through time, "evolution" is, at best, a twisted metaphor to explain the phenomena.

PBE is also related to the cellular automata models of early artificial intelligence (with the proviso that the models are physically realised). Cellular automata systems placed emphasis upon "interacting" entities, each operating according to their own rules. A focus is made upon the individual automata, although behaviour may "emerge" that demonstrates interesting "cooperation" between entities. In the cellular automata, there was no a priori specification of a constraint between particular entities, but frequently mutual behaviour emerged representing a constraint (such as the glider pattern that sometimes appears in Conway's "Game of Life" automata).

The physical realisation is the computation. It may seem that the reliance on "physical realisation" for computation means that principle-based engineering is the ultimate in "materialism," where the physical system is the ultimate point of reference (http://www.artsci.wustl.edu/~philos/MindDict/materialism.html) rather than the "non-material" in the abstract model of Turing machine computability. However, principle-based engineering does not entail the assertion that there is only the "material," it merely maintains that there is a "unity" between the physically realised and the mathematically modelled design. This is the incarnation. It may also seem that PBE is dualistic: where a distinction is made between the "material" and "immaterial." However, once again this is not the case. Principle-based engineering actually removes the distinction between the "immaterial model" and the "material realisation" by asserting that they are one and the same. In this sense, principle-based engineering shares some similarity with the double aspect philosophy (Davies, 1991) that has been used to explain human mind.

Paul Davies (1991) describes the "double aspect" theory of mind that sees a unification of "what is" as primary. There are various versions of the "double aspect" theory, ranging from that where "experience" and "consciousness" are primary in an almost existentialist framework, to that where there is some "neutral stuff" proposed, where mental events and physical events are both some aspect of that neutral stuff. Double aspect theory steps outside the prevailing dualistic/materialistic paradigm into one where there is a "unity" of substance. The philosophical paradigm shift also introduces difficulties in terminology since "mind" and "body," "spiritual" and "physical," and other descriptors come loaded with philosophical meanings from other schools because of the ontological divisions that have emerged in other schools. The absence of an appropriate "paradigm-free ontology" is part of the difficulty, together with agreeing upon the "aspects" that are part of the "unity." For example, double aspect may assume "material" and "immaterial" are all part of the same reality, but there is no reason why there may not be a three-fold ontology that identifies "mind," "body," and "soul" as components of the human reality: components that need to be melded into a unity in what we may call "triple aspect" theory. We may even decide that "will" is a separate "aspect" specific to human identity, that is, separate nature to mind, body, or soul, and require a "quadruple aspect" theory to unite the "categories." The main emphasis is that there is a unity.

Davies (1991) explains that advocates of "double aspect" theory have included Spinoza, Bertrand Russel, and David Hume. Spinoza thinks that there is only one type of substance, identical with the totality of what exists. Spinoza expounded his ideas in a series of five books, with the first claiming to demonstrate both the necessary existence and the unitary nature of the unique, single substance that comprises all of reality. Spinoza believed that "Deus sive Natura" ("god or nature") was the most fitting name for this being, and he argued that its infinite attributes account for every feature of the universe. Bertrand Russell also expounded a version of "neutral monism" with the idea that mental events and physical events are both to be reduced to aspects of some neutral stuff, which stuff considered by itself, is neither physical nor mental. David Hume considered that our sense perception gives us access to entities that are neither mental nor physical, and mind was essentially perceptions. These explanations are particularly associated with the connection between mind and body, although encompass general theories of "the reality that is." When considering the "mind-body" question, it is not possible to ignore the explanations that have specifically focused on the nature of the human being.

In this final category of the double aspect theory of mind is William James. In *Essays in Radical Empiricism*, James (1912) set out the metaphysical view most commonly known as "neutral monism," according to which there is one fundamental "stuff" that is neither material nor mental. James holds that mind and matter are both aspects of, or structures formed from, a more fundamental stuff-pure experience-that (despite being called "experience") is neither mental nor physical. Pure experience, James explains, is "the immediate flux of life which furnishes the material to our later reflection with its conceptual categories ... a that which is not yet any definite what, tho' ready to be all sorts of whats ... " Through this neutral monism he argues for a fourfold structure of self-entailing the material, the social, the spiritual, and the pure ego. The spiritual self is regarded as the awareness or consciousness that a person has of their perceptions. The concept of spiritual self is obtained by thinking of us as thinkers and is a product of reflection. It may simply be consciousness itself derived from introspection. With this perspective, the "thought computations" of the mind are the primary reality.

While some versions of double aspect theory postulate a different kind of "substance," principle-based engineering postulates an underlying universal "process," that of "entity interaction." This is the mechanism of constraint satisfaction. Thus, PBE refers to process, just as evolution is a process. The way that principle-based engineering "embeds" the process in the world, in a way that Turing machines can never be embedded, makes it a unique paradigm of "computation" for intelligent systems (or even "complex systems," in the mathematical sense of chaotic behaviours that sometimes defy mathematical explanation); one that goes towards solving the mind-body problem by asserting that it too is simply "computation" embodied in the world. The "embodiment" of the process of an intelligent system within the world is important for many reasons:

- The physical world is properly regarded as a part of the intelligent system, not just in terms of the inputs and outputs that the system makes, but its very situation within the universe is part of the system's "properties" that can never be modelled (see the existentialist philosophy of Heidegger (1996) with its emphasis on "being-in-the-world" or Dasein).
- The physical world within which the intelligent system exists cannot be modelled without "reproducing" the entire universe, and it is impossible to extract those key elements of the physical world that are "relevant" (although one may have the impression of being able to isolate key elements for a sorting algorithm or some less ambitious system, the concern of the whole enterprise of software engineering and database modelling).
- The "situation" provides a context and semantics for the intelligent system, whether the system perceives these or not is inconsequential (see the principles of "relevance" in natural language communication advocated by Grice (1989), where the essential feature of communication is the expression and recognition of intentions determined by contextual location).
- Physical realisation of a system through "components" that may fail, and so forth, is part of "computation" that may lead to "unpredictable" results or "non-determinism" in a way the mathematical model does not describe.
- There are physical phenomena that mathematical models just cannot describe, for example, chaotic weather patterns and other complex systems are part of the world for which there is, at best, a poor model, but whose "implementation" exists as the "experience" of daily life.
- The behaviour of people is difficult to describe "algorithmically," not just in terms of the difficulty in modelling it, but their autonomy and free volition.
- Embedding the computation within the world removes the distinction between "observer" and "observed." In terms of quantum mechanics, the "observer" is part of that which is "observed."

In this "incarnational shift" of PBE, we find theological themes emerge.

First, the focus on system description in terms of processes that are not necessarily "evolutionary" both broadens the scope of possibility for the underlying mechanisms, and challenges the Darwinian influence that has permeated artificial life. Evolution is a scientific theory, but one which does not adequately capture the "distinctiveness" of humanity as created "Imago Dei"; as such, it is incomplete, even if accurate in some aspects of physical emergence. In rejecting evolution as the ultimate "process" of the universe that may be modelled, and replacing that by constraint satisfaction, PBE may be seen to have theological themes.

Second, the importance of physically realising computation and the constraint-based model also has theological themes. It recognises the importance of "incarnation" in humanity. This is part of human identity: such a vital part that God became incarnate (in Jesus) in order to bring salvation to humanity. The central tenet of Christianity is that Jesus did indeed overcome physical death, rise to life, and thereby make provision for humanity to overcome and transcend this ultimate limitation. The "redemption" of fallen humanity includes this individual physical bodily resurrection. The importance of the "physical" cannot be lost. Dualistic philosophy has penetrated Western and Christian thought, suggesting people are "body and soul." Liberal theology also suggests that "resurrection" is somehow to be understood figuratively, and there is no "bodily" restoration. However, it is a decidedly theological theme that there is a "bodily resurrection," and that the physical is a vital part of what it is to be human. When we transcend the ultimate limitation of "death," we do not loose our physical bodies.

Third, PBE as situated, incarnated, constraint satisfaction gives a new nuance to computationalism. There can be no "disembodied AI" systems, devoid of contextual meaning, unrelated to the "social context" of the human world, operating in "unrelational" abstractions of the universe, and forcing that into a step-by-step procedure, with some series of states and an artificial mapping between the model and the realisation. PBE takes "unity" of substance as primary, and does not distinguish between material and non-material, spiritual and physical, but all such ontological distinctions are aspects of the same reality. PBE represents a philosophical shift from both dualism and materialism to "unity of substance." It challenges the possibility of abstraction of "algorithm" separate from its implementation; and the possibility of "intelligence" separated and isolated from its physical incarnation in a human being: a fundamental tenet of computationalism.

11.4 Constraint Systems and Evolutionary Systems

This section considers the similarities and differences between constraint-based systems and evolutionary systems as paradigms for intelligent systems. We outline the main characteristics of evolutionary theory, and the places where AI has adopted evolutionary principles: in artificial life systems, cellular automata, emergent systems, and genetic algorithms.

We start by outlining some of the evolutionary principles that underpin the evolutionary approach to AI. Evolutionary theory is not a cosmological theory: it is concerned with processes and not with origins of matter. However, its processes operate from the very first moment that such matter did exist. Darwin suggested the theory of evolution in the 19th century. He introduced his ideas in two separate treatises, with the first outlining the basic principles (1859) and the second applying them to humankind (1871). In his later work, *The Descent of Man,* he explained how humans shared a common ancestor with apes. This "common ancestor" extends to all creation, and is perhaps the most stunning tenet of evolution-humans and oak trees, whales and spiders are all related, coming from the same source-whose origin is outside the scope of the theory. "Evolution" stunned the world and Darwin's ideas rapidly gained popularity, despite some opposition from religious quarters.

Naturalistic evolution proposes life emerged from the primeval mass of subatomic particles and radiation. Some suggest the whole universe came into origin 14 billion years ago, 4 billion years ago the earth coalesced (others estimate it took some 20 billion years). Then life began as bacteria deep in rocks, and evolved to form the different species on earth. Biological evolution involves "large-scale evolution" — the descent of different species from a common ancestor over many generations-and "small-scale evolution" via changes in gene frequency in a population from one generation to the next. In large-scale evolution, a branching or splitting process splits off populations split from one another and gradually a new species is made. Then the species stop sharing genes and eventually, genetic differences increase until the group cannot interbreed. Thus, humans did not evolve from modern apes, but humans and modern apes shared a common ancestor, a species that no longer exists.

Thus, Darwin essentially suggested "descent" with "modification by natural selection" (incorporating "strict Darwinism" and "general Darwinism"). From these principles, we have various forms of evolution including Lamarckianism ("inheritance of acquired characteristics"), saltationalism (evolution proceeding by major leaps or jumps), gradualism (slow, uniform accumulation of modifications), punctuated equilibrium (periods of stasis followed by brief, intense periods of speciation), phyletic gradualism (speciation occurs gradually over a species' entire range), orthogenesis (evolution that follows a single direction or specific trend continuously, "straight- line" evolution, often appearing to be independent of natural selection). Often, when evolution is considered, it is used to refer to a mixture of these different ideas. Some of the "principles" of evolution, or the characteristics that are most closely associated with Darwin's original ideas include:

- The mechanism of evolution concerns biological stuff and revolves around changes in a gene pool; thus, it is not correct to speak of "evolution" outside a living biological context: the "evolution of a city" is not evolution.
- The mechanism of natural selection supposes survival of only the fittest, ensuring that similar forms are present in the next generation, and the survival of the fittest is for the benefit of the species, ensuring that it continues so there is an inbuilt assumption that the species wants to survive and continue.
- The environment is important in shaping the forms within it, and this environment is, itself, subject to evolutionary processes
- Evolutionary processes take many, many generations to be implemented (at least macroevolution). They are not "changes" that can happen within a couple of generations. Changes that we may witness in life-forms in a short span of time are adaptations and not true species mutation.
- There can be mutation between species to create a new species, and everything can be traced to the same common

ancestor and ultimately, to a piece of matter whose origin itself is left unexplained by the theory (since it is a not a cosmological account).

- Evolutionary principles suggest a slow path that is a "path of development," including from "simple" to "complex" organisms. There is a general increasing "order" in the universe, rather than decreasing order or cyclic order. But simply because something has a "history," it does not mean that it has "evolved."

Gould (1981) points out that Darwin liked to make a distinction between "the fact of evolution" and proposing a theory, that of natural selection, to explain the mechanism of evolution. Evolutionists have always acknowledged how far we are from completely understanding the mechanisms (theory) by which evolution (claimed "fact") occurred. The existence of "data" in the contemporary world includes fossils, skeleton remains, DNA comparisons of current species and many other scientific observations. The actual "theory" has undergone variations, and as "missing link" data has been discovered, the theory has changed to keep in line with the new data. Some parts of the predicted data are still missing, but that does not destroy the rest of the theory. Muller (1959) makes a similar point about the "uncertainty" of any scientific theory, pointing out that there is no certainty "the honest scientist, like the philosopher, will tell you that nothing whatever can be or has been proved with fully 100% certainty." We may say that there is "evidence," but accepting the theory still requires a certain amount of "belief" and "faith" and willingness to work within the limits of what the human can know, or does know from the data. So the "theory" is only a theory and not proved with 100% certainty: it is just a possible explanation of the data in the contemporary world. The details of the theory have undergone change, but the driving principle is "descent with modification."

Evolution is attributed to purely natural forces, including the survival of the fittest and random mutation. Recently, the union of molecular biology, genetics, and natural selection (Darwinism) lead to what is known as the modern synthesis, a theory about how evolution works at the level of genes, phenotypes, and populations, whereas Darwinism was concerned mainly with organisms, speciation, and individuals. Evolution is precisely defined as any change in the frequency of alleles within a gene pool from one generation to the next. The gene pool is the set of all genes in a species or population (http://www.skeptictank.org/hs/factfaq.htm). Conover and Voorhees (1990) produced an experiment where the environment in a population of fish was held constant (as water) and started with populations of fish that produced skewed sex ratios and ended with populations that produced balanced sex ratios. Since the environment was held constant, the change in the populations was therefore genetic. In other words, the gene pool changed over time. This is the definition of evolution.

The prime example of evolutionary methods in AI is found in genetic algorithms (Goldberg, 1989). Genetic algorithms explicitly model evolving populations. The genetic algorithm is a search and optimisation mechanism. Points in the domain space of the search are encoded as bit strings, called chromosomes, which represent "solutions." An initial population of random-bit strings is generated and valuated for their fitness or goodness in solving the problem. Successive populations are "evolved" from this initial one using three genetic operators: reproduction, crossover, and mutation, modelled on their biological counterparts. Members of a given population are selected with probabilities proportional to their fitness in order to generate the new population. Pairs of chromosomes in the new population are chosen at random to exchange genetic material, their bits, in a mating operation called crossover. This produces two new chromosomes that replace the parents. Randomly chosen bits in the offspring are flipped, called mutation. The algorithm repeats for some specified number of additional generations, evolving the population to contain more and more highly fit chromosomes. When there has been no significant further increase in the average fitness of the population, the best chromosome produced is decoded into the search space point it represents. Despite the biological analogy that this method seeks, there are obvious departures from the biological method.

The artificial life (Alife) program (Levy, 1992) studies the "emergence" of physical and biological phenomena, and how these may be simulated is also an example of "evolution." Alife studies "natural" life by attempting to recreate biological phenomena from scratch within computers and other "artificial" media. Alife amounts to the practice of "synthetic biology." The attempt to recreate biological phenomena in alternative media will result in not only better theoretical understanding of the phenomena under study, but also in practical applications of biological principles in the technology. Alife focuses on evolution, reproduction, morphogenesis, and metabolism. Brooks (2000) describes aspects of Alife, and has contributed a number of robotic experiments to demonstrate "emergent" principles. Rodney Brooks ANTS project (http://www.ai.mit.edu/projects/ants/) is just one example of a physically realised community of ant-like microrobot machines that are each programmed to respond to very simple light stimuli, search for food, and avoid obstacles. Each robot has 17 sensors including four light sensors, four IR (infrared) receivers, bump sensors, food sensors, and a tilt sensor. They communicate with each other using two IR emitters, one mounted on the front of the robot and one mounted on the top. From the collection of individual ants comes a very complex community of social interactions and behaviours. The community behaviours are entirely emergent, having no specification in any individual ant, or in an overall controlling program. This embodied emergence may make it possible to achieve behaviours from primitive components that cannot be specified, either within any one component or in a controlling simulation.

Clearly emergent communities can be simulated as Conway's Game of Life, popularised by Gardner (1970). This is a "cellular automaton" that illustrates how individual, but interacting, automata can evolve complex structures. A cellular automaton is any system in which rules are applied to cells and their neighbors in a regular grid. Life is played on a grid of square cells (like a chessboard but extending infinitely in every direction). A cell can be live or dead. Putting a marker on its square shows a live cell. Leaving the square shows a dead cell empty. Each cell in the grid has a neighborhood consisting of the eight cells in every direction, including diagonals. Various "patterns" emerge as the rules operate from generation to generation. Life can be played on other kinds of grids with more complex patterns. There are rules for playing on hexagons arranged in a honeycomb pattern, and games where cells can have more than two states (imagine live cells with different colors). Life is one of the simplest examples of what is sometimes called "emergent complexity" or "self-organizing systems," and shows how elaborate patterns and behaviors can emerge from very simple rules.

As paradigms for intelligent systems, we consider the following issues pointing to the weakness of evolutionary methods:

1. Some have questioned whether evolution could have produced an artefact such as the "human mind." Hamming (1980) finds there are aspects of the mind that have not arisen out of the purely physico-chemical processes of evolution. Although our bodies may well be the product of random mutation and selection, all the way from amoeba to man, our minds have some "unevolved" dimension. Hamming examines the human ability to comprehend mathematics and physics, finding two conclusions: (1) although it is a product of the human mind, mathematics is also involved in some strange metaphysical way at the deepest levels of physical existence and (2) there is no Darwinian explanation for the presence of mathematical abilities within the mind.
2. "Evolutionary" AI involves an implicit "design" behind a method that claims no "design." There is a "goal" in the system. There is an aim and purpose to produce that goal, whether this is the solution of a search problem or the recognition of an audio/visual signal, solving the Halting problem or simulating human reasoning. The idea of evolution not having a "target," other than that which is "most fit" for the environment, contradicts the "aims" of an artificial system that has a goal and purpose. Ultimately, evolutionary methods within an artificial system must face the contradiction that there is an implicit "design," the high level antithesis to evolution.
3. Metaheuristics that sometimes "constrain" evolutionary search spaces are just that, constraints. We do not have a truly evolutionary process, with random combinations, survival of the fittest, and other evolutionary principles. We have a system of constraints.
4. The evolutionary principle of "survival of the fittest" has been challenged by Richard Dawkins (1976) with the "selfish gene" principle. Dawkins suggests that evolution proceeds entirely for the sake of the selfish replicators, not for the good of the species. The genes are entirely selfish. Genes that are successful, spread, and those that are not, do not: the rest is all a consequence of this fact. Dawkins coined the term "meme" (appropriately doubling the "me"), using it to refer to evolu-

tionary information transfer, and gave rise to the field of mememics: the study of evolutionary models of information transfer.

5. Artificial evolutionary methods rarely bear a good resemblance to the natural evolutionary methods, other than maybe having some sense of "time," after which a "solution" emerges.
6. In artificial evolution, the environment is everything, and the "solution" that emerges is simply "most fit" for the environment (even in some "alternative" sense, as Dawkins may suggest). The environment — real or simulated — has to be created just right, so that these "desired products" emerge. This is simply placing a great burden on "getting the environment" right in order to "get the product right." There has, ultimately, been design, albeit of the environment. This is totally alien to evolution theory in the natural world, where the environment itself is subject to the same principles.

In each of these instances of where "evolutionary principles" have been applied outside the natural world, especially to AI, we see that important evolutionary processes and principles are disregarded, and evolution mutated to such an extent that we may question whether it can be regarded as evolution at all. In many instances, the "variations" of evolutionary theory actually point to the situated constraint-based nature of the underlying mechanisms: the importance of the environment or the constraints that operate at a "meta" level above the random workings of evolution.

The constraint-based approach has been applied within AI. It finds partial expression in symbolic AI, where it is a method of problem solving called constraint satisfaction. Constraint satisfaction entails making an abstract, formal, mathematical description of "conditions" that are to be satisfied in a problem. The operation of the system consists in searching for combinations of variables that satisfy those conditions, this being the solution.

As paradigms for intelligent systems, we consider the following issues pointing to the strengths of constraint-based:

1. There is evidence that the operation of the human mind can be regarded as "emergence" from constraint satisfaction between modules of the mind. Fodor (1975) proposed the process of "interacting modules" to explain elements of human cognition in the mind.
2. Constraint specification is theoretically more powerful in terms of the "languages" described, because it does not attempt an "enumeration" of the language, as does a rule-based description. The distinction between denumerable and non-denumerable numbers gives an example of some numbers that a computer could not represent, but which do have an alternative specification.
3. Constraint satisfaction is a natural way to embed a system within the environment, making the system and environment one constraint satisfaction system.
4. Constraint satisfaction is a more general process than evolution, since evolution could be regarded as a special form of constraint satisfaction.
5. Constraint satisfaction can be "simulated" in a generate-and-test procedure, and the "test" component is able to operate upon even that which cannot be generated.
6. Constraint satisfaction does not entail the step-by-step correspondence between abstract states and physical states, as implementation of a rule-based algorithm requires.

Thus, PBE, as a constraint-based understanding of computation, firmly situated as a physical system in the world, interacting with the world in that situation, is a more promising paradigm of AI. It is not symbolic AI, or sub-symbolic AI, or artificial life, but a new school in PBE. And underpinning PBE are some important theological concepts of (1) the importance of the physical in the identity of the human being, (evidenced in fall and redemption of that human), (2) the "unity-of-substance" philosophy that rejects both dualism and aterialism, and (3) the idea that evolutionary methods are not the ultimate mechanism of the universe (and frequently involve a contradiction in that there is implicit "design" in the evolutionary system, supposedly free of design).

References

Brooks, R. (2000). Artificial life — from robot dreams to reality. *Nature, 406*, 945-947.

Chomsky, N. (1986). *Knowledge of language: Its nature, origin and use* (Convergence Series). New York: Prager.

Conover, & Voorhees. (1990). Evolution of a balanced sex ratio by frequency-dependent selection in a fish. *Science, 250*, 1556-1558.

Darwin, C. (1859). *On the origin of species by means of natural selection*. London: John Murray.

Darwin, C. (1871). *The descent of man and selection in relation to sex* (2nd ed., revised and augmented). London: John Murray.

Davies, P. (1991). *Theories of the mind*. London: Penguin Books.

Dawkins, R. (1976). *The selfish gene*. Oxford University Press.

Fodor, J. (1975). *The language of thought*. New York: Thomas Crowell.

Gardner, M. (1970). Mathematical games: The fantastic combinations of John Conway's new solitaire game "life." *Scientific American, 223*, 120-123.

Goldberg, D. E. (1989). *Genetic algorithms in search, optimization, and machine learning*. Reading, MA: Addison-Wesley..

Gould, S. (1981). Evolution as fact and theory. *Discover*.

Grice, H. P. (1989). *Studies in the way of words*. Cambridge, MA: Harvard University Press.

Hamming, R. W. (1980). The unreasonable effectiveness of mathematics. *The American Mathematical Monthly, 87*(2).

Heidigger. (1996).

James. (1912). *Essays in radical empiricism*.

James, W. (1978). *Essays in philosophy*. Cambridge, MA; London: Harvard University Press.

Langendoen, & Postal. (1984). *The vastness of natural language*. Oxford: Basil Blackwell

Levy, S. (1992). *Artificial life: The quest for a new creation*. Pantheon.

Muller. (1959). One hundred years without darwin are enough. *School Science and Mathematics 59*, 304-305.

Scheutz, M. (1998). *Implementation: Computationalism's weak spot*. Retrieved from http://www.nd.edu/~mscheutz/publications/scheutz98conceptus.pdf

Spenceley, S. E. (1992). *The principle-based parsing of natural language in the engineering of intelligent systems*. Unpublished doctoral dissertation, Department of Computer Science, Reading, Berks, UK.

Stender, J., Addis, T. R., & Spenceley, S. E. (1993). Principle-based engineering : Theoretical background and economic applications. In J. Stender (Ed.), *Parallel genetic algorithms: Theory and applications* (pp. 117-128). Amsterdam, The Netherlands: IOS.

Chapter 12
Beyond Culture

"May you live in interesting times."

Old Chinese proverb

"It has become appallingly obvious that our technology has exceeded our humanity."

Albert Einstein

12.1 Introduction

In this final chapter, we conclude the examination of religion and technology. We have explored both how technology is impacting religion and, in the last few chapters, how theology impacts technology. We draw these strands together now in a consideration of impact upon society, where technology and religion not only coexist, but contribute mutual benefit to each other. In such a scenario, widespread through enough cultures and societies, we have what may be called a global techno-religious age. We start by describing the new global or "transcultural" culture that some people consider ICT technology is creating: a technoculture that transcends particular traditional cultures. We propose the Five-Is of information, immediacy, interaction, intelligence, and

Internet, as underpinning elements of computer-facilitated life in such a culture. We see the Five-Is as an important part of "transculture," and transculture as a "construction" that does indeed span across the globe as a framework for a techno-religious age.

In final conclusion, we evaluate where we would be without the contribution of this text, and where technology and religion would be without each other. From a religious perspective, we find that we would have a poorer comprehension of the phenomena of virtual religion; and indeed how technology may be creating a more authentic expression of religion; how virtual religion may be a "human construction," but one that no less gets in the way of the divine than the religion of Christendom. From a technical perspective, we find that theological input to the philosophy of technology answers some of the most important questions about how can human identity not be laid waste as technology increases; we find that the philosophy of AI and intelligent technologies benefits from attention to the theological explanation of the human being: their physical incarnation and moral nature (including the fall of this nature and the need to transcend the human condition through a salvation of this nature) and indeed the nature of "computation" that may permit this "humaness" to be achieved in a machine.

The objective of this chapter is to conclude the text; to draw together the dual strands of religion in technology, and technology in religion. We aim point to a techno-religious age where this synthesis is evident. Also, we aim to examine the consequences of not acknowledging the nexus of technology and religion.

12.2 A Transcultural World

In this section, we consider the idea of a transcultural world. Many see the 21st century as being a technologically dominated age, with influences of the technological West spanning the globe and all cultures. The idea that technology is bringing a new global culture or "transcultural" culture that transcends particular traditional cultures is related to Westernisation. The spread of Western values is, in turn, related to globalization; that "complex connectivity," the expansion of social ties across the planet.

Transculture is a mode of being at the crossroads of cultures. Mikhail Epstein (1995) says "The transcultural world lies not apart from, but within all existing cultures, like a multi-dimensional space which appears gradually over the course of historical time. It is a continuous space in which unrealized, potential elements are no less meaningful than 'real' ones. As the site of interaction among all existing and potential cultures, transculture is even richer than the totality of all known cultural traditions and practices." Transculture is seen as liberating, since within a culture, we are "prisoners," obliged to act and think in accordance with presumed traditions. A transculture supposedly frees humanity from culture itself. Transculture would appear to be both a "mingling" of cultures that eradicates differences between them, and a state in which the remaining multi-cultural can be appreciated without being a part of any particular culture. As a "transcendence of culture," the transcultural is, perhaps, part of the inevitable striving that drives technology.

To some extent, multi-culturalism is threatened by Westernisation, and Westernisation is often synonymous with technology (although many non-Western nations have contributed to technological developments, and in the earliest days of Christendom, it was not obvious that the Judeo-Christian peninsula of Europe would emerge as the power it did. China and Islamic countries were more developed, but somehow the religious constraints of Europe gave rise to the scientific West known today). While the use of technology sometimes does include adopting other Western values, there is no reason it has to. We explore characteristics of technological life in the Five-Is — information, interaction, immediacy, intelligence, and Internet — that do not necessarily eradicate underlying cultures. Epstein's reference to the transcultural lying "not apart from, but within all existing cultures," captures the Five-Is, overlaid upon a great variety of different cultures. The Five-Is provide a set of "expectations" that are manifest within the culture. They influence "expressions" of culture, but do not necessarily overwrite the culture or Westernise the culture.

Information is "data that has been interpreted, translated, or transformed to reveal the underlying meaning" (http://www.nrcan.gc.ca/cfs-scf/science/prodserv/kmglossary_e.html) or "any communication or representation of knowledge such as facts, data, or opinions in any medium or form, including textual, numerical, graphic, cartographic, narrative, or audiovisual forms" (http://www.gils.net/gilsappb.html). Information is typically the result of processing, manipulating, and organizing data in a way that adds to the knowledge of the person receiving it. Information can include deterministic, probabilistic, and quantum information. Information is fungible, which implies that its meaning can be identified regardless of the particulars of the physical realization. Technology has made information all pervasive, to the extent that the problem of "information overload" has been identified. The rapid rate of change in information augments the overload problem. It is estimated that every year, 250 megabytes of information is produced for each man, woman, and child on earth (Lyman & Varian, 2000). The reliability of information is also an issue. Humans are often faced with more information than they can process; they become unable to make decisions or take action. Information is part of the reality of the techno-religious age. It has its own negative and positive implications for this aspect of computer-facilitated life.

Intelligence is a concept related to information, but distinct from it. In reference to intelligence, we do not mean the strategic information that might be used by governments or businesses about their citizens or customers, or military surveillance methods. Rather, we mean the attempts to emulate, in some way, human intelligence in machines, to make them "smart" and behave in a human-like way. This is the domain of artificial intelligence. From visual information processing systems enabling face recognition, to communicating with natural language, intelligent technologies are making their impact upon society. Machine intelligence does not just emulate human behaviour, but has the potential to go beyond it. As we have seen, AI systems are often embedded in existing products, making the uptake of the technology particularly swift. There are not new products, just smarter and more efficient versions of already accepted products. The embedding of intelligence makes it very pervasive and invisible. It adds to the technological determinism problems that some philosophers see for society because of this inevitable way that technology is entwined as part of life.

There are two senses in which immediacy is used, one being the speed and quickness of event of action, the other being the emotional proximity of people. In terms of emotional proximity, immediacy is "(1) the degree to which a non-verbal message conveys liking or disliking; (2) Non-verbally, an expression of emotional attachment (or a feeling of closeness) to another person; (3) Signs that show heightened sensory stimulation, attentiveness, and liking" (Mehrabian, 1981). Anderson (1979) finds that immediacy promotes psychological closeness, being the degree of perceived physical or psychological closeness between people. Immediacy of ICT communication technology is an important aspect of the communication medium. In terms of pace, Merriam-Webster defines immediacy as "(1) the quality or state of being immediate, or (2) something that is immediate — usually used in plural." It is related to "instantaneousness," being the quickness of occurrence of event or action. The speed (at least potential speed) that computer-facilitated life offers is part of its immediacy: the "instantaneity" of life that technology brings. Communication technology enables messages to be instantly sent to people on the other side of the world, creating unique expectations for human communication. The instantaneous way that information can be retrieved also adds to the expectations of a fast-paced life.

Interaction is the paradigm of communication that replaces passive modes of exchange, such as television and radio and printed matter. In non-interactive modes of communication, people are "passive" recipients of information, and not "active" engagers. In interactive modes of communication, people expect to discuss and relate and be involved. Interaction means dynamically engaging with other people, and on occasion with machines, in order to complete a given "transaction." Interaction often occurs through the Internet. Interactivity is an important component of virtual communities, where some herald it as a new paradigm of "communication." Postman (1985) has divided communications history into three main epochs: the oral tradition, the literary tradition, and the visual tradition. Each of these traditions provides "ways of knowing" what is true and what is not. Summitt (1993) suggests that society is entering a fourth tradition, that of "interactivity," where the locus of interaction is cyberspace. People know what is true through "interaction." People are linked across cultural, social, economic, linguistic, and other borders, in a way never previously possible.

The Five-Is in a culture leads people to require or assume readily available information; there are intelligent devices to augment finding that information, and to facilitate every area of life;

interaction with intelligent devices and enhanced remote interaction with other people is assumed and required. Yet while technology does not have to change a culture, there is a subtle distinction between importing technology, and importing associated values that do change a culture. Advancement programs, such as the United Nations Development Programme (UNDP), are aware of the need to work with countries on their own solutions to global and national development challenges. It is vital to realise that technology does not necessarily mean other Western values-economic, social, political, religious, and so forth,are imposed. Often, the simple priority that material "problems" take — "eradicating poverty" and eliminating disease, attaining a certain transport infrastructure or attaining certain economic goals — reveals a cultural view, where the ultimate human realities that must be dealt with are physical. More spiritual concerns — human relationships and moral integrity — are often lost in a focus on material concerns. The transculture that many perceive emerging promises a "technological" age for the 21st century, not just in the West, but across the globe.

A "technological" age, with a uniform culture across the globe, where all religion has been rejected, would be a strange reversal from the Judeo-Christian origins of the technological society. In 1100 AD Europe, the centre of Christendom, was not a global technological leader. It had not yet spawned its colonies that were to be part of the driving force of science and technology. Dutch (2004) writes England was just emerging from the dark ages, having been overrun by advanced mainland neighbours, with a Creole language developing. The most technologically advanced countries were China, Japan, India, and the Middle East. But from this tightly controlled religious society of Christendom emerged the technological world of today. The initial conflict between science and Christianity gave way to mutual tolerance, with science dominant by the end of the 20th century. It was almost as if the persecution that religion inflicted upon the world of science stimulated it to greater ends. Through history, the roles of science and religion reversed, and perhaps only now are coming into equilibrium.

Today, the mutual drive for transcendence that people perceive in religion and technology is unlikely to go away. As this text has explored, technology is enabling many new expressions of religion, and people are still seeking that which the technological world cannot deliver. McGrath (2004) describes the decline in atheism as the irrelevance and dissolution overtakes it. The "Closer to Truth" forum also notices how there is an increased interest in fundamental and extreme religions in the contemporary world, paradoxically occurring with the increase in technology (The Kuhn Foundation, 2003). Technology has not eroded religion away. This text has also considered those ways that the technological questions within AI are impinging upon other domains: not just psychology and linguistics, mathematics and biology, philosophy or logic, but theology. AI aims to create human-like behaviour in machines. There are unescapable questions of humanity's nature that must be addressed: questions that are ultimately theological. Thus, from the nexus of religion and technology we find a "techno-religious" age emerging. It is a synthesis of those forces in Christendom that bore the technological society.

This "techno-religious age" represents an absence of conflict between "religion and science"; it recognises the undeniable presence of technology in society — "digital information," "virtual reality," AI, "biotechnology," WWW, "quantum computers," "genetic engineering," and many others that have permeated life in the Western world. This "techno-religious" age also recognises the undeniable importance of religion. Some find the "search for God" is intrinsic to humanity, see for example Gumble (2003). Religion's presence in virtual environments is a very real phenomenon. The techno-religious age finds "religion" and "technology" are undeniable partners in the 21st century world. While the idea of a techno-religious age may answer the question of how science and religion have finally come to coexist, even to mutual benefit, it also raises other questions, particularly, the question of how the techno-religious age will evolve; will the mutual coexistence of religion and technology thrive; or will there be a return to the Dark Ages, where the pursuits are perceived as fundamentally incompatible.

12.3 Without a Technology and Religion Synergy

In final conclusion, we evaluate where we would be without the contribution of this text. We evaluate the contribution to the three main areas: technology (in AI), religion (in Christianity), and the philosophy of technology (in answering technological determinism, and showing how humanity can influence technology), and where we would be without the contribution of this text.

From a technical perspective, we have reviewed the scope and nature of AI; we have examined its origins, the current state of art and possibilities for what will be important in the future in ambient intelligence and ubiquitous computing. We identified limitations of AI, and problems that are currently difficult for AI, including the question of "relational machines," the difficulty of ascribing semantics to machines operating in isolation from the human world, and the perpetual problem of human-machine communication. Our particular contribution has been to point out the limitations of AI, and implicitly the limitations of the current paradigms. In many instances, the approaches to AI have been narrowly focusing upon definitions of "intelligence" revolving around logical thought and narrow conceptions of what aspects of people are relevant in machine intelligence. More recently, "emotional intelligence" and the nature of human consciousness have been relevant to the questions of "real AI." However, there are still many unknowns in the attempt to recreate human ability and behaviour, and implicitly, human identity in a machine.

Without the observations of this text, there would still be three main schools of AI — the symbolic, sub-symbolic and artificial life — each with its inherent limitations. The symbolic school is locked into the formal representation of knowledge and reasoning. The limitations of formal systems have been documented, and point to the perpetual limitation of such AI systems to ever achieve "human-like" behaviour. The sub-symbolic school is narrowly focused on neural-based approaches to processing; ultimately, sub-symbolic computing is just another version of symbolic computing, although it has certain aims to be biologically plausible and mimic aspects of the human brain. The constraints to be biologically plausible, and the inherent constraints of formal systems, make this approach to AI, in some ways, even more limited than the symbolic school. Artificial life is a school of AI that developed in response to the limitations of the other two schools. Artificial life is based on the conceptions of evolution and emergence. It understands "evolution" as the most general process of the universe, which explains biological life, as well as cognitive functions. It mimics biological evolution in proposing general mechanisms (such as survival of the fittest). This text provides an alternative to these schools of AI, and an alternative to evolution being the explaining mechanism of the universe.

Without this text, the distinction and comprehension between constraint-based and rule-based systems would be poorer. There would be no alternative to challenge the rule-based understanding of computation, and no analysis of how rule-based systems and constraint-based systems might differ in theory. The assumptions of computationalism, and the ability of Turing machines and abstract automata to adequately capture human complexity, would have one less challenger. Turing's assumption that it is possible to abstract and represent complex "machine" operations in isolation from the world, and the "implementation" does not matter, would remain unquestioned — at least from the mainstream — even if branches of AI started to recognise that "consciousness" and other human abilities are beyond the explanation of formal models. Practically, this text calls for a renewed focus on the "interface" issues of machines and humans, and machines and the world; it reminds of the importance of "semantics" grounded in context, and life-setting, and other "human" factors that still defy formalisation.

From a religious perspective, without this text, we find that we would have a poorer comprehension of the phenomena of virtual religion. We would not have this precise analysis of the way that humanity strives to transcend through some of the major world religions, and how technology is impacting that striving in Christianity, Islam, Judaism, Buddhism, and Hinduism. We would not have considered how virtual religion may be a "human construction," but one that no less gets in the way of the divine than the religion of Christendom; indeed how technology may be creating a more authentic expression of religion through virtual communities that enhance aspects of human interrelation over face-to-face contact. We would not have the analysis of virtual Christianity by technical feature and ecclesial function being performed; not the distinction between the "theology of technology" and "cybertheology." The synergy of technology and religion explored means that religion is impacted by technology, both directly (in virtual religion) and indirectly (through the novel stimulants to community, new expressions of education, and new channels of communication for inherently spiritual activities such as prayer).

Primarily, we are brought face to face with the question of how 21st century "religion" can help humanity transcend its paradigm, or whether this is impossible, even with technology. We are led to wonder whether technology in religion simply represents a more sophisticated version of more primitive religion; whether "e-mail" and "virtual communities" offer anything more than the ancient pagan religions; whether technology really has changed superstitious ritual and human limitation. Or whether the intersection of technology and religion has changed a component of religion, and perhaps moved humanity a little closer to that transcendence which is sought. Some theologians would recognise that transcendence of the paradigm cannot be achieved through "religion"; they would recognise that "religion" actually gets in the way of the divine; and that great ideologies such as Christendom have only hampered humanity's efforts to know that divinity, divinity that Christianity teaches is beyond the human paradigm, yet which has entered it, and beckons it to transcendence of the ultimate human limitation. Transcendence, facilitated through "faith" in that divinity, that has called humanity into being.

As technology and religion combine in the techno-religious age, an ideology more helpful than Christendom may be created. In fact, within this ideology of a techno-religious age underpinned by the Five-Is, we see a transculture within which some of the poignant questions of the philosophy of technology are answered: questions of how can technology benefit and not destroy humanity, questions of whether technology is controlling society and determining humanity's course while laying waste essential humanity nature and identity, or whether technology is more controlled. In the way technology has impacted virtual religion, we see technology being used for a spiritual quest, helping humanity to fulfil its transcendence. In the "theology of technology," we find a way that "religious themes" can start to determine technology; there is a unique intersection of the scientific/technical and the theological/religious. The intersection determines the applications of science, and in AI, the types of technological artefacts that are produced are also uniquely influenced by theology. Both religion and technology are important human constructions.

Finally, without this text, the unique perspective about the "synergy" of religion and technology would not exist: that is, how each field can assist the other in their respective endeavours; how each field is furthered by the impact of the other, the way that religion is being enhanced by technology, and how technology may benefit from a broader basis. This synergy represents the mutual operation of two human constructions to transcend the human paradigm. Whether humanity is able to transcend its paradigm through the synergy is an open question: the techno-religious age may be more promising for doing so than an ideology such as Christendom, but there is no guarantee that humanity will overcome its limitations from within itself. The unique impact that religion makes upon technology in facilitating a "spiritual quest," remains one of the most distinguishing aspects of the 21st century. In this way, technology does not destroy what it is to be human, but facilitates a quest that ultimately reveals what it is to be human: a quest that shows what it is to be human in light of the machine and of the divine. Despite optimistic predictions of futurists, it is likely to show that transcendence of that human condition will not come from within the paradigm itself, but from beyond.

12.4 References

Anderson, J. F. (1979). Teacher immediacy as a predictor of teaching effectiveness. In D. Nimmo (Ed.), *Communication yearbook 3* (pp. 543-559). New Brunswick, NJ: Transaction Books.

Dutch, (2004). *The emergence of Western technology*. Retrieved from http://www.uwgb.edu/dutchs/westech.htm

Epstein, M. (1995). *Culture — culturology — transculture, after the future: The paradoxes of postmodernism and contemporary Russian culture*. Amherst: The University of Massachusetts Press. Retrieved from http://www.emory.edu/INTELNET/af.culturology.html

Gumbel, N. (2003). *Alpha — questions of life*. Hodder & Stoughton Religious.

The Kuhn Foundation. (2003). *Can religion withstand technology? Closer to truth*. Retrieved from http://www.pbs.org/kcet/closertotruth/explore/show_14.html

Lyman, P., & Varian, H. R. (2000). *How much information*. Retrieved from http://www.sims.berkeley.edu/research/projects/how-much-info/

McGrath. (2004).

Mehrabian, A. (1981). *Public places and private spaces*. (Japanese Trans.). Tokyo, Japan: Kawashima Shoten.

Postman, N. (1985). *Amusing ourselves to death: Public discourse in the age of show business*. New York: Penguin Books.

Summitt, P. (1993). *Future technology as religion*. Retrieved from http://www.summittnewmedia.com/Paul/nonfiction/Religion.htm

Glossary

Artificial identity (AI): conceptions of human identity range through the intellectual and rational, emotional and social, to the moral, to the relational and interactive components that uniquely distinguish people from other creatures and machines. The pursuit of 'intelligence' in AI is just a subset of the more general pursuit of artificial identity.

Artificial intelligence (AI): the scientific understanding of the mechanisms underlying thought and intelligent behaviour and their embodiment in machines

Artificial life (Alife): an approach to AI that emphasises the importance of emergent computing and evolutionary methods.

Christendom: the political organization of the Roman Empire which became the ideology dominating much of the Western world for over a thousand years.

Church: (1) a building, derived from Greek "kyriakon" meaning the Lord's house; (2) a local congregation of people, perhaps a whole denomination, perhaps the entire collection of people who call themselves Christian across the world.

Computable: A number is considered computable if its decimal can be written down by a machine; that is, they are real numbers whose expressions as a decimal are calculable by finite means. The class of computable numbers is very great, and in many ways similar to the class of real numbers, but it does not include all definable numbers. Turing presented the universal Turing machine as a mathematical model that could generate any computable sequence. Intuitively a task is computable if one can specify a sequence of instructions which when followed will result in the completion of the task.

Computationalism: this is the view that cognition essentially is a matter of computation. In particular, a mental state is a computational state embedded in a complex network of inputs, outputs, and other mental states.

Cybertheology: no single adequate definition; usages include the theology of the Internet and advanced technologies. Distinct from the "theology of technology".

E-world: the electronic world, often synonymous with virtual world, where computer facilitated communication, exchange, information and other transactions mediated through the Internet mimics elements of the actual human world.

Faith: faith is both (1) mental ascent to a body of doctrine; and also (2) an attitude, a lifestyle and a relational expression of 'trust' between personal entities.

Five-Is: information, interaction, immediacy, intelligence and Internet; the characteristics of technological life that do not necessarily eradicate underlying cultures but which impose upon them a "worldview" generating a transculture.

Internet church: an expression of Christianity that is located within the virtual world; arguably a community which does constitute that gathering of people functioning as the church. Maybe categorised by technological features and ecclesiological functions.

Internet congregations: conscious and intentional virtual religious communities, not just those who used discussion lists to talk about religious themes or find spiritual support.

Presence: the physical or social "connection" that exists between people in a computer facilitated communication environment.

Principle-based engineering (PBE): an approach to computation that is constraint-based, physically realised, contextualised and embodied within the human context. The constraint-based operation makes it distinguished from artificial life and approaches that posit evolutionary methods as the most general operating mechanisms of the universe.

Real AI: that AI which is pursued in isolation from ICT.

Religion: one important element of religion is its communal and social expression. This aspect is often used to distinguish religion from spirituality. Religion entails a belief in something higher than the individual human person (and this may be a personal god or a whole collection of supernatural beings, a "force" or even humanity itself).

Strong AI: the idea that human cognition may be, or has already been duplicated by machinery.

Technological determinism: the philosophical question of the influence that technology has upon society, suggesting that technology determines society; and that humanity is caught in a "juggernaut" of progress laying waste its nature.

Technology: an application of scientific knowledge, that as an application cannot be "neutral"; the craft or art or skill accompanying that application of knowledge. A tool and construction of humanity often aimed to transcend the limitations of humanity.

Techno-religious age: the "techno-religious age" recognises the undeniable presence of technology and religion as partners in shaping society; and partners that together answer the question of technological determinism where society is not just shaped by technology but the religious elements of society are able to shape the technologies.

Theology: theology is literally rational discourse concerning God including the study of the nature of God and religious truth; rational inquiry into religious questions. The science of the knowledge of God.

Theology of technology: the application of "conventional theology" to further the goals and aims of technology, and assist understanding, development and pursuit of technical goals without ceasing to be that which is "conventional theology".

Transculture: a mode of being at the crossroads of cultures. The transcultural world lies not apart from, but within all existing cultures, including technological cultures. As a "transcendence of culture" the transcultural is perhaps part of the inevitable striving that drives technology.

Virtual: "Virtual" is derived from the Latin word vertus, meaning truth; virtual looks like reality, but is not completely real. Thus the term "virtual" is often applied to the e-world of computer mediated communication — a world which is essentially intangible "information" and "interactions".

Virtual AI: the convergence of AI and information and communication technologies. Virtual AI both (1) augments the natural physical world in ubiquitous computing environments and (2) enhances the artificial virtual world through computer-facilitated life.

Virtual religion: religion that occurs in the virtual world; an expression mediated through electronic communication and Internet.

Weak AI: weak AI maintains that computers are doing no more than symbol manipulation. Generally weak AI does not seek any computational parallels with the human mind.

About the Author

Susan E. George received her BSc and PhD in computer science from the University of Reading, UK, and MSc in knowledge-based systems from Edinburgh University, UK. Dr. George has undertaken postdoctoral research at both the Department of Optometry and Vision Sciences, University of Wales, and the School of Computer and Information Science, University of South Australia. Her research interests lie within the field of artificial intelligence, especially artificial neural networks and pattern recognition in artificial intelligence with applications in a variety of fields.

Index

Symbols

D

E

T

U

V